THE AGE OF ECCLESIASTICAL ACCUSATION

Simon Demosthene

The Age of Ecclesiastical Accusation

© 2026 by Simon Demosthene

First Edition, 2026

Scripture Quotations

Cover design by Simon Demosthene

Library of Congress Control Number: 2026902222

ISBN: 979-8-218-92515-4 (paperback)
ISBN: 979-8-9948065-1-7 (hardcover)
ISBN: 979-8-9948065-0-0 (EPUB)

Trademarks and Permissions

The Age of Ecclesiastical Accusation is a trademark of Simon Demosthene. For permissions, ministry use, reprints, or study-edition inquiries, please contact demostsi@gmail.com.

Legal Notice

This work is intended for educational, theological, and pastoral purposes only. It is not intended to replace professional counseling, mental-health care, or medical treatment. Readers experiencing psychological or emotional distress are encouraged to seek qualified professional assistance in addition to prayer and pastoral support.

Printing Note

Minor corrections and editorial refinements have been made to the text after initial release. As a result, some copies may vary slightly from earlier printings. These changes do not alter the substance or intent of the work.

TABLE OF CONTENTS

AUTHOR'S STATEMENT

This book is written to help restore the Church's understanding of the ongoing tension between unseen spiritual realities and the lived faith of Christian believers—a tension often forgotten, misunderstood, or shaped by fear. Drawing from pastoral ministry, personal history, and sustained theological reflection, these pages are offered as a guide toward discernment, healing, and clarity. The aim of this work is to equip believers, address spiritual confusion, and encourage a renewed vision for the life and witness of the Church. Above all, this work is offered in love, for the Body of Christ and for all who seek to walk in freedom grounded in truth rather than fear.

DEDICATION

This book is dedicated to every servant of God who has chosen compassion over condemnation and truth over fear, to those who have stood faithfully in the light, resisting accusation and exposing fear in all its forms, and to those still learning to recognize and overcome it in the days ahead.

May your courage remind the Church that perfect love still casts out fear, and that grace remains stronger than accusation.

ACKNOWLEDGMENTS

Above all, I give thanks to God for His enduring grace, whose light has guided this work from beginning to end.

This work was made possible through the prayers, encouragement, and quiet faithfulness of believers and ministry partners who continue to model love and discernment in challenging times.

My heartfelt gratitude goes to my wife, Carine Demosthene, whose unwavering support, wisdom, and patience have strengthened every step of this journey. To my children—Maynard S. Demosthene, Pastor MacAlaire Demosthene, and Casiana Paul—you remind me daily that love is the true power of the Gospel and the deepest measure of faithful witness.

I am grateful to my colleague and friend, Reverend Dr. Ebzer L. Joseph, whose collaboration, wise counsel, and shared commitment to theological clarity and pastoral responsibility have contributed meaningfully to this work.

To my beloved congregation of Global Reach Evangelical Missionary Church (GREMC) in Boston, Massachusetts, thank you for walking with me through shared testimony, prayer, and growth. Your trust, perseverance, and faith continue to shape the heart of this ministry.

PREFACE

This book was not born in theory, but in the realities of lived ministry. Over the years, I watched relationships among pastors and leaders slowly change. Collaboration gave way to competition. Trust eroded into quiet suspicion. In some cases, the spiritual fall of a fellow servant no longer produced grief, but relief—sometimes even celebration. That realization was sobering.

I began to sense a shift in the spiritual atmosphere of the Church. What once united believers—the message of the Gospel of Jesus, the call to love, the hope of grace—was being overshadowed by fear and suspicion. It did not begin loudly. It emerged through whispers about motives, debates over who was "truly spiritual," and sermons that condemned more than they healed. Gradually, the pulpit that once broke chains began to build walls.

As a young minister, I had known persecution. But what I witnessed in recent years felt different. Discernment was increasingly confused with accusation. Authority was expressed through exposure rather than restoration. I found myself asking difficult questions: When did discernment become suspicion? When did deliverance become performance? When did we begin fighting one another instead of confronting darkness with unity and humility?

The answers did not come quickly. They came through prayer, Scripture, and lived encounters—one of which was the journey of Marie Michel.

Once deeply immersed in Vodou, Marie's deliverance was not a single dramatic moment but a long, quiet process marked by prayer, compassion, and perseverance. Those who stood with her were not celebrated figures, but faithful believers willing to love without fear.

Through that journey, I learned that deliverance without compassion becomes cruelty, and discernment without love becomes deception. True spiritual authority is not loud; it is steady. Freedom is not found in shouting at darkness, but in walking faithfully in the light.

This book was written from that place of conviction. I do not write as a critic standing outside the Church, but as a witness within it—one who has seen both the beauty of true deliverance and the damage caused by misused authority. These pages are offered in love, with the hope that the Church can recover discernment rooted in humility, courage shaped by compassion, and authority exercised for restoration.

READER'S ORIENTATION

This book is not written to sensationalize darkness, glorify spiritual conflict, or stir fear. It is written to restore clarity where confusion has become normal, compassion where suspicion has taken root, and biblical authority where counterfeit power has distorted spiritual life. *The Age of Ecclesiastical Accusation* is best read not as a manual for confrontation, but as a guide for discernment—one that invites careful reflection on the ways fear shapes faith, culture, language, and community.

What follows moves intentionally across Scripture, pastoral experience, cultural history, psychology, and spiritual theology. It does not proceed as a strictly linear argument built on isolated proof texts. Instead, it unfolds as a layered journey in which central themes—fear, authority, accusation, culture, and redemption—return from different angles. This is deliberate. Fear settles into individuals and communities gradually, and truth often must be encountered more than once before it reshapes perception, language, and practice.

Some sections are instructional, laying biblical and theological foundations. Others are narrative and reflective, drawn from lived realities and pastoral encounters. These accounts are not included for shock value, nor are they offered as models to imitate. They are here to humanize the discussion and to remind us that behind every doctrine, accusation, spiritual failure, or act of discernment stands a real person shaped by history, culture, suffering, and vulnerability.

Those from Afro-Caribbean, African, and diasporic backgrounds may recognize familiar spiritual language and inherited fears in these pages. Those from Western or secular settings may find the same realities unfamiliar, difficult, or unsettling. Neither response is accidental. This work intentionally stands between theological and cultural worlds that often misunderstand one another, calling each toward discernment grounded in Scripture rather than panic, denial, or fear.

At the same time, this book neither denies the reality of spiritual evil nor reduces every human struggle to demonic influence. It resists both superstition and denial. It asks the Church to remain sober enough to hold tension without rushing to conclusions, and humble enough to let Scripture—not culture, trauma, fear, or inherited assumptions—remain the final authority. Discomfort should not be mistaken for error, and agreement should not be forced too quickly. The goal is not instant consensus, but honest and disciplined engagement with truth.

Above all, this work is written from a pastoral posture. It challenges systems, not individuals. It confronts fear, not culture. It calls the Church back to a form of spiritual authority that heals without humiliating, corrects without condemning, and discerns without accusing. Read slowly. Reflect prayerfully. Keep Scripture at the center. And remember: the goal of discernment is not suspicion, but restoration.

WHO THIS BOOK IS FOR

I wrote this book for those willing to think carefully, discern patiently, and love deeply in an age when fear is too often mistaken for spiritual alertness. It is especially for believers—pastors, leaders, teachers, intercessors, and counselors—who sense, as I do, a shift in the spiritual atmosphere of the Church and Christian families. In many places, discernment once rooted in humility and truth has quietly given way to suspicion, accusation, and division.

It is for those who recognize that the greatest threat facing the Church today is not persecution from outside, unfamiliar cultures, or hidden powers lurking in every shadow, but fear itself—fear allowed to govern language, authority, and judgment.

This book is for readers who desire authority without arrogance, exposure without voyeurism, and conviction without hysteria. It speaks to those who understand that spiritual confidence does not require spectacle, volume, or panic, and that truth can be revealed without exploiting trauma or elevating darkness. The central thesis remains consistent throughout: fear-driven discernment has evolved into ecclesiastical accusation. What began as an attempt to guard holiness has, in many places, produced a courtroom culture where leaders suspect one another, language becomes weaponized, and wounded people are placed on trial rather than restored.

The structure and tone of this book are intentional. The narrative arc moves from architecture to manifestation, from exposure to restoration.

Theology precedes testimony, and pastoral responsibility governs every disclosure. Stories are used surgically, not sensationally—not to entertain or provoke fear, but to illuminate patterns, confirm truth, and reveal both the destructive and redemptive consequences of spiritual systems at work.

I am writing for readers who are willing to cross cultural and theological boundaries with humility. I seek to build a rare bridge between Afro-Caribbean spiritual realities and Western church pathology, showing how fear adapts to its environment—disguising control as holiness and suspicion as wisdom. I am not accusing cultures, nor targeting people. I am exposing fear as the true antagonist—the force that distorts perception, fractures community, and trains leaders to suspect before they understand.

The pursuit of mystical leverage or concealed spiritual advantage is not the aim. The aim is clarity disciplined by truth, sobriety shaped by humility, and healing grounded in light. When fear is institutionalized, accusation becomes inevitable. When love is permitted to govern, restoration becomes structurally possible.

AUTHOR'S NOTE

Every generation faces its own form of fear. In ancient Israel, fear often drove God's people toward forbidden substitutes for trust: omens, idols, and hidden powers that promised control while weakening the covenant. Those practices did not disappear with time; they changed form. Today, fear no longer bows before carved images, yet it still seeks control through spiritual shortcuts, mystical language, and misplaced authority, even within the Church.

The goal is not to produce anxiety, but maturity. As such, this work seeks to:

1. Help the Church distinguish between spiritual discernment and spiritual paranoia.
2. Restore compassion where fear has fractured relationships and ministries.
3. Equip believers with biblical and psychological wisdom that addresses the whole person.
4. Expose how fear empowers manipulation and false authority within ministry contexts.
5. Re-center the Gospel away from accusation and back toward restoration.

The Age of Ecclesiastical Accusation is both a warning and an invitation. It warns against a spiritual climate where fear masquerades as wisdom and suspicion replaces love. At the same time, it invites the Church to recover a form of authority that heals without humiliating, corrects without condemning, and discerns without accusing.

My prayer is that these pages will guide readers back to the freedom and confidence found in Christ—where fear has no home, and love remains stronger than accusation.

A NOTE ON LANGUAGE AND METAPHOR

The argument develops by weaving together multiple metaphor systems instead of relying on a single explanatory structure. These include, but are not limited to:

- Legal metaphors (jurisdiction, contracts, verdicts, authority, accusation, immunity)
- Architectural metaphors (altars, thresholds, infrastructure, confinement, foundations, strongholds)
- Familial metaphors (Father, adoption, home, inheritance, belonging)
- Medical metaphors (healing, trauma, restoration, symptoms, diagnosis, immunity)
- Military metaphors (warfare, weapons, siege, victory, exposure)
- Cognitive and perceptual metaphors (interpretation, distortion, inner ear, perception, memory)
- Technological metaphors (systems, networks, access, encryption, overwrite, signal)
- Pastoral and ecclesial metaphors (discipleship, formation, restoration, governance, care)

These metaphors are not decorative. They function as analytic lenses, allowing readers to perceive different dimensions of spiritual reality without collapsing them into a single explanatory model.

Why a Plurality of Metaphors Is Theologically Necessary

No single metaphor can faithfully carry the weight of spiritual reality. Scripture itself resists reduction by employing multiple, sometimes overlapping metaphors to describe the same truths. For example:

- Sin is described as debt, disease, captivity, and death.
- Salvation is described as adoption, redemption, healing, liberation, and new birth.
- The Church is described as body, bride, household, army, and temple.

This manuscript follows that biblical pattern deliberately. Each metaphor illuminates a specific aspect of spiritual life while remaining incomplete on its own. Together, they prevent distortion. The work avoids the theological danger of absolutizing metaphor by allowing no single image, whether warfare, legality, or power, to dominate and deform pastoral practice.

Metaphor as Translation, Not Ontology

None of the metaphors used in this book are presented as literal descriptions of the unseen realm's mechanics. They are analogical translations, not ontological claims.

- When legal language is used, God is not reduced to a judge alone.
- When architectural language is used, the soul is not reduced to a building.
- When technological language is used, the spiritual realm is not reduced to machinery.
- When medical language is used, healing is not reduced to technique.

Each metaphor answers a limited question:

- Legal: Who has authority?
- Architectural: Where does access occur?

- Medical: What requires healing?
- Familial: Where does belonging reside?
- Cognitive: How is reality interpreted?
- Pastoral: How is freedom sustained?

No metaphor is allowed to answer questions it is not suited to address.

Why Contemporary Metaphors Are Pastorally Responsible

Many readers of this manuscript come from:

- Occult systems that weaponize mystery
- Fear-based religious environments
- Communities shaped by accusation and suspicion
- Experiences of spiritual trauma and perceptual distortion

For such readers, ancient metaphors alone are insufficient. They often feel abstract or inaccessible.

Contemporary metaphors—technology, systems, networks, perception— allow readers to:

- Differentiate authority from intimidation
- Recognize access points without paranoia
- Understand why fear feels real even when power is broken
- Discern how captivity can persist internally after external deliverance

In this sense, metaphor becomes a tool of liberation, not confusion.

Safeguards Against Doctrinal Drift

The book maintains theological integrity through consistent safeguards:

1. Christ Is Always Personal, Never Procedural
   Regardless of metaphor, Christ remains relational, sovereign, and intentional—not a force, formula, or process.

2. Darkness Is Always Secondary and Derivative
    Evil is never portrayed as creative, autonomous, or equal. It exploits; it does not originate.
3. Fear Is Diagnosed, Not Exploited
    Metaphors are used to dismantle fear, not to dramatize darkness.
4. Deliverance Is Framed as Threshold, Not Fix
    Preventing triumphalism, dependency, or spectacle.
5. Discernment Is Communal, Not Private
    Guarding against paranoia, isolation, and subjective absolutism.

Why This Matters for the Book's Central Thesis

The central argument of The Age of Ecclesiastical Accusation is not about occult phenomena alone, but about how authority, perception, and accusation function across systems—spiritual, psychological, and ecclesial.

A single metaphor would fail to capture that complexity.

The multiplicity of metaphors mirrors the very problem the book addresses: captivity rarely announces itself in one form. It migrates, from altar to mind, from ritual to perception, from external power to internal authority.

This book's extensive metaphorical language is not excess; it is precision.

Each metaphor is a lens.

Together, they form a coherent theological vision that is:

- Biblically grounded
- Pastorally cautious
- Intellectually rigorous
- Spiritually liberating

The metaphors are not the message.
They are scaffolding—removed once the reader can stand securely in truth.

The foundation remains unchanged: Christ alone is Lord. Scripture alone governs authority. Love alone sustains freedom.

Throughout this book, terms such as architecture, landscape, and atmosphere are used relationally rather than competitively describing the same formative reality from different angles: structure (architecture), inheritance (landscape), and lived pressure (atmosphere).

PRELUDE

The sections that follow in this Prelude are not chapters in the traditional sense, nor are they intended to be read as isolated arguments. They function as conceptual foundations, architectural beams rather than finished rooms, designed to orient the reader to the spiritual, theological, and historical landscape in which *The Age of Ecclesiastical Accusation* has emerged. These sections establish patterns, language, and spiritual dynamics that will be explored, tested, and embodied throughout the chapters ahead. They are meant to prepare the mind and spirit rather than exhaust the subject, ensuring that what unfolds later is understood not as reaction or speculation, but as discernment grounded in structure, continuity, and truth.

Section 1: The Spiritual Landscape of the Modern Crisis

The crisis facing the modern Church did not begin in the visible realm. What we now experience as suspicion, accusation, fragmentation, and spiritual fatigue is the outward expression of deeper forces operating beneath perception. Scripture consistently teaches that what appears in history, culture, and community is often the final echo of something that has already taken shape in the unseen realm. "The things which are seen are temporal, but the things which are not seen are eternal" (2 Corinthians 4:18). "What is seen was not made out of what is visible" (Hebrews 11:3). These passages establish a governing reality: spiritual climates precede visible outcomes.

Conflicts that erupt publicly—whether in churches, families, or leadership structures—rarely begin as open hostility. They are first seeded quietly through influence, suggestion, distortion, and misinterpretation. What eventually manifests as division often begins as subtle pressure on perception. Human beings live at the intersection of the spiritual and the physical; what is embraced internally eventually expresses itself externally. Just as creation itself was spoken into existence before it appeared in time, many of the tensions confronting the Church today were conceived long before they became visible controversies. The Age of Ecclesiastical Accusation is not an accident of personality or culture alone; it is the fruit of a spiritual landscape that has been shaping thought, expectation, and interpretation beneath the surface. This section prepares the reader to recognize that the conflicts defining this age are not merely social or organizational failures, but reflections of an older spiritual architecture that has repeatedly shaped human history.

Section 2: Understanding Spiritual Confrontation, Oppression, and Resistance

Spiritual confrontation—referred to throughout this book interchangeably as spiritual warfare, spiritual attack, spiritual battle, or psychic assault—is one of the most frequently discussed yet least clearly understood realities of the Christian life. For some, these terms evoke dramatic encounters and overt manifestations. For others, the same reality is experienced quietly through fear, confusion, temptation, emotional pressure, persistent anxiety, or spiritual exhaustion. This book treats these expressions not as separate phenomena, but as different dimensions of the same underlying struggle.

At its core, spiritual confrontation describes the tension between God's purposes and forces that seek to distort, resist, or redirect them. This conflict unfolds across both visible and invisible realms and presses primarily upon the human mind and heart. Paul describes it plainly: "We wrestle not against flesh and blood" (Ephesians 6:12). The language of wrestling points not to spectacle, but to sustained pressure, resistance, and influence. In Scripture, spiritual conflict rarely advances through physical force; it advances through deception, misinterpretation, accusation, and the gradual erosion of trust. Jesus identifies Satan not as a warrior of violence, but as a liar and an accuser. The battlefield, therefore, is not first the body, but perception—how reality is interpreted, how motives are assigned, and how truth is remembered or distorted.

Section 3: Tracing Spiritual Warfare from the Beginning of Time

To understand the present climate of suspicion and accusation, we must look beyond the modern Church and return to the earliest contours of spiritual conflict. Scripture indicates that disruption in the unseen realm preceded disruption in the human story. Before humanity's fall, a rebellion had already taken place—one rooted in pride, self-exaltation, and resistance to divine authority.

That conflict enters human experience not through force, but through language.

"Did God really say…?" (Genesis 3:1)

This question marks the first human encounter with spiritual warfare. It is not a request for clarification, but an invitation to reinterpret reality. The strategy is subtle: doubt God's word, question God's character, distort perception, and invite agreement. Once agreement is secured, behavior follows.

From Eden forward, this pattern repeats. Spiritual influence moves from thought to emotion, from emotion to agreement, and from agreement to action. The earliest battles in Scripture are not won through domination, but through persuasion. Humanity is not overpowered; it is influenced.

This same pattern appears throughout the biblical narrative. Conflict emerges wherever perception is distorted, trust is weakened, and interpretation is reshaped under pressure. The struggle confronting the modern Church is not new; it is ancient, intentional, and deeply familiar to the biblical witness.

This section traces the continuity of that conflict without exhausting its examples, allowing the reader to recognize the pattern before encountering its modern expression.

Section 4: The Edenic Pattern: An Ancient Blueprint for Modern Crisis

The events of Eden reveal a sequence that continues to surface wherever spiritual and relational crises unfold. This pattern does not remain confined to Genesis; it reappears throughout Scripture and across generations. Its progression is consistent:

- Doubt enters perception.
- Confusion distorts interpretation.
- Division fractures relationship.
- Accusation assigns blame.
- Distortion reshapes memory and meaning.
- Agreement aligns the heart with deception.
- Destruction follows—not always immediately, but inevitably.

This sequence explains why conflicts often escalate faster than reason can correct them, why leaders are judged by suspicion rather than evidence, and why communities fracture under invisible pressure. The Edenic pattern does not announce itself as rebellion; it presents itself as discernment, caution, or self-preservation.

When leaders learn to recognize this pattern early, they stop reacting to surface behavior and begin discerning underlying influence. They cease fighting people and begin contending for clarity. They intervene before suspicion matures into accusation and before accusation hardens into spiritual damage.

The Edenic pattern is not a relic of ancient history. It remains active, shaping perception, culture, and leadership dynamics wherever fear is allowed to redefine discernment.

The ancient conflict traced in these sections did not disappear with time. It adapted. What once whispered in Eden now moves through modern systems, digital platforms, cultural ideologies, spiritual marketplaces, and wounded leadership structures. The same forces that distorted perception in the beginning have found new language, new speed, and new visibility.

With the spiritual architecture now established, we turn from the ancient pattern to its present manifestation. The question before us is no longer whether this conflict exists, but how it has come to define the current moment.

We now step into the reality of our time. What follows does not complete this architecture; it inhabits it.

THE AGE WE HAVE ENTERED

We are living through one of the most disorienting and spiritually unsettled seasons the Church has faced in modern memory. This is not theory, distant commentary, or social analysis dressed in religious language. It is lived reality, the reshaping of hearts, priorities, relationships, and spiritual habits in real time. What once appeared to be isolated excesses in a handful of ministries has spilled across nations, denominations, cultures, and generations. Something in the spiritual atmosphere has shifted, and it demands more than reaction. It requires discernment governed by truth rather than fear.

A new and troubling religious climate has emerged, marked by the multiplication of self-appointed prophets, apostles, and dream interpreters who promise instant miracles, overnight prosperity, and effortless access to the supernatural. Their voices dominate screens, saturate social media feeds, and increasingly shape what many believers think spiritual authority looks like. Messages are crafted to excite rather than transform. "Breakthrough" is marketed as immediate. "Anointing" is measured by intensity. And in the noise, the steady call to repentance, obedience, and mature discipleship is often drowned out.

For many sincere believers, the rise of the digital pulpit has shifted the center of gravity from spiritual formation to spiritual performance. Faith is no longer evaluated by the slow, hidden work of becoming like Christ, but by how quickly one can claim results, speak outcomes into existence, or "manifest" blessing. Quietly—almost imperceptibly—the central question of discipleship has changed from *Am I being transformed?* to *What can I obtain next?* When that shift happens, authority no longer rests in Christlike character and restoration; it drifts toward spectacle, technique, and persuasion. What appears powerful may not be true, and what is true may appear unimpressive.

The digital world has become its own altar. It streams sermons, prophecies, deliverance clips, and spiritual "warnings" that compete fiercely for attention. Algorithms reward urgency, certainty, and outrage, while humility and patience disappear into the background. Many pastors never imagined they would need to shepherd believers who are discipled more by livestreams, reels, and viral voices than by Scripture, community, and the slow labor of pastoral care. Yet here we are—living in a generation where faith must contend not only with deception, but with relentless distraction, and where attention itself has become a battleground.

In response to these pressures, many leaders have reacted in opposite but equally damaging directions. Some have taken up the sword of public confrontation—exposing false ministers and naming dangers in ways that may defend truth while quietly wounding the body. Others, bruised by betrayal and exhausted by chaos, withdraw into silence, caution, or isolation. Still others harden into suspicion, allowing discernment to collapse into vigilance without love. The result is a climate in which pastors suspect one another, leaders interpret disagreement as threat, and believers quietly wonder whom they can trust at all. This is how fear becomes a governing atmosphere: it does not merely frighten people; it trains them to interpret one another through threat rather than dignity.

Political ideology has only deepened the fracture. The gospel that once united believers across cultural lines now collides with partisan loyalties. Worship gatherings become arenas of tension. Conversations meant to heal often deepen division. Christians who once prayed shoulder-to-shoulder now argue over which political side "God endorses." In the name of righteousness, many have embraced rhetoric that breeds hostility rather than holiness. When fear governs language, accusation follows. And when accusation becomes normal, fellowship cannot survive.

In this swirl of confusion, this blending of anxiety, spiritual performance, digital pressure, and suspicion, one truth rises to the surface with sobering clarity: we have entered what this book calls the Age of Ecclesiastical Accusation. It is an era in which spiritual leaders have quietly and sometimes openly become each other's suspects; an era shaped not only by deception, but by mistrust; not only by error, but by fear. The defining danger of this age is not merely that falsehood exists, but that fear has trained the Church to respond to uncertainty with accusation rather than discernment, and to meet vulnerability with scrutiny rather than restoration.

Beneath what is visible lies another reality that many pastors know privately but hesitate to discuss publicly: deception rarely announces itself as darkness. It often arrives in familiar language, admirable confidence, and spiritual vocabulary that sounds orthodox enough to pass. These encounters taught me a vital truth that anchors this entire book: leaders must remain spiritually aware without becoming paranoid, and discerning without becoming suspicious of everyone. Scripture calls us to sobriety, not hysteria; maturity, not fear-driven hypervigilance. Discernment is not the art of looking for demons. It is the discipline of recognizing truth—holding Scripture, character, fruit, and community accountability together until clarity emerges. When discernment is severed from love, it becomes suspicion. When suspicion hardens, it becomes accusation. And once accusation governs a community, the wounded are no longer escorted into light—they are placed on trial.

There is also a dangerous silence I have observed, especially among ministers who understand how fear spreads through cultures and how occult ideas can infiltrate congregations. Many hesitate to teach these realities with biblical clarity because they fear stirring panic, feeding superstition, or being misunderstood. Yet silence is not discernment. Avoidance is not wisdom. Ignorance is not protection. To warn the flock is not fear-mongering—it is shepherding. This book is written to restore that proportion. It confronts systems, not people. It exposes fear, not culture. It calls the Church back to a form of authority shaped by truth, governed by compassion, and disciplined enough to restore without turning wounded people into defendants.

A central distinction runs throughout these pages: False Liberation versus true freedom in Christ. Many modern spiritual systems promise empowerment, healing, and clarity while quietly reinforcing fear, control, and dependence. This book names that pattern the Spirit of False Liberation. It offers relief without transformation, empowerment without surrender, and power without obedience. The gospel offers something fundamentally different: freedom rooted not in technique, spectacle, or spiritual shortcuts, but in the finished work of Christ and the steady formation of a life shaped by truth and love.

You will also notice that this book uses testimony, not as spectacle or proof of doctrine, but as witness. Theology comes first. Scripture governs authority. Stories serve as evidence of fruit where doctrine has already been established. In an age of digital exposure and spiritual entertainment, testimonies are often exploited—either to sensationalize darkness or to market power. This book refuses that posture. The aim is clarity, sobriety, and restoration.

As we move beyond this introduction, there are three chapters that function as key lenses for understanding the climate we are living in. First, *Clashing Truths*, where we examine the noise of clashing truths, digital saturation, political polarization, competing revelations, and how confusion retrains perception. Second, *A World Shaped by Modern Mystics*, where we trace how occult ideas and mystical practices have resurfaced in modern language, woven into wellness culture, entertainment, and identity, forming a new marketplace of spiritual shortcuts. Third, *The Root Beneath All Fear*, where we confront the deeper fear beneath accusation, mistrust, and division, the fear that shapes how people relate to God, interpret events, and assign motives to one another. Together, these chapters form a bridge between what we are watching unravel in plain sight and the spiritual and psychological dynamics that operate beneath the surface.

As you continue reading, take your time. Read slowly. Reflect. Pray. Allow the Holy Spirit to reveal not only what has been shaping our age, but what He is calling His Church to restore: discernment without suspicion, authority without fear, truth without spectacle, testimony without exploitation, and communities where restoration is the measure of maturity. Our journey into *The Age of Ecclesiastical Accusation* begins here.

CHAPTER 1

THE ROOT BENEATH ALL FEAR AND BIBLICAL BOUNDARIES

The journey into the Age of Ecclesiastical Accusation requires us to confront one of the deepest sources of human vulnerability: fear. Fear bends perception, feeds suspicion, and quietly retrains the way people understand God, authority, and one another. Before accusation becomes language and before division hardens into culture, fear has often already settled into the imagination. To understand the present crisis within the Church, we must first understand how fear works.

Some fears are easy to name: fear of falling, rejection, failure, loneliness, sickness, or being misunderstood. These fears have familiar faces and often arise from identifiable experiences. Yet beneath them lies a quieter and more persistent fear: the fear of what cannot be measured, controlled, or immediately explained. It is the fear of unseen forces, hidden enemies, spiritual attacks, and powers believed to operate beyond ordinary human sight. Left unexamined, this fear can mature into constant vigilance, and constant vigilance can eventually become a desire to control people, spaces, and interpretations.

This deeper fear has shaped human behavior across centuries and cultures. Though its expressions vary, its core remains the same. In many African and Caribbean societies, and among their diasporas, the invisible world is often treated as close, active, and deeply involved in daily life. People pray not only for blessing, but for protection. They speak of spiritual attack, hidden enemies, intercepted destinies, inherited threats, and unexplained opposition. In such contexts, fear is not merely an emotion. It becomes a way of interpreting life. It trains people to explain misfortune, assign blame, and evaluate relationships through the possibility of unseen interference.

The word sorcery carries particular weight in these settings. It is not only a reference to ritual practice or spiritual attack. It can become a lens through which vulnerability is understood. When illness strikes, relationships fracture, progress stalls, or strange patterns repeat, the imagination may begin searching for an unseen cause. The mind reaches for a familiar explanation and gives it a name: sorcery. At its deepest level, this fear is not only about magic. It is about the anxiety of losing control in a world where suffering cannot always be explained.

Across generations, the fear of sorcery has functioned as both explanation and inheritance. It has been carried through stories, prayers, warnings, family memories, and community assumptions. Sometimes it grew out of real spiritual bondage. Sometimes it grew out of distorted interpretation. Sometimes it was intensified by history, trauma, secrecy, and the confusion produced when different spiritual practices were placed into one frightening category. Over time, fear became embedded in the imagination of families and communities. It was not always taught as formal doctrine. Often, it was passed down as instinct. The wound, therefore, is not only spiritual. It is also historical, emotional, and psychological.

Long before modern cultures named this fear, Scripture addressed it directly. God warned His people against sorcery, divination, and occult power, not to terrify them, but to protect them. In Deuteronomy 18, God draws a clear boundary between trusting Him and seeking hidden power through forbidden means. The purpose of this boundary was never to magnify darkness. It was to preserve confidence in divine authority.

"I will cut off sorceries from your hand, and you shall have no more tellers of fortunes" (Micah 5:12).

"Behold, they are like stubble; the fire consumes them; they cannot deliver themselves from the power of the flame" (Isaiah 47:14).

These declarations are not expressions of fear. They are declarations of supremacy. God does not warn His people because He is threatened by darkness. He warns them because He knows its deception. His response to fear is not panic, but truth. He gives knowledge instead of hysteria, discernment instead of suspicion, and trust instead of spiritual confusion.

Fear, however, rarely remains honest. It adapts. What once appeared through ancient ritual can reappear through spiritual sensationalism, exaggerated deliverance practices, and teachings that magnify demonic activity more than divine authority. In such environments, believers begin to see danger everywhere. Vigilance hardens into paranoia. Compassion gives way to suspicion. Discernment quietly mutates into accusation.

That is the deeper danger: fear can borrow spiritual language and present itself as wisdom. It urges separation where restoration is needed. It interprets misunderstanding as malice and difference as threat. It teaches believers to protect themselves from one another instead of testing truth with patience, humility, and love. Over time, fear reshapes the posture of the Church itself, turning communities inward and leaders against one another.

Jesus never led through fear. He confronted darkness directly, but He restored the afflicted with dignity. He rebuked unclean spirits, but He did not humiliate the wounded. True discernment, as modeled by Christ, always moves toward redemption. It clarifies without cruelty. It exposes without destroying. It protects without dehumanizing. Where fear governs, however, deliverance becomes performance and authority becomes spectacle.

This chapter is not written to deny the reality of spiritual evil or to dismiss the experiences of those who have encountered darkness. It seeks instead to name fear as one of the deeper forces beneath much of what people attribute to sorcery, spiritual attack, or hidden manipulation. Fear enlarges shadows into giants. It turns uncertainty into accusation. It causes people to see enemies where there may be confusion, weakness, immaturity, or pain.

I have witnessed families and churches fracture under the weight of rumor, untested prophecy, and fear-trained interpretation. Homes have been divided and reputations damaged without evidence, conversation, or prayerful discernment. Humiliation has been mistaken for deliverance. Accusation has been mistaken for spiritual authority. Yet the Gospel was never given to shame the accused. It was given to heal the wounded, restore dignity, and bring people into the freedom of truth.

Fear thrives where ignorance remains unchallenged. Knowledge grounded in Scripture and guided by the Holy Spirit restores proportion. When believers understand what the Bible truly teaches about spiritual authority, fear begins to lose its grip. Hysteria gives way to peace. Suspicion yields to wisdom. Accusation is replaced by intercession.

"Behold, I have given you authority… and nothing shall by any means hurt you" (Luke 10:19).

Authority in Christ does not need to shout. It stands. It does not panic. It rests. A believer anchored in this truth does not tremble before curses, rumors, threats, or unseen powers, because light has already triumphed over darkness. Where fear once governed interpretation, faith restores clarity.

Because fear often imitates wisdom, it must be named carefully. Not every warning is fear. Not every boundary is insecurity. Not every concern is suspicion. Wisdom can recognize danger without being governed by it. Caution can establish boundaries without withdrawing from love. Discernment can test what is false without becoming cruel toward people.

Fear operates differently. Fear rushes to certainty. It magnifies threat. It treats uncertainty as danger. It does not wait for truth to become clear. It fills silence with assumption and calls the assumption revelation. Without this distinction, believers may misname maturity as fear and mistake fear-driven reactions for spiritual insight.

Fear left unnamed becomes the soil in which confusion, superstition, and the misuse of authority grow. But fear does not exist in isolation. It is sustained, and often justified, by misunderstanding what Scripture teaches about spiritual power, divine boundaries, and human responsibility.

To move from naming fear to dismantling its justification, we must now examine the lines God has drawn in the sand. These biblical boundaries were not given to restrict the people of God, but to protect them from unauthorized power and to preserve their confidence in Him.

BIBLICAL BOUNDARIES

Having named fear as a governing force, we now examine the boundaries Scripture establishes to restrain its influence.

Fear does not sustain itself on imagination alone. It survives where truth is unclear, distorted, or selectively taught. When Scripture is misunderstood, or reduced to fragments pulled from their covenantal context, fear finds room to justify itself. Practices meant to be rejected become mystified. Boundaries meant to protect become sources of anxiety. If the Church is to confront fear honestly, it must return to the clarity of God's Word, not as a weapon, but as a foundation. Only then can discernment be restored without suspicion and authority exercised without panic.

Understanding begins with truth. Before the Church can minister wisely or confront darkness with confidence, it must be anchored in what Scripture actually teaches. Every divine prohibition in Scripture functions as protection, not punishment. When God forbids something, He is not restricting life; He is preserving it. Boundaries in Scripture are not expressions of fear, but declarations of order.

The biblical commands concerning sorcery, divination, and occult practice are often misunderstood. They are not warnings issued from anxiety, nor attempts to magnify the power of darkness. They exist to draw a clear line between trusting God and pursuing power apart from Him. Where that line is crossed, confusion follows, not because God withholds authority, but because counterfeit authority always seeks control rather than relationship.

When Israel prepared to enter Canaan, they encountered nations that depended on magicians, mediums, and spirit consultants for healing, guidance, protection, and prosperity. Spiritual power was treated as a commodity, something accessed, negotiated, or manipulated. God's command was direct and uncompromising:

"Let no one be found among you who practices divination or sorcery, interprets omens, engages in witchcraft, casts spells, or consults the dead" (Deuteronomy 18:10–11).

This command was not rooted in superstition. It was rooted in covenant. Israel was called to trust the Lord directly, not through hidden intermediaries. To pursue spiritual power outside of relationship with God was not curiosity. It was rupture. Covenant trust cannot coexist with transactional spirituality.

At its core, sorcery is not defined by ritual alone. It is defined by motive. It is the attempt to achieve spiritual outcomes through manipulation rather than submission. Whether through incantations, charms, symbols, secret knowledge, or spiritual technique, the objective remains the same: control. Scripture consistently exposes this posture because it contradicts the nature of faith itself.

The account of Simon the Magician in Acts 8 reveals this clearly. After witnessing the apostles impart the Holy Spirit, Simon attempted to purchase that authority. Peter's rebuke was severe, not because Simon desired power, but because he attempted to turn grace into transaction. "You thought you could buy the gift of God with money" (Acts 8:20). The issue was not curiosity. It was posture. Sorcery reduces spiritual authority to leverage.

This is why Scripture draws a sobering connection between rebellion and witchcraft. When King Saul rejected God's command, the prophet Samuel declared, "Rebellion is as the sin of witchcraft, and stubbornness is as iniquity and idolatry" (1 Samuel 15:23). The comparison is precise. Witchcraft and rebellion share the same root: self-will. Both reject divine authority in favor of personal control. Both seek outcome without obedience.

Sorcery, then, is not confined to ancient ritual or occult ceremony. It emerges wherever human will attempts to override divine order. This is why Scripture treats it so seriously, not because it threatens God, but because it fractures relationship. Trust is replaced with technique. Surrender is replaced with strategy.

Yet Scripture does not end with prohibition. It moves decisively toward victory. "Having disarmed the powers and authorities, He made a public spectacle of them, triumphing over them by the cross" (Colossians 2:15). The cross is not only forgiveness. It is dethronement. Every claim to spiritual authority outside of Christ has already been stripped of legitimacy.

When this truth is understood, fear begins to lose its authority. Believers no longer interpret every hardship as evidence of spiritual attack, nor do they dismiss spiritual realities altogether. They live from assurance rather than anxiety. Darkness may exist, but it does not reign.

Scripture also warns that sorcery does not always remain outside the walls of religion. Whenever prayer becomes formula, fasting becomes leverage, or offerings become transaction, faith begins to imitate magic. Jesus addressed this distortion directly: "When you pray, do not keep babbling like pagans, for they think they will be heard because of their many words" (Matthew 6:7). Prayer is not incantation. It is communion. God responds to surrender, not technique.

This is why Paul's instruction in Ephesians 6 is so revealing. Believers are not told to hunt darkness, expose hidden enemies, or obsess over demonic hierarchies. They are told to stand. Each piece of the armor counters a counterfeit posture: truth replaces deception; righteousness guards integrity; peace steadies the heart; faith extinguishes suspicion; salvation protects the mind; the Word anchors authority; prayer sustains communion. Spiritual warfare, in Scripture, is not aggressive superstition. It is disciplined faithfulness.

Modern spirituality often repackages ancient deception in new language: manifestation, energy alignment, ancestral activation, and spiritual shortcuts. The vocabulary has changed, but the posture has not. The same lie persists: you can become your own source. Christ offers something fundamentally different. He does not offer energy to manipulate, but relationship to inhabit. The Holy Spirit is not a force to control. He is a person to know.

Scripture reveals these truths not to cultivate fear, but to restore confidence. When believers understand what God forbids, and why, they stop interpreting every obstacle as witchcraft and stop denying the reality of spiritual influence altogether. Balance is restored. Proportion returns. Authority settles.

Fear loses its grip where truth is understood. The believer anchored in Scripture does not tremble before unseen threats. They walk with calm assurance, knowing that Christ reigns. Yet biblical clarity alone does not erase the cultural lenses through which people interpret spiritual power. Truth may be established, but fear often survives through inherited language, history, and lived experience.

To minister wisely, the Church must now confront not only what Scripture says, but how culture has taught people to see. That journey requires an examination of the language of power itself: how meaning is assigned, how fear is transmitted, and how authority is understood long before Scripture is applied.

Truth is rarely received in a vacuum. It is filtered through the stories and histories of our ancestors. To understand why fear persists even in the presence of truth, we must step into the cultural landscapes that taught us how to interpret power in the first place.

CHAPTER 2

CULTURE, THE LANGUAGE OF POWER, AND CLASHING TRUTHS

Scripture may establish truth, but truth is always received through interpretation. Even when biblical boundaries are clearly taught, fear can persist through inherited language, memory, and cultural habit. The Church does not minister to abstract people; it ministers to people shaped by history, pain, family memory, and collective imagination. To understand why fear can survive even where Scripture is preached, we must examine how culture teaches people to interpret power long before theology is applied.

Every people group learns to explain reality through the stories it has inherited. Culture becomes a lens, a way of assigning meaning to suffering, success, danger, and hope. It shapes how authority is understood, how causality is imagined, and how the unseen world is perceived. No culture approaches spiritual reality as a blank slate. Long before Scripture is opened, assumptions about power are already in place.

When Christianity enters a cultural context, it does not arrive in a vacuum. It encounters an existing language of power: symbols, rituals, taboos, ancestral memory, and spiritual explanations embedded deep within the imagination. Some of these expressions may reflect humanity's longing for God. Others may become places where fear, bondage, or confusion take root. Wisdom in ministry requires the ability to distinguish between cultural inheritance and spiritual captivity. Without that discernment, the Gospel can be filtered through fear rather than received through truth.

This distinction is especially important in communities where the unseen world is treated as active, personal, and constantly influential. In such environments, spiritual explanations are rarely treated as symbolic only. They are often understood as immediate and relational. Power is not abstract. It is experienced, negotiated, and feared.

In the Haitian experience, history and spiritual imagination have often stood close together. The nation was shaped through unimaginable suffering: slavery, violence, displacement, and relentless survival. Enslaved Africans carried not only physical wounds, but inherited spiritual languages that had helped preserve identity, cohesion, and resistance before and during colonial domination. In that context, spiritual expression was not merely religious. It was connected to survival, dignity, memory, and the struggle to remain human where humanity had been violently denied.

Drums, chants, invocations, and ritual gatherings could function as sources of unity and courage. They helped a wounded people make sense of pain and endurance. Yet over time, what began as a language of survival could also become a system of spiritual exchange. Vodou came to function for many not simply as folklore, but as a way of seeking protection, healing, leverage, and influence over unseen forces. The spirits were not approached only for meaning, but also for outcomes.

This development matters. What begins as survival can become dependence. When power is understood as something to negotiate rather than something to surrender to God, fear can quietly become the governing logic.

Vodou operates through relationship, ritual, and reciprocity. Power is not understood as freely received; it is often maintained through exchange.

Offerings are given for protection. Rituals are performed to influence outcomes. Authority is measured by access to spirits and the ability to activate them. In this way of seeing the world, neutrality is difficult to imagine. Every event has a cause, and that cause is often understood as personal.

This transactional logic shapes interpretation. When progress appears, alignment is credited. When misfortune strikes, suspicion searches for interference. Loss is rarely received as random; someone or something is often believed to be responsible. Fear thrives in such systems because control is never complete. Assurance remains conditional.

Colonial domination did not merely seize land; it also affected how spiritual meaning was judged, named, and transmitted. Many Haitians, Christian and non-Christian alike, recognize that certain elements of Vodou involve real spiritual danger, bondage, and demonic influence, not merely symbolic or cultural expression. Yet colonial power often failed to make careful distinctions. African healing traditions, ancestral reverence, cultural memory, and overt occult practice could be grouped together under one condemnatory lens. As a result, ancestral memory was stripped of clarity and rewritten through fear. Over time, this produced a double wound: systems entangled with genuine bondage retreated into secrecy and suspicion, while

Christianity, when filtered through colonial fear rather than biblical proportion, absorbed an exaggerated demonology that sometimes replaced discernment with reflexive accusation.

The result was an inheritance of fear passed down through generations. Spiritual language became charged. Symbols once associated with community could be read only as threats. Fear was no longer simply a response to danger; it became a reflex shaping prayer, interpretation, and expectation.

When this inherited fear remains unexamined, it reshapes Christian discernment itself. Scripture is read through anxiety rather than authority.

Spiritual leadership becomes associated with confrontation instead of clarity. Power is measured by intensity rather than fruit. Accusations arise quickly. Dreams are scrutinized. Motives are questioned.

Community life becomes fragile, governed more by fear of contamination than by confidence in Christ.

This does not mean culture is irrelevant or disposable. It means culture must be redeemed rather than denied. The Gospel does not erase culture; it purifies it. Christ does not call His followers to abandon cultural awareness, but to submit cultural interpretation to divine truth.

Jesus demonstrated an authority that transcended cultural fear. He did not deny the reality of spiritual forces, yet He refused to operate within systems of transaction or suspicion. He did not negotiate with darkness; He displaced it. He did not rely on ritual to prove power; His presence restored order. When He encountered those labeled unclean or dangerous, He did not withdraw; He drew near (Mark 1:21–27; Mark 5:1–20; Luke 4:18–19).

This posture matters. Where culture trains fear, Christ restores proportion. Where inherited language fuels suspicion, Christ redefines authority through love, truth, and restoration.

I have witnessed individuals accused of witchcraft, sorcery, or spiritual manipulation without evidence, conversation, or compassion. Families have been marked by suspicion rooted not in Scripture, but in inherited fear. In those moments, culture, not Christ, was governing interpretation. That is not discernment; it is fear wearing religious language.

Redemption begins when language is clarified. In Scripture, power flows from relationship, not ritual. Authority is rooted in obedience, not intimidation. Protection is found in communion with God, not in constant vigilance against imagined threats. When believers understand this, fear loosens its grip. Culture is no longer denied but reinterpreted through Christ.

Biblical boundaries establish what God has forbidden. Cultural patterns reveal how fear reshapes meaning. When these forces interact over time, they generate environments where clarity weakens and spiritual life grows noisy. In such conditions, authority is no longer formed in stillness, but under pressure. The Church finds itself navigating not only belief, but confusion itself.

And where confusion becomes normal, voices multiply.

This discussion does not present Vodou or any culture as the source of *The Age of Ecclesiastical Accusation*. It shows how inherited fear, carried through history and language, can become a lens through which authority is misread, both inside and outside the Church.

Inherited fear, once woven into the language of faith, cannot be contained in shadows. It echoes through the Church as a chorus of confusion. Ultimately, the Church arrives at a crossroads where it must choose between the ghost of fear and the light of Christ.

THE NOISE OF CONFUSION AND THE CHURCH AT THE CROSSROADS

When cultural lenses shape how power is interpreted, confusion does not remain theoretical. It becomes atmospheric. What is first learned quietly through inheritance eventually expresses itself publicly through language, behavior, and expectation. When fear-trained meanings collide with biblical claims of authority, the result is not open rebellion, but noise—layers of voices competing to define reality. It is within this atmosphere that the Church now finds itself standing. I sense this noise—this confusion—everywhere, even among those who struggle to name it. Our time is no longer marked by simple disagreement, but by saturation. Social, political, spiritual, and emotional signals flood daily life, competing for attention and demanding reaction.

What once promised clarity now produces instability. What claimed to heal division often deepens it. Awareness multiplies, yet understanding thins. Conviction grows brittle. Trust steadily erodes. This confusion does not remain neutral. It cuts across politics, religion, culture, and identity, feeding on crisis narratives and emotional rhetoric. Absolute truth is questioned, moral anchors are loosened, and long held convictions are reframed as threats or relics of the past. In the absence of shared grounding, spiritual pluralism flourishes. New spiritual blends emerge, borrowing language from psychology, mysticism, ancestral memory, and self-actualization, often detached from Scripture and unmoored from historic faith. Biblical truth is rarely rejected outright; it is diluted, reframed, and reinterpreted through lenses foreign to its authority.

Modern societies no longer operate within a single worldview. They function through ideological hybrids layered in contradiction. Individuals are shaped simultaneously by competing systems—politically secular, spiritually eclectic, morally relativist, culturally tribal. These frameworks coexist within the same person, producing internal tension and external instability. What is confessed in worship often collides with what is absorbed through media, education, and digital life. Faith becomes fragmented, lived in compartments rather than coherence.

This shift is deeper than misinformation or borrowed narratives. It is formative. Emotion is triggered before reflection has time to settle. Fear rises first, followed by anxiety, suspicion, and defensiveness. The consequences ripple outward—straining families, distorting relationships, reshaping faith communities, and quietly retraining culture. Beneath the surface, people begin asking urgent questions: What does this mean for me? What might I lose? What must I defend?

In moments of instability, many seek guidance—from elders, pastors, trusted voices, or what they perceive as inner conviction. Yet instead of clarity, they often emerge more conflicted than before. Counsel is filtered through memory, past wounds, cultural conditioning, and inherited fears. Guidance is no longer received as truth; it is evaluated as either threat or confirmation. Others withdraw altogether, choosing silence over dialogue and isolation over discernment. Confusion intensifies where conversation disappears.

A familiar pattern follows. Some adapt prematurely, reshaping convictions to survive the moment. Others entrench defensively, fortifying positions that feel safe while quietly wounding the soul. In both cases, fear governs the response. Discernment is displaced. Survival replaces sight.

The Church is not immune to this pressure. Prayer, praise, teaching, and obedience remain visible, but their meanings have shifted. Prayer signifies different spiritual sources. Praise is driven by emotion rather than truth. Teaching absorbs ideology before Scripture. Obedience is redefined to fit personal conviction rather than divine command. Noise fills worship while confidence in God's sovereignty quietly erodes.

Authority becomes divided. Platforms rival pulpits. Opinions move faster than wisdom. Allegiance shifts from local shepherds to distant voices amplified by algorithms. Shepherding gives way to scrutiny, and where healing should flourish, suspicion takes root. The Church, called to be a living expression of God's love, finds itself strained by competing loyalties and fractured trust.

Yet in the midst of this confusion, something unexpected is unfolding.

The Gospel advances through voices many did not anticipate—former Satanists, former Vodou priests and priestesses, former New Age adherents, and ex-occult practitioners. They come without platforms or credentials, carrying testimony rather than technique. They do not accuse the Church; they expose darkness by contrast. Having served counterfeit systems from the inside, they testify that everything those systems promise—power, peace, identity, salvation—is false.

Two such lives frame this work with particular weight: my father, Reverend Jean Maxi Demosthene, once known as Baron, and the evangelist Marie Michel. Their testimonies stand not as spectacle, but as evidence. In an age saturated with noise, God still restores. He redeems without panic. He exposes without humiliation. He rebuilds patiently, life by life.

When confusion becomes constant, it no longer feels disruptive; it feels normal. People learn to live among competing versions of truth rather than confront them. And where clarity fades, authority is reshaped often in ways that promise certainty while quietly cultivating fear.

When this atmospheric confusion settles, it does not leave us in silence; it produces a world of clashing truths, where the loudest voice, rather than the truest one, begins to govern our perception of reality.

CLASHING TRUTHS

When confusion becomes normal, people do not stop searching for truths. They begin searching for certainty. In an atmosphere filled with competing voices, authority is no longer formed through patience, prayer, and testing, but through volume and confidence. What speaks loudest begins to feel truest. It is here, where noise and fear meet, that clashing truths take shape and begin to train perception.

I remember the early days of the COVID-19 pandemic, when the world seemed to tilt without warning. News screens stayed on constantly. Images of empty streets and rising death counts filled the airwaves. Government officials, medical experts, commentators, and spiritual leaders spoke with confidence, yet often with different conclusions. Guidance changed quickly. Certainty dissolved. Fear accumulated. At one point, overwhelmed, I stepped outside simply to breathe. Yet even walking felt dangerous. Every passerby appeared as a possible threat. Every sound carried weight. I was not sick with the virus; I was saturated by the atmosphere.

That season reshaped behavior not only through personal experience, but through sustained exposure. What entered the mind altered posture, judgment, and interpretation. It revealed something we now live with constantly: information often travels faster than discernment can process it. Every day, political narratives collide, medical claims compete, spiritual commentary multiplies, and opinions are delivered with the authority of fact. The sheer volume can overwhelm reflection. People react before they reflect, panic before they pray, and mistrust grows because so many voices claim final authority.

In such an environment, truth does not disappear. It competes. Media institutions, cultural movements, spiritual influencers, and personal convictions all try to define reality. Each presents its version as urgent, necessary, and superior. The result is not clarity, but collision. Truth becomes something to defend before it is something to discern. People begin gravitating toward the version of truth that calms their fear, affirms their identity, or protects their sense of control.

These clashing truths do more than shape opinions; they shape people. They can alter how families communicate, how marriages handle conflict, how communities interpret disagreement, and how churches understand spiritual authority. Beneath the surface, a quiet exhaustion settles in. Many live in constant tension, uncertain of what is real, who is credible, or which voice deserves trust.

I recognize this exhaustion personally. I grew up in a Christian home in Haiti, surrounded by a mosaic of beliefs: Vodou practices, Catholic traditions, Jehovah's Witnesses, Seventh-day Adventists, and various Christian movements. Later, in the United States, I spent decades in academic environments shaped by competing ideologies and cultural perspectives. Alongside this, pastoral ministry placed me close to lived human struggle: marriages breaking under pressure, leaders navigating conflict, and individuals wrestling with addiction, illness, loss, and disappointment.

Across classrooms, boardrooms, and sanctuaries, I began to notice recurring patterns. People were not merely confused; they were being trained by contradiction. Beneath the cultural fog lay a deeper struggle, a battle for perception itself. Scripture warns that deception rarely announces itself as deception. It often arrives dressed as enlightenment, compassion, or even holiness. Our age mirrors Paul's warning that "Satan himself is transformed into an angel of light" (2 Corinthians 11:14).

In this climate, discernment becomes essential, not as suspicion, but as spiritual survival. The conflict we face is not simply between opinions, but between truth and the imitation of truth; between the voice of God and voices that mimic His tone while denying His nature. When this distinction blurs, authority can shift quietly from Scripture to spectacle.

Modern media often intensifies this pressure. News is frequently designed for reaction. Digital platforms tend to reward outrage, certainty, and emotional intensity. What is loud spreads quickly; what is measured often disappears. People can become conditioned to view disagreement as threat. Public discourse becomes adversarial. Loyalty becomes a test. Identity becomes territory to defend.

The Church can absorb this pressure almost unconsciously. Believers enter worship carrying the conflicts of the week. Pastors feel cultural weight pressing down on their congregations. Slowly, the language of politics can begin shaping the language of prophecy. The rhythms of the news cycle can begin shaping the rhythms of the pulpit. Without intention, the same forces dividing society can begin dividing the Body of Christ.

I witnessed this firsthand in a small congregation in Massachusetts. A Haitian-born pastor preached faithfully from Scripture, yet his teaching gradually absorbed the vocabulary and posture of partisan ideology. From the pulpit, political narratives began to replace pastoral discernment. Nothing doctrinal appeared to shift, yet something relational fractured. Families felt unseen. Others felt pressured to defend ideology as proof of loyalty. Eventually, people left, not because of heresy, but because competing truths had displaced unity.

This is how clashing truths operate. They distort perception. They fracture fellowship. They elevate suspicion over love. And in that environment, Ecclesiastical Accusation finds fertile ground. Leaders begin to interpret disagreement as disloyalty. Believers learn to watch one another carefully. Trust becomes conditional.

Where truth fragments, a vacuum forms. And where a vacuum appears, alternative spiritual voices often rush in to fill it. In seasons of instability, mystics, dream interpreters, and digital prophets may rise with confidence. They offer shortcuts, hidden explanations, and supernatural certainty. Their influence expands not during times of clarity, but during seasons of confusion.

We have seen this vividly in Haiti. After seasons of political collapse, foreign intervention, natural disaster, and repeated disappointment, spiritual hunger often intensifies. Public mysticism may flourish. Spiritual explanations can multiply. In such conditions, occult systems do not appear foreign to many people; they appear helpful. They offer answers where institutions have failed and certainty where leadership feels absent.

These voices do not remain outside the Church. They enter through the doors, shaping expectations, fears, and interpretations of authority. When truth becomes unstable, people do not simply seek answers; they seek voices that sound decisive. And where decisiveness replaces discernment, authority begins to take on dangerous forms.

This is the landscape in which the Church now ministers: a world of clashing truths, trained reactions, and exhausted discernment. To move forward, we must confront not only false ideas, but false authority itself: systems that promise clarity while cultivating fear, and voices that claim insight while quietly detaching people from the steady ground of truth.

What emerges next is not merely confusion, but a counterfeit form of power, one that feeds on fear while presenting itself as liberation.

CHAPTER 3

A WORLD SHAPED BY MODERN MYSTICS AND THE EPIDEMIC OF FEAR

When truth fragments and authority becomes unstable, power does not disappear—it is relocated. In a climate trained by fear and contradiction, people begin searching not for understanding, but for control. They want voices that sound certain, methods that promise results, and systems that bypass waiting. What emerges in such moments is not a rejection of spirituality, but a reengineering of it. This is the world now shaped by modern mystics.

We are living in a moment not unlike ancient civilizations—Egypt with its magicians, Babylon with its sorcerers, Greece with its oracles—except the mystics of our age no longer gather primarily in temples, sacred groves, or hidden sanctuaries. They gather on livestreams, phone screens, podcasts, wellness retreats, and digital platforms. What was once whispered in secrecy is now broadcast with lighting, branding, and algorithms. The tools have changed, but the influence has not.

People today are increasingly drawn to what can be called spiritual technology: systems of supernatural shortcuts promising instant breakthrough, effortless power, and rapid transformation while bypassing the slow, cruciform work of discipleship. Authority is no longer something to be embodied through relationship with God; it is something to be accessed through technique. In this marketplace, spirituality becomes functional rather than relational, transactional rather than covenantal.

Language shifts accordingly. The Holy Spirit is quietly replaced by impersonal substitutes—vibrations, alignments, universal energy, ancestral activation. If prayer feels slow, divination is offered as efficient. If obedience feels costly, manifestation is presented as empowering. The ancient deception reappears with modern polish: outcomes can be secured without surrender.

Beneath this revival of mystical curiosity lies a shared human wound. Many are tired, disappointed, and quietly afraid that life will never come together. Doors close repeatedly. Systems fail. Promises collapse. When effort no longer guarantees stability, the soul begins looking for alternate paths. What once felt questionable now feels necessary. Any doorway labeled breakthrough starts to resemble hope.

I have seen this hunger expressed in countless ways: a young man convinced fame is the only remaining path to security; a graduate whose degree sits unused while applications go unanswered; a single mother drowning under rising costs, terrified that one bill will undo everything; immigrant families frozen by uncertainty, unsure whether their lives will be uprooted overnight; couples consulting psychics and tarot readers to learn whether love will stay or leave; leaders—even politicians—quietly seeking mystical reassurance to preserve influence. Different stories, the same pressure. When people feel trapped, shortcuts gain credibility.

As introduced earlier in this book, altars are formed wherever attention, fear, and hope converge—and few spaces gather those forces more consistently than digital platforms.

The digital world has accelerated this shift. Online spaces have become altars—places where attention, trust, emotion, and allegiance are offered daily. Occult practices have been democratized through apps that promise instant revelation for a subscription fee. Aesthetic spirituality packages engineered belief as self-care. Influencers curate rituals, crystals, journals, and guided meditations, presenting spiritual manipulation as wellness. Authority is measured by visibility rather than character, by engagement rather than fruit.

The mystics of our generation rarely resemble the figures my family once feared. They look approachable—therapeutic, empowering. Their language is gentle, inclusive, and carefully framed. Yet beneath the surface lies the same ancient posture: power without repentance, empowerment without surrender, authority without accountability. What once demanded ritual now demands attention. What once required sacrifice now requires loyalty.

This is not merely a cultural trend; it is a spiritual reorientation. We are witnessing a quiet drift away from the God who speaks through Scripture and toward systems that promise peace without transformation. The result is a generation fluent in spiritual vocabulary yet unfamiliar with the character of Christ. Many can explain their energy alignment more confidently than they can describe the fruit of the Holy Spirit. The serpent no longer whispers from a tree; it speaks through curated feeds and trending language.

The Church now ministers within this environment. Pretending this is harmless curiosity or a passing phase is no longer an option. This is the world our children scroll through, the world our congregations absorb daily, and the world shaping expectations of spiritual authority. Yet many churches remain uncertain how to address it. Some leaders hesitate, fearing that naming spiritual deception may generate panic. Others avoid the topic altogether, hoping silence will preserve peace.

Neither response is sufficient. Panic feeds the very fear these systems exploit. Silence leaves people untrained and vulnerable. What is required is clarity strong enough to name deception without dramatizing it, authority rooted in relationship with Christ rather than reaction, and compassion that remembers that behind every ritual is often a person tired of feeling powerless, invisible, or unsafe.

This moment exposes a deeper reality. As occult altars multiply in digital form, fear quietly migrates into religious spaces. The same hunger that draws people toward mystical shortcuts can, when left unaddressed, reshape the pulpit itself. The line between exposure and exploitation begins to blur. And when fear is allowed to govern spiritual authority, the stage is set for something even more dangerous—not merely counterfeit power, but counterfeit liberation.

As we have seen, the hunger for shortcuts draws seekers toward modern mystics. However, when this same hunger enters the sanctuary unaddressed, it creates a spiritual epidemic—relocating the operating logic of the sorcerer's altar directly into the prophet's pulpit.

THE EPIDEMIC OF FEAR

When power is pursued without surrender to God, fear can become the currency that sustains it. What begins in occult spaces does not always remain there. Fear travels. It adapts its language, changes its clothing, and relocates its altar. When spiritual hunger is left unformed by truth, the same mechanisms that once governed sorcery can quietly migrate into religious environments, carrying their logic with them. This is how an epidemic takes form: not suddenly, but gradually, as fear learns to speak the language of faith.

There was a time when fear was easier to recognize because it wore a visible form. It appeared embodied in figures publicly associated with the manipulation of unseen forces: the sorcerer, the houngan, the mambo, the *bòkò*, the medium, and the psychic. Their spaces were marked by ritual objects, prescribed gestures, symbolic vessels, and carefully guarded knowledge. Nothing about the setting pretended neutrality. The atmosphere itself signaled danger, secrecy, and power held at a cost.

People came to these figures not out of curiosity alone, but out of desperation. They sought relief from persistent illness that medicine could not explain, answers to misfortune that felt patterned rather than random, insight into future outcomes, protection against perceived enemies, or control over fragile romantic, political, or religious relationships. Others came simply because fear had been inherited, taught long before reason or Scripture had time to intervene. In each case, vulnerability became the entry point.

The exchange often followed a familiar logic. Fear was first awakened, then interpreted. A diagnosis was given: an angry spirit, a neglected obligation, a jealous rival, a broken covenant. Threat was personalized. Consequences were named. And once danger was established, a solution was offered, often conditional and never final. Rituals had to be repeated. Offerings had to be renewed. Payments had to be made. Assurance remained temporary, because permanence would have ended dependence.

The environment was dark, but the transaction was clear. Power was framed as accessible, but never free. Relief could be negotiated, but only through compliance. Fear was not merely present; it was structured, cultivated, and sustained. It functioned as both the diagnosis and the fuel of the system. Without fear, the altar lost its authority. Without threat, the entire economy collapsed.

What I have described so far is not theory. It is not a distant critique of systems observed from the outside. Long before I could name these patterns theologically or pastorally, I encountered them personally. Fear did not first reach me through preaching or doctrine, but through proximity, through space, relationship, and lived experience. What follows is not offered as spectacle or accusation, but as witness: a formative encounter that revealed how fear operates long before it becomes language, belief, or authority.

I remember, as an adolescent, how much I enjoyed visiting my favorite aunt on my father's side. Among my father's siblings, she was the only one he trusted enough to allow us to visit freely, even though she was a Vodou priestess. His trust did not rest on agreement with her spiritual practices, but on her character. She carried herself with restraint and ethical consistency that earned his confidence, and for a time, that distinction mattered.

Whenever I visited her small dwelling within the family compound, I always left with something: a kind word, a small gift, or simply the warmth of being received. Her presence felt familiar, almost comforting, and nothing about those early visits stirred fear in me. She remained, in my mind, an aunt before she was anything else.

One day, however, I went to visit her and found the door closed. When I asked about her whereabouts, another aunt explained that she had moved into the *peristil*, a Vodou temple nearby. Without hesitation, and without understanding what that truly meant, I decided to go there to see her.

Her room was located directly within the altar area, the inner space where objects dedicated to the *lwa* were kept. The moment I stepped inside, I sensed a shift. This would be my first and last time entering such a place. Something in me recoiled immediately, long before I could name why. I never wanted to return.

The chamber was dimly lit by a single kerosene lamp. Its weak flame cast uneven light across the weathered concrete walls, creating shadows that seemed to move on their own. The air was heavy, thick with incense and an underlying metallic scent that suggested rituals performed repeatedly over time. It was not dramatic or theatrical. It was oppressive in its stillness, charged with an energy that unsettled rather than announced itself.

At the center stood a wooden altar table, worn by age and stained by substances I did not want to identify. Its surface bore carved symbols, deep, deliberate marks, alongside images of Catholic saints, each representing a different spiritual power or entity invoked within the system. Flickering candles surrounded the altar, their flames casting long, wavering shadows that stretched across the room, giving the impression of movement where none existed.

Scattered throughout the space were objects whose meanings were unfamiliar to me but instinctively disturbing: bottles, jars, ritual tools, a machete resting where it did not belong. The walls were marked with chalk and painted symbols, layered and overlapping, as though the room itself had been written on again and again. Nothing felt incidental. Everything seemed assigned, intentional, and watchful.

What struck me most was not curiosity, but fear, not the kind born of imagination, but the kind that rises uninvited, before reasoning has time to intervene. The environment did not invite questions; it demanded caution. In that moment, something in me understood that whatever comfort I once associated with my aunt could not survive in that space.

I left with a clarity that needed no explanation. I never returned to visit her there. The fear that settled in me that day did not come from stories or warnings; it came from direct encounter. It marked the end of my innocence regarding such places and quietly planted the awareness that fear, when embedded in space and ritual, does not need to shout to be effective. It simply waits to be felt.

Only later did I understand that what unsettled me was not imagination, but exposure to a system in which fear was embedded in space itself.

Today, that same fear often appears in more familiar and respectable forms. In some churches, it has learned religious vocabulary and begun to quote Scripture. It has moved from hidden shrines into public spaces, from the *peristil* into the pulpit. What once controlled people through ritual intimidation now seeks influence through spiritual authority. This fear does not always look dramatic or aggressive. It often appears confident, organized, and convincing. That is precisely why discernment is now more necessary than ever, not to accuse, but to protect, to heal, and to guide people back to the peace found in Christ.

Many who once served at altars of darkness may leave the physical space without fully unlearning its system. They may have left the *hounfò*, but still carry its operating logic into the sanctuary. The instruments change. The language softens. Yet the strategy can remain intact: control through fear, manipulation through revelation, and dependency through urgency. Power is still measured by the ability to terrify consciences and dramatize danger.

In Haiti, testimonies from former practitioners such as Bachon and Marie Michel help illustrate how this system can function. Marie Michel's testimony has circulated widely in publicly recorded videos, while Bachon was personally known within my family circle. Their accounts, along with similar testimonies I have heard over the years, point to a recurring pattern: when people arrive seeking healing or relief, fear often becomes the entry point.

A person may be told that a spirit is angry, that an obligation has been neglected, or that misfortune is the result of hidden interference. Neglecting ritual obligations may be framed as an invitation to sickness, loss, or death. Others may be warned that a neighbor has bewitched them, or that a child's soul has been captured and requires immediate intervention. The narratives vary, but the movement often follows the same path: awaken fear, create dependence, and offer relief at a cost.

Fear was the economy. Without it, the altar lost its authority. Without threat, the system collapsed.

What is deeply troubling is how easily this same economy can reappear within Christian spaces. Some self-proclaimed prophets, apostles, and deliverance ministers now operate using the very logic they claim to oppose. The vocabulary has changed: witchcraft attack, monitoring spirit, ancestral covenant, spirit spouse. Yet the effect can remain unchanged. Believers are not led toward confidence in Christ; they are trained to panic. Instead of freedom through truth, they receive bondage through fear.

The pulpit, once meant to proclaim liberty, can become a stage for emotional coercion. Congregations are told their sickness comes from enemies, their finances are blocked by curses, their delays are proof of spiritual sabotage. And before understanding has time to settle, a solution is offered, often urgent, public, and transactional. "Sow now." "Act immediately." "Do not miss this moment." The structure mirrors the sorcerer's altar too closely to ignore. Fear is manufactured, danger is dramatized, and escape is monetized.

This is not discernment. It is intimidation baptized in religious language.

WHAT FEAR IS NOT

Because fear so often disguises itself as spiritual seriousness, wisdom, or vigilance, it must be clearly distinguished from the qualities it imitates. Not every warning is fear. Not every hesitation signals panic. Not every boundary reflects insecurity. Without this distinction, discernment itself becomes suspect, and maturity is quietly mislabeled as weakness.

Fear is not discernment. Discernment seeks clarity through patience, testing, and proportion. It remains open to examination and correction. Fear, by contrast, rushes to certainty and resists scrutiny. Discernment can wait; fear cannot.

Fear is not wisdom. Wisdom responds to complexity without exaggeration and addresses risk without surrendering peace. Fear magnifies threat and trains the mind to expect harm even where none has been demonstrated.

Fear is not caution. Caution establishes boundaries to preserve integrity while remaining open to relationship. Fear erects barriers to avoid vulnerability altogether. Where caution protects, fear isolates.

Fear is not conviction. Conviction produces humility, repentance, and transformation. Fear produces defensiveness, control, and self-protection. Conviction draws people toward truth; fear drives them toward accusation.

This distinction matters because fear, when misnamed as discernment, does not merely distort judgment; it prepares the ground for mistrust. Once fear becomes the lens through which motives are interpreted, relationships can no longer rest in good faith.

Such dynamics help explain why trust among leaders has become fragile. Pastors hesitate not because they lack love, but because they have seen too much misuse of authority. Scandals erupt without warning. Titles outpace character. Exposure spreads faster than verification. In this climate, discernment easily slips into suspicion, and caution hardens into distance. The Church learns to watch itself nervously.

This is the tragedy of the age we are living in. Accusation travels faster than truth. Rumor gains authority before evidence. Spiritual confidence is mistaken for arrogance, and intimidation is confused with anointing. Many sincere leaders move carefully, guarding their hearts not out of pride, but out of exhaustion. They have seen fear weaponized too often.

From a pastoral perspective, fear can function like trauma. It narrows perception and isolates people from reason. When individuals are repeatedly told that every hardship is demonic and every delay is an attack, they lose the ability to interpret life through faith and maturity. Suffering is no longer formative; it becomes suspicious. Growth is replaced by vigilance. Peace becomes elusive.

This is not only a theological problem; it is a deeply human one. Prolonged exposure to fear-based spirituality can damage trust, erode discernment, and fracture identity. People become hyper-alert, spiritually anxious, and emotionally dependent on authority figures who promise protection. In such conditions, the Gospel's invitation to rest can begin to sound irresponsible, even dangerous.

Yet Christ never governed His followers through panic. He did not keep them alert with threats. He formed them through truth, presence, and trust. Where fear spreads contagiously, love restores proportion. Where intimidation multiplies, clarity heals.

This discussion does not accuse individuals; it exposes a system. Fear can move from occult altars into religious structures, not because the Church is weak, but because fear adapts wherever it finds influence. To confront it, the Church must recover authority that rests rather than reacts, discerns without dramatizing, and restores without humiliating.

Exposing fear does not immediately heal its effects. When fear has governed authority for long enough, it leaves behind a residue that reshapes how people interpret motives, read intentions, and relate to one another. Even after intimidation is named, trust does not automatically return. What fear normalizes next is mistrust. To understand the damage fear inflicts beyond pulpits and platforms, we must now examine how it retrains relationships, erodes confidence, and quietly reorganizes the Church around suspicion rather than communion.

CHAPTER 4

THE BREAKDOWN OF TRUST IN A FEAR-FORMED ENVIRONMENT

In the previous section, "The Epidemic of Fear," we examined fear not as an occasional emotion, but as a governing atmosphere, one capable of shaping perception, decision making, and collective behavior. Fear, once normalized, no longer announces itself as fear. It presents itself as caution, discernment, even wisdom. What remains to be examined is its relational consequence. Fear does not remain abstract. It does not stay internal. It reshapes trust.

Fear is often treated as a private struggle, something personal to be managed through prayer, discipline, or the support of medical and mental health professionals. Scripture, however, consistently treats fear as a force that reshapes communal life. When Paul writes that God has not given us "a spirit of fear, but of power, love, and a sound mind" (2 Timothy 1:7), he is not merely addressing emotional stability. He is naming the conditions under which trust can exist. Power, love, and a sound mind are relational foundations. When fear replaces them, trust does not simply weaken. It reorganizes itself around caution, suspicion, and self-protection.

I remember a time from my childhood, in my parents' birthplace, when trust was not something discussed or defended. It was assumed. Doors remained open throughout the day. At night they were closed, not with locks, but with a simple device, more symbolic than defensive. There was no electricity, and in the darkness, people could not always tell who was who, yet fear did not govern the community. The absence of light did not automatically produce mistrust. What protected those homes was not technology or vigilance, but relationship. People lived with a shared confidence in one another that made constant suspicion unnecessary.

That shared confidence feels increasingly distant today. There was a time when people answered their phones without hesitation. A ringing phone meant connection, familiarity, or need. Today, in communities saturated with scammers, automated fraud, and relentless digital sales tactics, people hesitate even to answer their own devices. Trust has eroded to the point that the very tools designed to connect us are treated with suspicion. Many no longer feel free to speak openly, unsure who, or what, is listening on the other end. Conversations feel monitored. Speech feels exposed. Even ordinary communication now carries an undercurrent of risk.

This erosion of trust does not stop with technology. Patients trust their doctors less. People trust priests and pastors less. Clients trust their lawyers less. Parents trust teachers less. These shifts are not merely institutional failures or professional shortcomings. They reflect a broader cultural condition in which fear has trained people to expect deception, exploitation, or hidden agendas even in relationships once assumed to be safe. Trust has become provisional everywhere, extended cautiously, withdrawn quickly, and rarely restored.

Socially, this marks a shift from relational confidence to defensive interaction. Trust is no longer assumed; it is negotiated. Authority is no longer received; it is scrutinized. Institutions once held together by shared expectation now operate under suspicion. Fear does not merely protect against harm; it restructures social life, conditioning people to anticipate betrayal where trust once lived. The result is rarely dramatic collapse.

More often, it is quiet hardening. Relationships become transactional. Communication becomes guarded. People remain connected, but not bonded. What disappears is not order or efficiency, but mutual confidence, the invisible trust that once sustained communal life.

Scripture names this condition with unsettling clarity. "The fear of man brings a snare," Proverbs tells us (Proverbs 29:25). The snare is not immorality; it is relational entanglement. Fear reshapes expectations. People no longer ask first whether something is true or loving, but whether it is safe. In such an atmosphere, trust erodes quietly. Fellowship gives way to monitoring.

Self-protection displaces mutual care. Communities do not always fracture openly. More often, they thin out emotionally, relationally, and spiritually.

Digital formation intensifies this breakdown by removing the conditions under which trust is normally formed. Trust requires proximity, consistency, and shared life. Scripture assumes this. Paul describes his ministry as being "gentle among you, like a nursing mother taking care of her own children" (1 Thessalonians 2:7–8). Authority, in the biblical imagination, grows out of presence. Trust develops where people are known, not merely heard. Digital spaces invert this logic. Voices are encountered without history. Claims circulate without relationship. Influence becomes detached from accountability. In such an environment, trust shifts from relational to transactional. Messages that confirm fear are trusted. People who complicate it are not. Knowledge increases, but confidence in one another diminishes, confirming Paul's warning that "knowledge puffs up, but love builds up" (1 Corinthians 8:1).

Engineered spirituality accelerates this shift by redefining trust as dangerous unless tightly controlled. Discernment, which Scripture presents as relational and humble, is reframed as constant vigilance. Believers are indeed called to "test the spirits" (1 John 4:1), but that testing is meant to occur within love, patience, and self-examination. Fear-formed systems remove those restraints. People are evaluated before they are understood. Trust is withheld until alignment is proven. Even then, it remains provisional. Community becomes a space of quiet surveillance rather than shared care, contradicting the biblical vision of a body in which "the members may have the same care for one another" (1 Corinthians 12:25).

The most dangerous moment arrives when mistrust is no longer recognized as loss but celebrated as wisdom. Suspicion is reframed as discernment. Distance is renamed holiness. Withholding trust is praised as maturity. Scripture warns that even the most impressive spiritual gifts become hollow when separated from love (1 Corinthians 13:2). James confronts this distortion directly, tracing conflict not to doctrine, but to formative desires at work within communities (James 4:1). When trust collapses, communities do not always divide loudly. More often, they freeze. People remain present but guarded. Conversations lose depth. Vulnerability disappears. Confession becomes unsafe, despite Scripture's insistence that healing flows through mutual openness (James 5:16).

Truth cannot function as God intends where trust has eroded. Scripture assumes relational safety as the medium through which truth operates. Paul's call to "speak the truth in love" presumes an environment where love makes truth bearable and life-giving (Ephesians 4:15–16). When trust collapses, truth is experienced not as healing, but as threat. Exposure increases while restoration diminishes. Authority hardens because it is no longer anchored in shared life. The tragedy is not disagreement, Scripture anticipates disagreement, but the loss of shared reality, where good faith is no longer assumed and love no longer governs correction.

Restoration does not begin with heightened vigilance. It begins with the courage to name fear rather than sanctify it. Scripture is unambiguous: "There is no fear in love, but perfect love casts out fear" (1 John 4:18). Trust cannot be commanded, but it can be rebuilt slowly through presence, humility, patience, and embodied accountability. These are not secondary virtues. They are spiritual disciplines.

The Church was never meant to resemble a courtroom or a content feed. It was meant to be a household, "the household of God" (Ephesians 2:19), where trust and truth coexist, where authority protects rather than intimidates, and where fear does not determine the terms of relationship. Until trust is restored, the Church remains vulnerable to accusation, not because truth is weak, but because relationship has been starved.

It is this relational vulnerability, this atmosphere of suspicion and guardedness, that opens the door to forces Scripture does not treat lightly. What happens when fear shapes trust, and trust collapses, is not merely social; it is spiritual. We must now turn to the specific warnings issued by the Apostle Paul regarding the spirits of Authority and Dominion that thrive wherever trust has been starved.

CHAPTER 5

AUTHORITY, DOMINION, AND FALSE LIBERATION

From the Early Church to Today

When trust collapses under the weight of fear, the damage is never merely social or psychological. Scripture insists that something deeper is at work. The apostle Paul repeatedly warned that distorted atmospheres create openings, not only for confusion, but for spiritual influences that thrive where discernment is weakened and love is displaced. These forces are not always crude or obvious. They do not announce themselves as evil. They often enter through fear that feels justified, caution that feels wise, and vigilance that feels faithful. What Paul names as "spirits" should not be reduced to abstractions or moods; they are powers that shape how people think, judge, accuse, and relate.

They become especially active when trust has eroded, community has thinned, and fear has been allowed to set the terms of interpretation.

Fear does not only distort emotion; it distorts authority. When panic becomes spiritualized, it creates an opening for imitation power, forms of authority that sound biblical, appear ordered, and promise freedom, yet quietly reproduce bondage. This is the danger Paul addressed when he warned the early Church about principalities, powers, rulers of darkness, and spiritual wickedness in high places. He was not describing forces removed from daily life. He was naming a spiritual reality that could operate within the life of the Church itself.

The first-century sanctuary became a gathering place for diverse converts, including Greeks and Romans, who did not arrive as blank slates. They came to Christ carrying assumptions, habits of thought, and inherited worldviews shaped by prior spiritual practice. These patterns did not simply disappear at baptism. They could linger in how authority was understood, how freedom was imagined, and how power was expected to function.

Many Greek converts came from cultures shaped by oracles, mystery traditions, and philosophical speculation. In cities such as Corinth and Ephesus, religious and intellectual life had trained many people to associate spiritual power with secrecy, initiation, and elevated knowledge. For some, this background could express itself as fascination with hidden wisdom and intellectual transcendence. The Gospel could then be subtly reframed as a new philosophy rather than a call to surrender. This posture fed what I describe as the *Spirit of False Liberation*, the belief that secret revelation, ecstatic experience, or higher insight can bypass the offense of the cross and the discipline of obedience.

Roman converts carried a different set of assumptions, shaped by empire, hierarchy, and household structure. Authority had often been understood through the figure of the emperor, who represented order, power, and public loyalty. This mindset could translate into the elevation of human leaders within the Church, where apostles, teachers, or spiritual figures might be treated with devotion that quietly rivaled allegiance to Christ. Alongside this stood the memory of household gods, the *lares* and *penates*, ancestral spirits believed to guard the home. Even after conversion, some may have feared that abandoning these observances would expose their families to danger.

The Roman structure of *pater familias* further intensified this distortion. Absolute household authority had been normalized in the wider culture, allowing spirits of control to cloak themselves in the language of spiritual covering. Shepherding could harden into religious domination. Authority could become something exercised over people rather than responsibility carried for them.

Paul understood that these spirits did not enter the Church only through pagan streets or external persecution. They could also enter through pulpits, routines, and respected structures, disguising themselves as spiritual insight while preserving old chains. Among the principalities he named, few are more destructive than the spirits of Authority, Dominion, and False Liberation. They do not always announce themselves with chaos. They operate through imitation. They hide behind order, present themselves as revelation, cling to position rather than truth, and maintain control while appearing orthodox.

The greatest threat was never only pagan altars outside the Church. It was the imitation of divine authority within it.

These spirits are strategic. They adapt their presentation to the culture they are addressing. The names change. The language shifts. The packaging evolves. But the product remains the same: dependency, fear, and spiritual abduction.

In Haiti, a nation forged through struggle and marked by deep economic vulnerability, this product is often marketed as liberation from poverty. False Liberation exploits survival anxiety, offering rituals, sacrificial giving, or ancestral agreements as pathways to unlock destiny or protect against hidden enemies. The branding is hope and prosperity, yet the outcome can be deeper spiritual and financial bondage.

In Western contexts, the same spirits rarely present themselves as religion. They often emerge through wellness culture, therapeutic language, self-optimization, and technological convenience. Spiritual practices are reframed as tools for balance, productivity, and healing. What once required altars and visible allegiance is now often rebranded through concepts such as energy alignment, manifestation, abundance, consciousness expansion, ancestral healing, and total well-being. God is not always openly rejected; He is quietly displaced, as the inward self becomes healer, interpreter, and final authority.

In post-colonial societies marked by historical erasure and trauma, the product may be marketed as cultural authenticity and ancestral sovereignty. The spirits whisper that biblical faith is a foreign imposition and that true power lies in reclaiming generational contracts and blood-sealed rituals. What claims to restore heritage can instead forge new chains, binding descendants to spirits they never personally chose to serve.

In Western cities, the strategy remains constant. The goal is always the same: to move the believer away from freedom that requires surrender to Christ and into systems that require only agreement with deception. Freedom is promised, but obedience is removed. Identity is celebrated, but submission is resisted. Power is offered, but truth is displaced.

We have already seen how these spirits manifest in our current era through digital platforms and modern movements.

We must now move from their outward expression to their inner strategy. The power of the spirits Paul named is anchored most clearly in the deception of the *Spirit of False Liberation*. It promises freedom while quietly reconstructing bondage. It offers empowerment while forging dependency.

To restore true freedom, this system must be exposed at its core.

We now turn to unmasking the anatomy of the Spirit of False Liberation.

THE SPIRIT OF FALSE LIBERATION

False liberation never announces itself as captivity. It arrives sounding like rescue. After authority is distorted and fear is internalized, liberation becomes the next vulnerability. People no longer ask whether something is true; they ask whether it feels relieving. It is into that longing that the *Spirit of False Liberation* speaks. Not every voice that calls itself a liberator comes to set people free. Some come only to exchange one set of chains for another. The system behind those voices is deliberate. It exploits fear, disguises bondage as empowerment, and demands allegiance through agreements sealed in ritual, vow, or blood.

The *Spirit of False Liberation* does not lead with threats. It leads with promises, quiet promises shaped to fit the wounds of each generation. Cultural promises. Emotional promises.

Identity-shaping promises. Its voice echoes the ancient lie first whispered in Eden, yet it adapts its tone to history, trauma, and longing. To some it says that strength is found in ancestral spirits. To others it insists protection lies elsewhere. In other spaces it claims identity is rooted in tribe, ritual, or reclaimed heritage. Destiny, it whispers, is unlocked not through surrender, but through action, through a key, a formula, a practice that bypasses waiting on God.

To people living under fear, loss, historical erasure, and oppression, these promises feel like oxygen. They sound like hope, like restoration, like meaning regained. Yet the same spirits that offer identity quietly lay claim to everything: finances, time, emotional energy, geography, and allegiance. What begins as empowerment slowly becomes dependency. What feels like movement becomes exhaustion. What is presented as freedom becomes an endless cycle of striving. This is the nature of false liberation: it gives quickly, but it never finishes the work.

I have seen this repeatedly in pastoral life. I have seen people who know almost nothing about Christian doctrine send thousands of dollars to self-proclaimed prophets and spiritual healers in desperation for their problems to be solved. In some cases, the problem appears to resolve, only for a few weeks or a few months, before another crisis emerges. Relief comes, but it never lasts. Peace is promised, but it never settles. Each solution demands another offering, another instruction, another emergency response.

I have also known believers who live in a constant cycle of fasting: three days, seven days, twenty-one days, forty days, only to begin again and again, searching for liberation that never stabilizes. Often this pattern unfolds under the guidance of digital prophets or online spiritual healers, even while these individuals continue attending local churches faithfully. Outwardly, nothing seems amiss. Inwardly, they are exhausted, anxious, and quietly convinced that if they stop striving, something terrible will happen. Liberation has become labor. Faith has become pressure.

This is not discipline; it is spiritual panic disguised as devotion. When fasting, prayer, and sacrifice are driven by fear rather than trust, they quietly shift from obedience into transaction. The believer is no longer resting in Christ's finished work; they are attempting to secure safety through repetition. The *Spirit of False Liberation* thrives in this environment because it does not need to deny Christ. It only needs to keep Him perpetually insufficient.

In ancestral systems such as Vodou, blood is never symbolic. It is contractual. Blood seals agreement. Blood marks territory. Blood binds generations. Through blood rituals, the *Spirit of False Liberation* extends beyond the individual who enters the covenant. Descendants who never chose the agreement may still live under its weight. Families may experience oppression, confusion, or spiritual instability not because of personal rebellion, but because of vows made long before they were born. The spirit moves quietly, first shaping household habits, then embedding itself into culture, then redefining identity until it becomes part of national consciousness. False liberation always works from the inside out.

Haiti's history reveals this pattern with painful clarity. Independence was won through courage, brilliance, strategy, and unimaginable sacrifice. Blood was poured out in quantities history rarely records. Yet generations later, after political collapse, instability, natural disasters, foreign interference, and persistent poverty, the spirits once credited with liberation remain silent. They cannot offer the freedom once attributed to them because they were never true liberators. They functioned as unseen colonizers. The serpent's promise has not changed. It still claims power, freedom, and restoration. And its deception remains intact: the freedom it offers enslaves, the empowerment it grants demands bondage, and the identity it provides is maintained through fear.

False liberation does not always enter through ceremony. Sometimes it enters through vocabulary, through a reclaimed word, a cultural slogan, or a symbol polished until its spiritual origin is forgotten. In November 2025, while visiting family in Florida, I found myself in a long conversation with a cousin, a committed Christian and respected deacon, about the Haitian Creole word *ayibobo*. He insisted it was merely a harmless cultural expression, equivalent to "amen." His confidence startled me. In that moment, I recognized the *Spirit of False Liberation* at work, not through rebellion, but through normalization.

My understanding of that word is not academic. I grew up hearing it shouted during Vodou ceremonies near our home. It was never casual. Today, however, it is being sanitized and celebrated as cultural pride across the diaspora. A ritual cry becomes fashion. A spiritual invocation becomes identity. And just like that, agreement is formed without awareness. What is reclaimed linguistically becomes reintroduced spiritually.

This is how the *Spirit of False Liberation* operates pastorally. It does not force people into captivity; it persuades them. It repackages disobedience as enlightenment and bends truth just enough to make bondage look desirable. Chains become culture, heritage, or empowerment. Its two primary tools remain accusation and fear. Accusation attacks identity, shaming those who resist deception. Fear threatens loss, harm, or generational consequence. Together, they weaken discernment and erode courage while maintaining the illusion of choice.

The *Spirit of False Liberation* is not merely a doctrine; it is a pattern. It shaped Eden. It shaped empires. It shaped Haiti. It has shaped families, churches, and spiritual movements. Its methods evolve. Its language shifts. Its disguises change. But its objective never moves. It leads people away from freedom that requires surrender to Christ and into bondage that requires nothing but agreement.

Recognizing that pattern is not condemnation; it is the beginning of healing. Paul called this system philosophy and vain deceit. Today, we recognize it as engineered spirituality, a structure designed to feel empowering while quietly dismantling trust, rest, and freedom. Freedom is promised, but obedience is removed. Freedom becomes bondage. Empowerment becomes dependency. To restore true liberation, this system must be exposed not only theologically, but pastorally, where fear, fatigue, and identity intersect.

Only then can the Church reclaim freedom without deception and authority without chains.

What we have examined so far is not a collection of isolated failures. These patterns point to something more organized: a form of spirituality that manages fear, produces dependency, and disguises control as power. To confront false liberation fully, we must now examine that design.

CHAPTER 6

ENGINEERED SPIRITUALITY

What we have uncovered so far is not a collection of isolated beliefs, cultural curiosities, or personal excesses. The patterns seen in false liberation, endless striving, fear-driven urgency, *transactional devotion*, and identity reshaped through persuasion do not emerge randomly. They are produced. Behind repeated cycles of spiritual exhaustion lies a carefully assembled structure that blends theology, psychology, culture, authority, and fear into something that feels elevated while quietly redirecting allegiance. To understand why false liberation reproduces itself so efficiently, we must now examine the design that sustains it. This is the realm of *Engineered Spirituality*.

Engineered Spirituality describes a manufactured form of spiritual life in which power, meaning, and transformation are pursued through technique, atmosphere, performance, and control rather than through surrender to God, obedience to Scripture, and the slow formation of Christlike character. It is spirituality designed to produce results, impressions, and dependency, often by shaping perception, emotion, and behavior in ways that appear spiritual while bypassing truth, humility, repentance, and love.

There are moments in Scripture where Paul's language feels almost surgical, as though the Holy Spirit draws back the covering over culture, religion, and human emotion to expose the machinery operating beneath them. In letters such as Colossians, Ephesians, and Timothy, Paul does not speak in abstraction or speculation. His words function like diagnostic instruments. He is not merely teaching doctrine; he is identifying systems of influence designed to appear wise, liberating, and spiritually elevated while quietly separating believers from the living Christ.

Paul names these forces with startling precision: philosophy, vain deceit, the tradition of men, the rudiments of the world, seducing spirits, doctrines of devils, the course of this world, the spirit that now worketh, and the prince of the power of the air (Colossians 2:8; 1 Timothy 4:1; Ephesians 2:2). These were not theoretical dangers to the early Church. They were active pressures shaping teaching, worship, morality, and perceptions of authority. Some influence arrived from outside the community of faith, but much of it emerged from within. Teachers promised higher revelation. Philosophers clothed unbelief in refined language. Mystical experiences felt powerful and enlightening while quietly carrying poison. Beneath all of it echoed the ancient question first whispered in Eden: *Has God really said?* (Genesis 3:1).

False liberation always begins with the promise of more: more freedom, more access, more insight, more spiritual depth. Yet it loosens the believer's grip on Christ one subtle thread at a time. What Paul confronted in the first century has not disappeared. It has adapted.

When Paul warns, "Beware lest any man spoil you through philosophy and vain deceit," he is not condemning intelligence, inquiry, or thoughtful engagement with ideas (Colossians 2:8). The danger is not depth itself. The danger arises when human wisdom becomes the doorway through which spiritual abduction enters. Philosophy becomes destructive when understanding is elevated above surrender, insight replaces obedience, and spirituality is detached from Christ as its anchor.

Engineered Spirituality does not appear in only one form. It adapts itself to the hunger of each age. In one setting, it may appear as intellectual enlightenment. In another, as emotional healing. In another, as cultural recovery. In another, as personal empowerment. The names change, but the movement remains the same: the soul is invited to seek transformation through something other than surrender to Christ.

The Spirituality of the Self

One of its most common expressions is the spirituality of the self. In this form, the human person becomes the center of power. Manifestation teaching, the law of attraction, self-help spirituality, and forms of quantum mysticism often promise that destiny can be unlocked by thought, speech, energy, or mental alignment. These ideas can sound empowering, especially to people who feel wounded, overlooked, or trapped. They offer language for hope. They tell the person, *You are not powerless.* Yet beneath that promise, a quiet exchange takes place. Prayer becomes visualization. Faith becomes vibration. Surrender becomes self-command. The self replaces God. God is not always openly denied; He is slowly replaced by the authority of the inner self.

The Spirituality of Hidden Knowledge

A second expression is the spirituality of hidden knowledge. This appears wherever secret insight, higher consciousness, mystical experience, or special revelation is treated as superior to simple obedience. In Paul's day, certain teachers presented spiritual maturity as access to deeper mysteries beyond the plain sufficiency of Christ. In our time, similar patterns appear through New Age spirituality, mystical universalism, and teachings that promise awakening without repentance. The language may be gentle, compassionate, and intellectually attractive. Yet the danger remains: Christ is repositioned. He becomes one guide among many, one expression of truth among others, one voice inside a larger spiritual system.

Once Christ is reduced, the cross is no longer central, repentance is no longer necessary, and obedience becomes optional.

Paul pairs philosophy with vain deceit, exposing a lie polished to appear profound (Colossians 2:8). Vain deceit carries emotional resonance, spiritual flavor, and psychological appeal, yet it remains hollow. It promises fulfillment but delivers restlessness. This deception often surfaces in teachings that sound elevated, therapeutic, or empowering while quietly detaching the soul from Christ. They may speak of awakening, abundance, consciousness, or alignment, but the pattern remains recognizable. The believer is offered a way to feel spiritually expanded without being spiritually surrendered.

The same pattern existed in the early Church through ascetic, mystical, and anti-body teachings that promised liberation but produced exhaustion and confusion. Vain deceit always advertises elevation, yet it leaves the soul thirsty, the conscience unformed, and the believer disconnected from the true power and presence of God.

Paul then exposes the danger of the tradition of men, systems built from inherited religious habits, cultural spirituality, or human wisdom that gradually overshadow a living encounter with Christ (Colossians 2:8). These traditions feel safe because they are familiar and socially reinforced. In our time, this danger may appear through mystical universalism, the gentle religion of the modern age. It insists that all paths lead to God, elevates intuition above Scripture, experience above revelation, and desire above divine command. God is not denied; He is reshaped into a reflection of preference. What feels compassionate quietly removes repentance, holiness, and submission to Christ.

Paul's phrase "the rudiments of the world" points to something deeper than cultural habit (Colossians 2:8). It exposes unseen forces shaping what feels reasonable, normal, and self-evident. These rudiments influence assumptions about identity, morality, purpose, and truth. In our generation, secular humanism stands as one of their strongest expressions. It teaches that humanity is the highest authority, reason replaces revelation, and God becomes optional. Faith is tolerated only if it remains private and non-disruptive.

The Spirituality of Alternate Mediation

A third expression is the spirituality of alternate mediation. Here, the soul seeks protection, healing, identity, or power through ancestors, spirits, energies, rituals, or cosmic forces. This may appear through ancestral veneration, spirit guides, neo-shamanic practices, or religious systems that assign spiritual authority to intermediaries other than Christ. The appeal is understandable. People want connection. They want roots. They want healing from historical wounds and family pain. But when identity is rebuilt around spiritual agreements outside Christ, healing becomes another doorway into bondage. What is presented as recovery can become reattachment. What is offered as heritage can become allegiance.

The early Church faced similar pressure. Many believers came from cultures shaped by astrology, ancestral veneration, and political ideology fused with spiritual loyalty. Households honored ancestral spirits believed to guard destiny. Even after conversion, some feared that abandoning these practices would invite harm. This is why Paul addressed food offered to idols in Corinth and warned believers not to treat spiritual allegiance lightly (1 Corinthians 8:1–13; 10:19–22). He also warned the Colossians against the worship of angels, practices tied to spiritual intermediaries (Colossians 2:18–19). Peter names this struggle directly when he speaks of redemption from "vain traditions received from your fathers" (1 Peter 1:18). Paul's response was liberating: in Christ, no ancestor, spirit, or intermediary holds final authority over the believer's destiny. Christ alone stands as head over every power and principality (Colossians 2:10, 15; Ephesians 6:12).

The danger remains subtle. A believer may retain Christian language while adopting a non-Christian worldview. Christ remains on the lips while culture becomes the interpreter. *Engineered Spirituality* does not demand rejection of Jesus; it requires only redefinition.

Paul's warning to Timothy introduces an even deeper threat: "some shall depart from the faith, giving heed to seducing spirits, and doctrines of devils" (1 Timothy 4:1). These teachings rarely appear hostile. They often arrive therapeutic, empowering, and transcendent. In our time, this pattern can surface through Eastern mysticism detached from Christ, *kundalini* awakenings, yoga framed as ascension, meditation aimed at dissolving the self into universal consciousness, or other practices that promise spiritual expansion without submission to the lordship of Christ. They may also appear through neo-shamanism, where ancestral rituals and spirit guides promise healing and identity.

These experiences can feel profound. They may stir emotion, peace, and a sense of power. Yet when they redirect the believer away from repentance, holiness, and lordship, they become spiritually dangerous. The most dangerous doctrines are not always those that deny God, but those that redefine Him in ways that require no obedience.

Paul describes life before Christ as walking according to "the course of this world," under "the prince of the power of the air," and influenced by "the spirit that now worketh in the children of disobedience" (Ephesians 2:2). This course functions like a current, steady, subtle, and powerful. Few choose it deliberately; most drift. Modern expressions include self-help spirituality and quantum mysticism, which teach that destiny lies within the self. Prayer is replaced by affirmation, Scripture by mindset, and God by self-belief. Any form of Christianity that never collides with the current of its age is already being shaped by it.

Paul then names the force energizing this drift: "the spirit that now worketh in the children of disobedience" (Ephesians 2:2). This is not mere stubbornness; it is an atmosphere that forms rebellion. In Corinth, sin was celebrated as liberty. In our time, boundaries are often dismissed as oppression. Desire becomes doctrine. Authenticity replaces obedience. Once holiness is optional, identity collapses.

Finally, Paul unveils the architect behind the entire system: "the prince of the power of the air" (Ephesians 2:2). This influence operates like atmosphere, unnoticed and inhaled constantly. Each generation receives a tailored deception. Legalism binds one era. Mysticism binds another. Universalism binds another. Our age is often bound by self-deification. The enemy is indifferent to the method, so long as believers feel spiritual while being detached from Christ. The whisper has not changed: *You shall be as gods* (Genesis 3:5).

When Paul's vocabulary is taken together, a complete map of deception emerges. These forces weakened the early Church from within, and they operate with equal subtlety today. Our generation is spiritually active but not anchored, hungry for transcendence, resistant to surrender, seeking power without the cross and identity without holiness.

These expressions do not need to look identical to belong to the same system. Some appear religious. Others appear therapeutic. Others appear intellectual, cultural, or technological. But each carries the same inner design. It promises transformation while avoiding surrender. It offers power while loosening obedience. It speaks of freedom while detaching the soul from the lordship of Christ. This is why Paul's warning remains urgent. *Engineered Spirituality* is not merely false belief; it is a patterned system of influence that trains people to feel spiritual while being quietly moved away from the truth that sets them free.

The danger no longer lives outside the Church. It can sing in worship, preach from pulpits, circulate through prayer groups, and flow through *digital prophecy*. It sounds familiar, yet it carries another spirit. The question before us is no longer whether *Engineered Spirituality* exists, but whether the Holy Spirit is allowed to expose it before it reshapes us entirely. In an age thick with this atmosphere, we must ask whether we are breathing the breath of God or adapting to air engineered by another source. That question is no longer theoretical. The cost of living inside this atmosphere is already being paid by the modern believer.

LIVING INSIDE THE ENGINEERED ATMOSPHERE

Once a system is exposed, the question is no longer whether it exists, but how it is lived inside. What Paul identified as spiritual forces pressing against the early Church now helps us understand the atmosphere surrounding believers today. In our generation, *Engineered Spirituality* presses against people at the most personal level. It no longer operates only through teachings and institutions, but through daily habits, quiet choices, and unseen influences shaping thought and desire. I encounter it not only in sermons or books, but in conversations, counseling sessions, prayer lines, and whispered confessions.

Because of this engineered atmosphere, I now meet people, young and old, educated and uneducated, churched and unchurched, who carry some degree of occult exposure. For some, it belongs to the past. For others, it remains active in the present. What was once hidden behind temples, secret societies, or cultural rituals is now carried in pockets, streamed through videos, and packaged in the language of wellness, empowerment, and personal growth. Spiritual influence has become mobile, accessible, and normalized.

What is most striking is how ordinary this exposure has become. It is increasingly rare to speak with someone without discovering a point of contact. Tarot cards tried out of curiosity. Astrology consulted for direction. Crystals worn for protection. Energy healing explored during emotional distress. Ancestral rituals inherited without examination. Spiritual practices absorbed through music, wellness culture, or social media. Much of this did not enter through deliberate rebellion against God. It entered through availability, through language that sounded harmless and systems that promised insight, healing, or empowerment without requiring repentance or submission to Christ. Because curiosity often precedes conviction, many do not realize a door has opened until peace begins to erode.

The internet has dramatically accelerated this reality. What once required a priest, a shrine, or a cultural lineage now arrives through a screen. Occult practices have been democratized, simplified, and sanitized. They are presented not as religion, but as tools; not as worship, but as self-care; not as devotion, but as personal growth. The danger is not only that these practices exist, but that they are framed as spiritually neutral, as though a believer can engage them without consequence. In this way, *Engineered Spirituality* rarely pushes people to curse Christ. It simply trains them to seek comfort, guidance, and power without Christ as their anchor.

By biblical definition, many who engage these practices are participating in what Scripture identifies as sorcery, even if they would never accept the label. Scripture defines sorcery not primarily by intention, but by source and function. Seeking spiritual knowledge, protection, power, or guidance apart from God, through intermediaries, symbols, energies, or rituals, places a person within a system that competes with the lordship of Christ. Pastoral wisdom, however, requires discernment here. Not everyone who touches these practices touches them with the same heart. Some pursue control. Others stumble through ignorance. Many are not rebels or predators, but wounded people attempting to satisfy spiritual hunger with substitutes that cannot heal.

This is where the Church's posture matters deeply.

Alongside widespread occult exposure, I have witnessed another phenomenon rise with equal force: accusation. Some of the most compelling evidence of Christ's dominion comes through the testimonies of men and women who were once deeply embedded in occult systems. Supported by firsthand accounts from trusted colleagues, some former Vodou priests themselves, these testimonies stand as undeniable proof of Christ's power. These individuals come from Haiti, across Africa, and throughout the United States. They were once sorcerers, high-ranking Vodou practitioners, former Satanists, mediums, and ritual specialists. Today, they preach Christ with clarity and conviction.

I have had the privilege of knowing some of them personally. Listening as they recount the rituals they performed, the spiritual authorities they once served, and the very real power they once wielded is both sobering and faith-building. Their stories leave no doubt that spiritual conflict is real. But their testimony does not end with conversion.

Almost without exception, they describe the pain they encountered inside the Church they ran to for refuge. Instead of immediate embrace, many were met with suspicion. Instead of shepherding, they encountered distance. Some were openly accused of being spies or spiritual plants. Fear shaped the response of believers who did not know how to interpret redemption that emerged from such darkness. The result was isolation. They were treated as risks rather than as wounded soldiers coming home.

They consistently testify that, if it had not been for the unmistakable grace of God that drew them out, the rejection they experienced inside the Church could have driven them back into the familiar, yet deadly, systems they had escaped. This is a sobering truth. When fear governs the Church, restoration becomes fragile.

At the same time, a culture of suspicion has intensified in many Caribbean and African contexts. Accusations of sorcery now travel quickly and with little restraint. Families fracture under suspicion. In-laws accuse one another. Pastors accuse members. Members accuse prophets. What once passed as discernment has often devolved into fear-driven labeling. The word sorcerer becomes both explanation and weapon. Once spoken, it stains reputations, destroys trust, and ignites conflicts that far outlive the original issue.

This is not evidence of spiritual strength. It is evidence of spiritual anxiety. When *Engineered Spirituality* saturates a culture, people become spiritually exposed without being spiritually formed. They sense the presence of unseen forces but lack the clarity to interpret them through Christ. Fear replaces wisdom. Suspicion replaces shepherding. Naming an enemy feels easier than walking someone patiently through healing, repentance, deliverance, and restoration.

Pastoral correction must begin here. The Church is not called to deny spiritual reality, nor to dramatize it. It is called to interpret reality through the finished work of Christ. True discernment restores proportion. It names danger without multiplying fear. It confronts darkness without reproducing its methods. Where *Engineered Spirituality* trains people to react, the Gospel trains them to remain grounded.

To understand the full danger of an atmosphere that normalizes compromise while breeding accusation, we must look back to a moment in Scripture when idolatry hid itself within sacred space. Just as our age is thick with invisible influence, there was a time when Israel spoke the language of covenant while practicing the rituals of seduction. The reign of King Josiah reveals what happens when holiness is breached, and how restoration begins when hidden compromise is brought into the light.

CHAPTER 7

WHEN HOLINESS IS BREACHED

Fear Attacks the Church from Within

When spiritual compromise becomes normalized, it rarely announces itself as rebellion. It settles quietly into sacred space, adopts familiar language, and learns to coexist with worship. After examining how Engineered Spirituality shapes the atmosphere of the modern Church, we must look backward to understand how deeply this pattern runs. Long before Paul confronted infiltration within the early Christian communities, King Josiah faced a strikingly similar tragedy in Judah, one that reveals how corruption survives not by opposing God openly, but by living comfortably alongside devotion.

Judah had not abandoned Yahweh. The people still claimed loyalty. They still gathered at the Temple. The rituals of the covenant continued uninterrupted. Yet beneath the language of worship, corruption had taken root. It did not enter through open defiance, but through routine, tradition, and the gradual dulling of spiritual sight. What was familiar went unquestioned. What was inherited went unexamined. Holiness was assumed rather than discerned.

Inside the Temple itself stood altars to Baal. Asherah poles rose within sacred courts. Astral symbols were painted on walls consecrated to the

Lord. Shrine prostitutes occupied chambers built for priestly service. Child sacrifice occurred within walking distance of the sanctuary (2 Kings 23:4–7, 10–12). Judah had not lost belief; it had lost discernment. This is how spirits of authority, domination, and false liberation operate. They normalize what God never approved, disguise compromise as strength, and occupy the very spaces where true worship should reign. Even Josiah, faithful, sincere, and devoted, could not see the corruption until Scripture exposed it.

When the Book of the Law was rediscovered and read aloud, Josiah tore his garments (2 Kings 22:8–13). The words of God shattered the illusion of holiness he had inherited. In that moment, he realized he had been standing inside a defiled system. This did not mean Josiah himself was corrupt. It meant the structure he inherited was spiritually diseased. A sincere heart can function within a polluted environment without recognizing its condition. A leader can love God deeply and still minister among altars that no one has yet named. What Josiah experienced is what many leaders quietly face today.

The idols of Josiah's time were carved and visible. The idols of our time are clothed in religious language. They appear as prophetic theatrics, fear-driven authority, ancestral spirituality reframed as identity, traditions elevated above Scripture, and suspicion masquerading as discernment. The symbols have changed, but the spirits behind them have not. What Josiah dismantled physically, Paul confronted doctrinally. What Paul exposed theologically, modern leaders must now confront spiritually.

Josiah was righteous, yet the Temple was infiltrated. Paul was faithful, yet his congregations were manipulated. Many pastors today love God sincerely, yet minister within systems weakened by fear, superstition, and confusion. This reality does not condemn leaders; it clarifies their assignment. Josiah needed Scripture to uncover hidden altars. Paul needed revelation to confront counterfeit authority. We need the Holy Spirit to cleanse the structures we have inherited.

Josiah's story teaches that worship can coexist with corruption when no one examines the foundation. Paul's letters teach that spiritual authority can be imitated when leaders fail to discern the spirit behind the manifestation. Scripture warns that Satan can disguise himself as an angel of light, and that his servants can appear as servants of righteousness (2 Corinthians 11:13–15). Together, these warnings reveal a sobering truth: corruption thrives quietly when fear replaces discernment and when false liberation replaces truth. If idols could live inside the Temple unnoticed, and if false apostles could infiltrate Paul's churches undetected, humility demands that we ask where compromise may be hiding in our sacred spaces today.

Josiah was a God-fearing king, but he was also the son of a nation spiritually compromised long before he ascended the throne. His father, Amon, and his grandfather, Manasseh, did not merely introduce idolatry; they reshaped Judah's spiritual identity. For more than fifty years, Baal worship, Asherah devotion, and astral practices were woven into the language of the covenant. The people learned to speak holiness while practicing mixture. Faith sounded intact, but it was animated by another spirit.

The priests suffered from the same blindness. Formed under idolatrous kings, they spoke the language of covenant while carrying out rituals shaped by Baal. Their incense rose from the right altar, but with corrupted hearts. Their sacrifices kept familiar forms, yet lacked the holiness Yahweh required. Until Scripture was found again, they could no longer tell the sacred from the seductive. What had become normal was no longer seen for what it truly was.

Josiah's awakening was so violent because Scripture cut through generations of mixture. What appeared sacred was revealed as compromised. Light separated darkness. The people had forgotten what holiness looked like and therefore could not recognize its absence. This is the danger of prolonged exposure to *Engineered Spirituality*: when compromise becomes familiar, holiness feels extreme.

This danger is not confined to history. A colleague pastor once shared with me a sobering incident that unfolded within his own congregation. Following a misunderstanding over a sermon that displeased a church member, someone secretly placed a brown bag beneath a pew. Inside were objects that appeared to be witchcraft fetishes. The intention was clear, not devotion, but intimidation. When the bag was discovered, fear spread rapidly. Panic took hold. Church leaders were shaken. The atmosphere of worship was instantly replaced with suspicion and alarm.

Nothing supernatural needed to occur for damage to be done. The mere suggestion of occult presence was enough to destabilize the community. Fear accomplished what no altar ever could. This is how breached holiness manifests in modern spaces. When fear is allowed to interpret reality, the sanctuary itself becomes vulnerable. What should have been handled with discernment and calm authority was instead absorbed as threat, revealing how quickly sacred spaces can be psychologically invaded when fear replaces confidence in Christ.

Josiah's reforms reveal more than historical idolatry. They expose a system shaped by political power, cultural blending, generational compromise, and spiritual forces skilled at hiding beneath worship language. It produced people who felt spiritual without becoming holy, devoted without transformation, religious without reverence. The Temple still stood, but its atmosphere had changed.

We must now move from the historical Temple to the modern pew. When a system becomes spiritually diseased, the battle shifts from abstract doctrine to lived atmosphere. What begins as external pressure eventually seeks a voice within the sanctuary. Peace is disrupted. Trust erodes. Fear enters quietly and begins to interpret reality. A place meant for rest becomes a site of unseen invasion.

It is here, inside the congregation, among sincere believers, that fear begins its most destructive work. We now turn to what happens when fear no longer waits outside the Church, but begins attacking it from within.

WHEN FEAR ATTACKS THE CHURCH FROM WITHIN

What competes with the Gospel today is not always open disbelief, but convenient spirituality, practices that appear modern and harmless while quietly recycling ancient deceptions by offering direction without relationship and healing without surrender. After witnessing how holiness was breached within the Temple during Josiah's reign, we now face a more unsettling reality: fear no longer waits outside sacred spaces. It enters with the people who carry it. And once inside, it begins to speak.

This is where the next battle emerges. As modern mysticism rose around us, confident, polished, and wrapped in soft promises, I began noticing something I had not fully understood before. People were not pursuing these practices because they hated God. Many were pursuing them because they were wounded, tired souls searching for meaning in a world that kept robbing them of it. What I did not yet grasp was this: storms that form outside the Church do not always remain at the door. Eventually, they follow the people who carry them inside.

I remember a young woman who came to me deeply shaken, struggling to articulate what had happened to her. She spoke cautiously, as though even describing the experience might invite its return. What began felt innocent. A friend had given her tarot cards as a gift, no darkness, no warning, only curiosity. She handled them casually, studied the images, and treated the experience as harmless exploration.

Soon after, something changed. She began noticing shadows moving at flash speed, mostly in her peripheral vision, quick enough to startle her, gone before she could focus. At first, she dismissed them as fatigue or imagination. But they returned, accompanied by an unease she could not explain, a pressure that felt external rather than emotional.

As her engagement with the cards continued, the experience intensified. The images no longer felt like ink on paper. She described impressions forming in her mind, ideas arriving uninvited, carrying an urgency that did not feel like her own thoughts. What began as curiosity crossed into intrusion. Something felt imposed rather than chosen.

Then she described the moment that terrified her most. She felt as though something entered her, an inward invasion she could not control. A voice began speaking inside her mind, distinct from her inner dialogue. At times, her mouth twisted involuntarily, pulling to one side, as though her body no longer fully obeyed her will. She was conscious, aware, and frightened, trapped between fear and confusion as control slipped away.

I listened carefully, not to dramatize her experience, but to understand it. No experience, spiritual or otherwise, that fragments a person's sense of self, steals peace, or interferes with bodily control should ever be normalized. What struck me most was not the imagery she described, but her vulnerability. She was not seeking darkness. She was seeking meaning, connection, and understanding. What she encountered instead crossed boundaries that should never be crossed.

Her story stands as a sober reminder that when the mind is opened without discernment or protection, what enters can overwhelm rather than enlighten.

I once believed the sanctuary would be a refuge, a place where the weary could breathe again. But people rarely arrive with empty hands. They come carrying hunger and fear. They bring wounds they cannot name, dreams they cannot interpret, memories that refuse to stay buried, and spiritual residues inherited long before they could choose their own path. These invisible histories do not remain silent. They lift hands in worship while trembling beneath the surface. They kneel in prayer while whispers linger beneath their breath. And when truth does not confront them, fear learns to speak louder than faith.

It was inside the Church I loved that I learned a lesson no seminary ever taught me: fear does not only haunt individuals; it seeps into the atmosphere of a congregation. Once fear enters the house of God, it finds a voice. It questions motives, bends perceptions, reshapes relationships, and misinterprets the very work God is trying to heal. That was the moment I stepped into without knowing it, the moment when fear began speaking from within the Church. Nothing about my calling, my prayer life, or my understanding of spiritual conflict would ever be the same.

When I opened the doors of Global Reach Evangelical Missionary Church in 2009, I did not imagine leading a congregation through a war with fear. My vision was simple: to build a place of hope, community, and spiritual direction for immigrant families, young adults, and long-time believers. After nearly two decades in Baptist contexts and years shaped by Pentecostal environments, I felt prepared. I imagined joyful worship, prayer, fellowship, and steady growth. But almost immediately, that expectation fractured.

People came ready to worship, yet carried heaviness they could not explain. Moods shifted without warning. Some grew uneasy when prayer intensified. Others shut down at the reading of Scripture. At first, I assumed it was cultural stress, emotional strain, or the weight of diaspora life. But beneath the surface, something else was moving, quiet, persistent, and deeply unsettling.

I tried community. Shared meals. Familiar language. Stories of home. These moments brought warmth, but beneath them I sensed another presence, something that did not shout but breathed, something that fed on fear. It surfaced in anxieties, reacted to prayer, shaped behavior, and whispered through memories people could not interpret. I realized this was not trauma alone. It bore the signature of inheritance, something passed down, not chosen, shaping spiritual vulnerability long before conscious belief was formed.

Inside GREMC, I encountered realities outside every framework I had learned. People lifted hands in worship while carrying invisible agreements. Others resisted prayer without knowing why. Scripture stirred tears, agitation, or collapse. These reactions were not emotionalism or culture shock. They were manifestations of inherited spiritual residue. God had not placed me there to entertain or condemn, but to help people untangle shadows that had followed them into the sanctuary.

As I stepped deeper into this calling, I felt the limits of my preparation. I could preach, teach, and counsel, but I could not yet diagnose spiritual residue disguised as habit, trauma, or personality. I knew how to guide people through loss and conflict, but not how to help someone fight a battle they inherited but never invited. I felt like a surgeon holding the wrong instruments. Yet this was where God began teaching me again, through experience, revelation, and the lives entrusted to me.

I listened to former *houngans* and *mambos*, people who understood Vodou not academically but experientially. They spoke of rituals as contracts, of spiritual authorities governing identity, of bondage masquerading as personality, of manifestations mistaken for anxiety or mood. Their stories did not frighten me; they clarified what I was already witnessing. Scripture began speaking louder, especially passages I once skimmed without urgency. The seven churches of Revelation suddenly became a mirror rather than a metaphor.

Transitioning from occult-shaped environments into the life of the Church is far more complex than many recognize. People do not simply leave old worlds behind; they enter new ones carrying shame, fear, stigma, and unresolved conflict. The Church becomes both refuge and battlefield. Many fear judgment if their past is known. Others feel spiritually unclean without accusation. Some struggle to trust leadership after manipulation. Many must relearn what spirituality truly means. Loving Jesus does not immediately erase fear of His people.

Digital spirituality has made occult exposure easier to encounter and harder to recognize. Practices once tied to formal ritual spaces are now repackaged as wellness, guidance, or personal growth, often reaching wounded people before they understand the spiritual cost. In this environment, many are trained to seek comfort, direction, and power without Christ as their anchor.

As I began teaching these truths, fear surfaced. Some withdrew. Others grew nervous. Some trembled, not resisting truth, but terrified by it. Truth awakened them, and fear awakened with it. Suspicion replaced discernment. Normal frustrations became spiritual threats. Without intending to, I had fed fear. Truth without grounding becomes a storm. Revelation without Christ becomes a burden.

So, I changed course. I moved teaching into Bible study, then into smaller gatherings, then into private counsel. People did not need more information about demons. They needed a deeper revelation of Christ.

Over time, I learned an uncomfortable truth: there are witches in the Church. Not always malicious. Not always aware. Some come seeking freedom. Some carry attachments from past environments. This is not accusation; it is reality. Modern witchcraft often enters through curiosity, trauma, digital influence, or relationships. Deliverance is not spectacle. Collapse may be a beginning, but never the end. True deliverance requires discipleship, repentance, healing, accountability, and time.

Oppression rarely begins with ritual. It begins with a door, an agreement, a vulnerability, a permission. Ancestral covenants linger. Cultural traditions become bridges. Trusted objects become doorways. Trauma whispers lies. Unforgiveness anchors pain. Digital spirituality disciples without consent. Deliverance is not merely expelling spirits; it is untangling a life.

When fear enters the Church and begins to speak, it demands more than authority to silence it. It demands formation. Leadership alignment determines whether a sanctuary becomes refuge or battlefield. Accusation does not arise in a vacuum; it forms where atmosphere and leadership intersect.

To lead faithfully in this contested space, we must learn to distinguish voices, those called, those formed, those self-appointed, and those dangerous. We now turn to examine the many faces of spiritual leadership and the authority they produce.

THE MANY FACES OF LEADERSHIP: CALLED, FORMED, AND DANGEROUS

At this stage, ecclesiastical accusation can no longer be understood merely as a breakdown in relationships. It must be recognized as a deeper crisis of leadership formation, shaped by fear, misused authority, and an identity that has not been honestly examined. Accusation does not thrive only because people are wounded. It thrives when leadership lacks formation, when authority is assumed rather than received, and when fear is allowed to govern the atmosphere of the Church.

The posture of a leader determines whether accusation withers or finds room to grow.

Every church has leadership. Every church has atmosphere. But when the wrong atmosphere meets the wrong kind of leadership, accusation begins to breathe. It does not appear suddenly; it accumulates. Fear softens the soil, confusion waters it, suspicion takes root, and wounded people unknowingly fertilize it. Then an unformed or unhealthy leader gives it permission. What appears to be a single moment of conflict is often the final stage of a process that has been quietly unfolding for months, sometimes for years.

Accusation thrives where leadership is weak, prideful, unhealed, defensive, or divided. It survives on silence, grows through misunderstanding, and matures wherever spiritual discernment is replaced by emotional reaction. Accusation does not rise in a vacuum. It forms within the atmosphere a congregation inhabits, an atmosphere shaped by fear, confusion, unresolved pain, and spiritual pressure. Leadership, more than any other influence, determines whether that atmosphere becomes a place of healing or a breeding ground for ecclesiastical attack.

Called and Formed Leaders

Called leaders often become targets of accusation precisely because they carry the burden of God rather than the approval of people. Their obedience irritates spiritual forces that prefer the Church to remain bound. Their transparency disturbs those who have learned to survive by appearance. Their compassion exposes the coldness others have learned to call wisdom. A called leader's integrity becomes a mirror, and mirrors tend to trouble those who do not want to face what remains wounded within them. Many accusations against called leaders do not begin with evidence, but with discomfort, the unease that arises when someone refuses to perform, manipulate, or conceal.

Theologically formed leaders also become targets, especially when teaching touches generational wounds. In communities shaped by trauma, superstition, or syncretism, correction can feel indistinguishable from control. What was intended to heal is interpreted as an attack. Fear begins whispering that the leader is judgmental, disconnected, or unsafe. Over time, even faithful teaching becomes filtered through unresolved pain. Accusation rarely begins as a deliberate lie. More often, it begins as misinterpretation, a wounded heart attempting to protect itself from the discomfort of truth. Yet the most volatile form of accusation emerges when authority is assumed rather than received.

Self-Appointed and Unsubmitted Leaders

Self-appointed leadership must therefore be addressed carefully. Not all self-appointed leadership is destructive. Many churches and organizations are born through leaders who step forward before formal structures exist. In its healthier form, self-appointment arises from perceived calling, unmet need, or innovative vision. Scripture offers examples of such initiative exercised under God's authority rather than personal ambition, as seen in Nehemiah, whose leadership was birthed in prayer, submission, and communal discernment rather than self-promotion (Nehemiah 1:3–11; 2:11–18). When self-appointed leadership remains teachable and submitted to formation, it functions as a transitional stage rather than a permanent claim to authority.

There is, however, another form of self-appointed leadership, one that does not emerge from vision, but from dissatisfaction. This leader does not need a pulpit to cause spiritual damage; influence alone is sufficient. Scripture warns of leaders who rise through grievance rather than calling, such as Absalom, who positioned himself by exploiting unmet expectations, flattering the discontented, and quietly "stealing the hearts of the people" (2 Samuel 15:1–6). This form of leadership emerges when zeal is present, but submission is absent. Unsubmitted zeal is never neutral. It produces quiet rebellion or public accusation (Numbers 16:1–3; Jude 1:11).

These leaders arise where affirmation outpaces discipleship, where gifting matures faster than character, and where wounded identity seeks validation rather than surrender. They gather people around shared grievances instead of common obedience. They do not build altars; they build audiences. They do not submit to authority; they compete with it. Scripture repeatedly warns that authority assumed rather than received leads to exposure and loss rather than legitimacy, as seen in Saul's unauthorized actions and in the sons of Sceva's attempt to exercise borrowed spiritual authority (1 Samuel 13:8–14; Acts 19:13–16). Left unformed and unchecked, this kind of self-appointed leadership often reproduces suspicion, division, and spiritual harm.

Opportunistic and Charismatic Leaders

Opportunistic leaders understand something dangerous: fear makes people vulnerable. They recognize that accusation spreads most quickly in wounded environments, and they exploit that vulnerability to build platforms. Their concerns sound pastoral, their critiques sound spiritual, their warnings feel urgent, yet beneath the surface lies a hunger for power. Accusation becomes their currency, fear their strategy, and division their harvest. Like Absalom standing at the gate, they whisper to wounded people, promising better leadership that never truly materializes.

Charismatic leaders become another open door when charisma replaces character. Such leaders draw crowds and generate momentum, yet when grounding is absent, emotion begins leading in the place of the Holy Spirit. Congregations then misinterpret spiritual conflict as personal conflict. Giftedness is exalted above submission, and accountability is reframed as persecution. The enemy favors charismatic atmospheres without structure because reaction replaces discernment, and intensity substitutes for truth. Even healthy charismatic leadership, however, can awaken resistance.

Transformational and Relational Leaders

Transformational leaders often face accusation precisely because transformation threatens comfortable dysfunction. Whenever leaders confront generational bondage or spiritual residue, accusation rises. Scripture reflects this pattern repeatedly. Moses faced accusation when deliverance began. Josiah encountered resistance when reform exposed mixture. Nehemiah endured slander when rebuilding threatened corrupt comfort. Accusation does not always arise because a leader is wrong, but because darkness resists exposure.

Even within legitimate leadership, different styles carry distinct vulnerabilities, and the enemy exploits those vulnerabilities with precision. Visionary leaders are targeted because they live in tomorrow while others remain anchored in yesterday. Vision arrives before readiness, and stretching feels like threat. Whispers begin: the leader is moving too fast, does not care, is reckless, or is prideful.

Servant leaders are targeted because humility is mistaken for weakness. Compassion is misread as inconsistency. Kindness is interpreted as a lack of authority. Crisis leaders are targeted because crisis exposes immaturity; they must make difficult decisions while others panic. Their urgency is misinterpreted as control, and their calm as coldness. Mentor leaders are targeted because close investment is easily misunderstood. Fear may mistake intentional formation for favoritism. Innovative leaders may also face resistance because new approaches can unsettle what feels familiar. To some, innovation feels too fast; to others, it feels risky; and to those deeply attached to tradition, it can feel like betrayal.

Persecuting and Dangerous Leaders

Persecuting leaders, the most dangerous of all, do not merely fall into accusation; they cultivate it. They weaponize Scripture, shame the vulnerable, spiritualize pride, and train followers to imitate suspicion. Under their influence, accusation becomes culture, and entire congregations can burn beneath the authority of a single destructive voice.

The antidote to accusation is not stronger leadership in the worldly sense; it is formed leadership. The leader God is still forming is the leader least usable by the spirit of accusation. Accusation finds no resting place in a heart that is genuinely surrendered. Formed leaders react less and trust more. They do not interpret conflict as threat. They do not need to win every moment. They do not feed suspicion to protect their image. Accusation begins to lose oxygen when leaders are governed by obedience rather than insecurity.

Unauthorized and Misaligned Authority

Conversely, the spiritual realm exploits leaders operating outside their calling. Whenever a leader ministers through ambition, pressure, or identity instability, the enemy exploits the gap. A teacher striving to function as a prophet, or a pastor chasing apostolic status, creates vulnerability. Scripture's warning through the sons of Sceva still speaks: authority cannot be borrowed, and spiritual reality does not respect imitation. Leaders without calling often imitate others and build ministries to heal personal wounds. When identity is unstable, counterfeit identity becomes attractive.

Not every vision is divine. Some are born from comparison, pressure, or unresolved trauma. When vision does not originate with God, the foundation becomes engineered, and collapse becomes inevitable. Scripture repeatedly warns against unauthorized authority, including kings who acted beyond their assignment. Saul forced a sacrifice he had no right to offer. Uzziah entered the Temple to burn incense and was judged for assuming priestly authority that did not belong to him (1 Samuel 13:8–14; 2 Chronicles 26:16–21). The spiritual realm recognizes authentic authority instantly, and counterfeit authority even faster. When leaders minister from desire rather than obedience, they open doors without covering.

In many cases, persistent struggle reveals misalignment more than external attack. Misalignment becomes the seedbed for ecclesiastical accusation through disappointment, whispering, and hidden resentment. Unauthorized leadership often produces unauthorized messages: truth without grace, correction without compassion, confrontation without healing.

Spiritual authority cannot be copied. It grows through brokenness, intimacy, and obedience. Ministries birthed through enthusiasm rather than divine instruction often collapse because God does not protect what He never birthed. Unauthorized authority, as seen in Saul, Uzziah, and Diotrephes, becomes an open door to deception. Staged manifestations and theatrical deliverance often signal authority assumed rather than received. The enemy favors unassigned leaders because they are easily manipulated, allowing accusation to spread and instability to become normal.

The real victims are wounded believers, seekers, and new converts who cannot distinguish counterfeit authority from genuine care. Accusation wounds the sheep more than it wounds the shepherds. Yet even here, God's purpose is not shame. God exposes misalignment to rescue leaders, not to destroy them. Alignment restores protection. Obedience restores clarity. Accountability restores safety. Ecclesiastical accusation loses power when leaders return to the voice that called them in the first place.

The Leadership of Speech

While the character and alignment of a leader form the foundation of authority, the most potent tool entrusted to them, and the most dangerous when mishandled, is speech. Accusation may begin in the heart, but it finds life through the mouth. Words do more than communicate; they consecrate. They can heal or harm, liberate or bind, restore order or summon chaos. In environments already shaped by fear, the tongue becomes a spiritual instrument capable of either reestablishing peace or intensifying destruction.

The Church cannot address ecclesiastical accusation without confronting how language itself is used, weaponized, and spiritualized. What was designed for worship is often repurposed for manipulation. What should release life is redirected to sow fear. Authority is reinforced or undermined not only by action, but by speech, repeated, endorsed, and normalized. To understand how accusation gains momentum and why words carry such spiritual consequence, attention must now turn to the altar that forms every atmosphere long before actions follow: the tongue itself.

WHEN THE TONGUE BECOMES AN ALTAR

Long before accusation becomes a movement, it becomes language. Long before division manifests publicly, it is rehearsed privately. The tongue is the most underestimated spiritual instrument in the Church, not because Scripture is unclear about its power, but because familiarity has dulled our fear of God where speech is concerned. We speak as though words are neutral, forgetting that Scripture treats them as vessels. Jesus taught that words reveal the heart and that people will give account for careless speech (Matthew 12:34–37). James warned that words can ignite entire forests (James 3:5–6). Proverbs declares that life and death travel through the tongue (Proverbs 18:21). Yet in practice, we often speak carelessly while praying fervently, unaware that we are dismantling with language what we ask God to heal through prayer.

In spiritually charged environments, words do more than describe reality; they shape it. What is spoken repeatedly becomes normalized. What is normalized becomes defended. And what is defended eventually becomes doctrine. Spiritual climates are rarely formed by sermons alone. They are shaped by conversations, by whispers in hallways, exchanges in prayer circles, leadership discussions, and digital messages passed quietly from person to person.

This is where a subtle and dangerous form of sorcery can enter the Church, not through candles or rituals, but through speech that manipulates rather than heals, labels rather than shepherds, and intimidates rather than restores. It does not announce itself as witchcraft. It calls itself discernment.

Biblically, sorcery is not limited to theatrics; it is also concerned with source, intent, and the attempt to influence spiritual realities apart from submission to God. Whenever language is used to control rather than serve, to dominate rather than protect, or to instill fear rather than faith, it crosses a spiritual boundary. Words can begin functioning like spells, not because they are mystical, but because they are coercive.

This occurs when phrases such as "God showed me," "The Lord told me," or "I discerned a spirit" are used not to invite accountability, but to silence dialogue. Once spoken, such language becomes a shield. It discourages questions, bypasses process, and creates intimidation rather than clarity. The listener is no longer responding to a person, but to a presumed divine verdict. This is not prophecy; it is pressure clothed in reverence.

When this language circulates unchecked, fear is sanctified and silence is mistaken for submission. The tongue becomes an altar, not of worship, but of influence, where words are offered to shape perception, secure loyalty, and eliminate opposition. No blood is spilled, yet reputations bleed.

No demon is named, yet bondage multiplies. And because the language sounds spiritual, it often escapes challenge.

One of the most dangerous confusions in the Church is the blending of gossip with intercession. Gossip speaks about people without responsibility; intercession speaks for people with burden. Yet many prayer gatherings have become sanctuaries for sanctified rumor. Conversations begin with concern and end with contamination. "We need to pray for…" becomes a socially acceptable way to release suspicion into the atmosphere.

Once released, words do not remain idle. They travel. They recruit agreement. They shape assumptions. When enough people agree with a suspicion, it begins to feel like confirmation. This is how accusation gains momentum without evidence, process, or love. Jesus warned that every idle word will be accounted for, not because God is harsh, but because words generate consequences long after the speaker has moved on (Matthew 12:36–37).

True intercession costs something. It requires restraint, humility, and trust that God can address what we cannot control. Gossip feels powerful because it offers insight without responsibility. One restores; the other rehearses. One builds covering; the other builds consensus. And the enemy prefers consensus over truth, because consensus does not require repentance, only agreement.

Words do not only affect the spirit; they imprint the soul. Fear-saturated language reshapes how people see themselves, their leaders, and even God. When sermons emphasize danger without anchoring safety in Christ, believers begin scanning their lives for threats rather than fruit. When correction is framed as exposure, vulnerability becomes unsafe. When spiritual language is used recklessly, people begin fearing discernment instead of trusting shepherding.

In such environments, suspicion is internalized. Believers question their salvation, mistrust leadership motives, and hesitate to confess struggles. The Church becomes a place of surveillance rather than sanctuary.

Slowly, spiritual sobriety gives way to spiritual paranoia. People become fluent in naming demons but illiterate in naming grace. This is not maturity; it is anxiety baptized in religious vocabulary.

One of the most destructive uses of the tongue in the Church is labeling. When people are reduced to words, witch, Jezebel, rebellious, dangerous, unsubmitted, their humanity is eclipsed. Labels simplify what requires shepherding. They shortcut discernment. They replace patience with verdicts.

Scripture reveals that even when correction is necessary, God deals with people personally and redemptively. Jesus confronted sin without stripping dignity. Paul corrected error without assassinating identity. Labeling, by contrast, freezes people in their worst moment and denies the possibility of repentance, growth, or healing. It is spiritual power exercised without love, and power without love always becomes abuse.

Words spoken without responsibility can function like curses, even when no curse is intended. They shape how communities treat individuals, how leaders are perceived, and how fear spreads. This is why Scripture repeatedly warns against reckless speech, not because words are harmless, but because they are powerful.

The remedy is not silence, but sanctification. God does not call the Church to speak less, but to speak truer. Speech surrendered to the Holy Spirit produces clarity rather than confusion, conviction rather than condemnation, and healing rather than fear. When the tongue is yielded, discernment regains its purpose: to protect without wounding, to expose without humiliating, and to correct without destroying.

Over years of ministry, I have learned that many spiritual battles are not lost through a lack of prayer, but through a lack of restrained, sanctified speech. I have watched people proclaim forty-day fasts with digital pastors while their daily conversations with family cut like knives. There is a tragic contradiction when intense spiritual discipline coexists with careless language. One cannot fast for breakthrough while simultaneously wounding others with words.

Before accusation becomes culture, it is born in private conversation. Before it becomes movement, it begins as whispered suspicion. Before it hardens into doctrine, it is rehearsed as careless speech that we mistakenly call discernment. The Church is already living with the consequences of words spoken too quickly and guarded too little. Until the holiness of speech is recovered, the cycles of conflict we have traced will continue reproducing themselves.

The climate surrounding the Church today is not neutral. Mistrust has become ordinary. Suspicion has become reflex. Leaders watch one another. Believers brace for exposure. This is not merely a communication problem; it is an era defined by accusation. This is the atmosphere in which ecclesiastical accusation becomes more than an occasional failure; it becomes a governing culture, reshaping the sanctuary into a courtroom and turning discernment into suspicion before restoration has a chance to speak.

CHAPTER 8

THE AGE OF ECCLESIASTICAL ACCUSATION

From Sanctuary to Courtroom

We are living in what can no longer be described merely as a season of disagreement, doctrinal tension, or cultural strain. We are living in an age marked not by the absence of spiritual activity, but by the dominance of accusation as a governing force within the Church. The sanctuary, once understood as a refuge of mercy, formation, and restoration, has in many places assumed the posture of a courtroom. Fear functions as prosecutor, suspicion as evidence, and spiritual language as the weapon of choice.

This shift did not happen overnight. It emerged gradually as fear displaced discernment and exposure replaced restoration. Where persecution once came from outside the Church, it now often arises from within. The adversary no longer relies primarily on violence or exclusion; suspicion alone now suffices. The result is an ecclesial environment in which leaders watch one another cautiously, believers brace for judgment, and silence is mistaken for wisdom. This posture becomes normalized not because truth has disappeared, but because interpretation has been hijacked by fear.

Scripture names this pattern clearly. Satan is identified not first by force, but by speech: "the accuser of our brethren," accusing them day and night (Revelation 12:10). When accusation could no longer stand in the courts of heaven, it found fertile ground in earthly spaces. And when the Church lost confidence in Christ as Advocate, she slowly assumed the role of prosecutor.

How Accusation Forms

Accusation rarely begins with malice. More often, it begins with discomfort. An experience is felt but not interpreted. Fear rushes in to explain what formation has not prepared the believer to discern. Sensation precedes reflection. Interpretation follows without testing. Agreement forms. Only then does accusation surface.

This is the defining pattern of this age: experience first, explanation second, accusation third.

When spiritual literacy weakens, people may still encounter conviction, authority, clarity, and holiness, but they often lack language to interpret them rightly. Discomfort becomes evidence. Exposure becomes threat. What should invite self-examination instead redirects attention outward. The question shifts quietly from *What is God revealing in me?* to *What was done to me?* And once that shift occurs, accusation has already begun its work.

The Age of Ecclesiastical Accusation is sustained not by increased evil, but by misdirected fear. Authority is judged by sensation rather than fruit. Leaders are evaluated by emotional reaction rather than character. Stability is mistrusted. Peace becomes suspect. Holiness unsettles what remains unhealed, and rather than naming the wound, fear assigns blame.

To understand why this pattern has intensified in our time, we must examine how theological authority itself has been quietly reconfigured.

Theological Authority in an Age of Accusation

The age of ecclesiastical accusation has altered not only how believers speak to one another, but also who is granted theological authority and why. As confidence in inherited structures weakens, alternative sources of legitimacy rush in to fill the vacuum. These figures do not emerge at random; they arise from identifiable pressures: fear, disappointment, exposure culture, and the fragmentation of trust. Together, they represent overlapping tendencies now exerting significant influence within and around the Church.

Shifting Sources of Authority

The first group may be described as theologian-evangelists whose authority is rooted less in formal theological education than in lived spiritual rupture. Many are former Vodou priests or priestesses, occult practitioners, Satanists, Freemasons, New Age adherents, or atheists whose conversions are dramatic and publicly narrated. Their credibility flows from testimony. Having crossed visible spiritual boundaries, they are seen as possessing insider knowledge of both darkness and deliverance. This form of authority can be powerful because it comes through lived experience rather than institutional credentialing. In many Christian communities, especially in Pentecostal and postcolonial contexts, such experiential authority can become doctrinally persuasive, even when it functions without sustained communal discernment or theological accountability.

Alongside this group stands a second tendency that functions differently but often overlaps in influence. These figures display impressive fluency in biblical language. They quote Scripture rapidly, move quickly across texts, and construct arguments that appear airtight, especially to believers who lack deeper biblical grounding. Yet their theology is frequently detached from ecclesial accountability, historical interpretation, and pastoral patience. Scripture is treated as though it can be handled apart from the wider wisdom of the Church, the slow work of formation, and the humility required by spiritual leadership. Such approaches rarely produce maturity. Instead, they can foster fragmentation, suspicion, and doctrinal instability. In an accusatory age, this style of theology thrives because it equips believers not to be formed, but to expose, turning Scripture into a weapon rather than a means of communion.

A third pattern arises less from confrontation than from disappointment. Many believers, disillusioned with their local congregations or frustrated by pastors they perceive as slow, traditional, or insufficiently responsive, seek formation elsewhere. Digital platforms, artificial intelligence, and social media now offer immediate answers, curated insights, and endless theological content. Authority migrates from embodied community to networked platforms, where learning often occurs without submission and knowledge without relationship. Compared with algorithmic efficiency, the slow rhythms of pastoral teaching, rooted in repetition, worship, and incremental discipleship, can appear outdated. Over time, formation becomes detached from place, and theology becomes a matter of consumption rather than covenant.

Accusation, Importation, and Lived Consequences

A fourth tendency must also be named, though it requires careful distinction and pastoral restraint. In recent decades, broader cultural movements, particularly those centered on gender, sexuality, race, and social power, have increasingly pressed against ecclesial boundaries, often seeking theological validation or institutional recognition within the Church. This includes women advocating for expanded roles in leadership, as well as ideological movements such as LGBTQ activism and Black Lives Matter, each carrying its own moral vocabulary, narratives of justice, and claims to authority. Within ecclesial life, these dynamics are often experienced less as dialogue and more as pressure. In an atmosphere already shaped by accusation, disagreement is easily reframed as exclusion, silence as violence, and theological hesitation as moral failure. What emerges is not merely debate over doctrine, but contestation over who has the right to define faithfulness itself.

In such a climate, even those sincerely called by God are not immune to entanglement.

The problem is not always rebellion against faith, but the uncritical importation of interpretive lenses that quietly reshape authority, identity, and discernment. Certain ideologies and movements that originated within specific Western historical conditions did not remain confined to their original settings. As they traveled across cultures, they were often detached from the legal, social, and theological contexts that gave them meaning. Once transplanted, they can cease to function as instruments of healing or justice and instead become lenses of suspicion, rivalry, and accusation within communities they were never designed to govern.

I observed this dynamic firsthand in January 2026 during a widely viewed debate on the YouTube channel Echo Bleu. The host, Joana Cesar, moderated a tense exchange between two respected Christian leaders, Apostle Jeff and Apostle Esther Pierre. Jeff argued that women should not serve as pastors or apostles, while Esther contended with equal conviction that women are called to preach, teach, and lead within the Church. Both presented their cases with theological sophistication and emotional force. At one point, Esther turned directly to the camera and urged women viewers to "open their eyes" and claim their rightful place in ecclesiastical leadership. The exchange was compelling, yet it also revealed how quickly theological disagreement can shift into public accusation, summoning entire groups to take sides rather than inviting patient discernment.

A similar pattern emerged thousands of miles away in Abidjan, Côte d'Ivoire, during a live televised program titled "Point d'Accord." A husband contacted the show's hosts, Pastor Tumou and Roland Sambo, seeking help for a marriage unraveling under spiritual strain. His wife, who had become a pastor in a church they founded together, Église Paix et Amour, had begun referring to him publicly as "my son" and "one of my members." She explained that the conflict arose because he refused to submit to her pastoral authority.

According to her, she now stood as his supreme spiritual authority, appointed to shepherd and govern him, and his resistance constituted rebellion not only against her but against God. She went further, claiming divine revelation that God would take his life if he continued to resist. What began as a conversation about calling and leadership devolved into a climate of fear, accusation, and spiritual coercion, fracturing marital trust and violating social, cultural, and theological boundaries.

The *Echo Bleu* channel later aired another episode revealing yet another face of this age of accusation. It featured a figure known online as Zamex, a vocal Jesus mythicist who appeared with Bible in hand, confidently asserting that Jesus Christ was not a historical person, was never born, and was never foretold by any prophet. By selectively quoting Scripture, he presented his claims as biblically grounded while dismissing centuries of historical and Christian witness. Similar arguments circulate widely in the United States, where proponents of the Christ Myth Theory use the Bible itself as a weapon against Christianity, often without engaging serious historical method or responsible theological interpretation.

The Vacuum of Silence and the Rise of Testimony

Theorists who operate without theological accountability or historical discipline can wield disproportionate influence over the public imagination. Their impact is not merely intellectual; it is formative. By presenting fragments of Scripture, selective history, or emotionally charged narratives as "hidden truth," they cultivate confusion where discernment once belonged. They destabilize trust in authority without offering a credible alternative, leaving entire generations suspicious of inherited structures. Once trust collapses, interpretation becomes radically individual, intuition replaces communal wisdom, and faith is no longer received but endlessly interrogated.

These theorists also collapse complexity into accusation. Rather than teaching believers how to hold tension between text and context, faith and history, authority and humility, they reduce disagreement to moral failure. Dissenters are portrayed as blind, manipulated, or complicit. Scripture itself is weaponized, treated not as a coherent witness formed within history and community, but as a quarry of isolated verses extracted for demolition rather than formation. Digital platforms accelerate this fragmentation, rewarding certainty over wisdom and provocation over patience, shaping theological identity through exposure rather than discipleship.

The result is a generation fluent in suspicion yet impoverished in wisdom, confident in critique yet uncertain in faith. What is lost is not merely doctrine, but the capacity to discern truth without fear, authority without domination, and freedom without fragmentation.

Many pastors, theologians, and historians with deep biblical and historical training intentionally refuse to engage such theorists in public debate. Their refusal is rarely rooted in fear or intellectual incapacity, but in discernment. They recognize that these debates are often structured in bad faith, dependent on selective citation, shifting definitions, and rhetorical traps rather than shared standards of evidence. To participate is frequently to legitimize a framework that already rejects the rules required for meaningful dialogue.

Yet this principled silence carries unintended consequences. By withdrawing, credible voices leave behind a wide interpretive vacuum. Into that space step confident personalities armed with fragments of Scripture, simplified narratives, and media-savvy delivery. For audiences unfamiliar with historical method or theological formation, silence is easily mistaken for concession, and restraint misread as inability to respond. What was intended as wisdom becomes, in practice, a quiet surrender of the public square.

It is precisely within this vacuum that something remarkable has occurred. God, revealed as El Shaddai, the All-Sufficient One, has raised a different kind of witness: testimonial authorities whose legitimacy is forged not in academic halls but in lived spiritual rupture. These are former insiders, once practitioners, skeptics, or opponents, now authoritative critics of the systems they left behind. Grounded in spiritual power, authenticity, and undeniable calling, they step into arenas where theologians and historians often will not go, confronting Jesus mythicism and radical biblical skepticism that denies the historical existence of Christ, even as the unseen world trembles at the mention of His name.

These four tendencies, experiential authority, rhetorical biblicism, digital formation, and sociopolitical pressure, do not function independently. They intersect within a shared spiritual climate marked by fear, urgency, and suspicion. Together, they reveal how theological authority is being renegotiated in the contemporary Church, often outside the slow, communal processes through which discernment has historically been cultivated. Understanding these patterns is essential if the Church is to respond not with reaction or retreat, but with renewed clarity, humility, and fidelity to truth grounded in love rather than accusation.

A Narrative Diagnosis of a Hidden Ecclesial Pattern

One of the quietest, yet most revealing, ways ecclesiastical accusation is forming in our time is rarely discussed publicly. It does not erupt through sermons, Sunday school, platforms, or overt conflict. It moves quietly from one believer to another, carried through whispered interpretations of personal experience. Because it is uncomfortable and difficult to name, it is rarely addressed through discipleship. Yet I have encountered it repeatedly in pastoral ministry.

I have encountered it under different circumstances, but the description is often the same. A believer speaks of feeling weak, unsettled, or strangely disoriented after a brief handshake, an embrace, or a moment of close interaction with a spiritually grounded leader. The sensation itself is real. The damage begins not in the experience, but in the interpretation. Some describe it as "energy theft." Others conclude that the brother or sister involved must be practicing witchcraft in secret, siphoning spiritual power through touch.

I first noticed this pattern in 2002 during a conflict in a church where I served as a leader. For a season, the pastor abruptly stopped giving or receiving handshakes, not only with congregants, but even with his deacon corps. At the time, I did not know what to make of it. No explanation was given. Gossip spread quickly, like fire through dry straw, and suspicion filled the vacuum where pastoral clarity should have been.

Years later, in 2009, I observed something similar among fellow ministers. A few colleagues deliberately avoided handshakes after services with a particular brother. Eventually, I learned the reason: fear. They were afraid of feeling what they described as a sudden "zap," like a battery being discharged. Their suspicion centered on this individual, whom they quietly accused of occult involvement. Yet this man was widely respected, faithful in service, and without reproach in the community for years. Still, interpretation overtook evidence, and fear outran discernment.

It did not take long before I myself became a suspect.

Several years later, in my own church, I noticed that a young woman who had been baptized only weeks earlier hesitated to shake my hand after services. Soon after, she avoided shaking hands with my wife, Carine, with a deacon, and with my associate pastor. Her behavior was noticeable and consistent. Rather than allowing assumptions to grow, I chose to ask her directly. I wanted to understand the fear.

She explained that after certain handshakes she felt sudden weakness in her legs, so intense that she struggled to remain standing. She described the sensation as being drained of strength, as though her energy had abruptly left her body. These episodes, she said, occurred specifically after physical contact with us.

At the time, I did not know what to make of her explanation. My mind returned to earlier encounters I had witnessed over the years. One memory, in particular, surfaced with clarity. Early in my ministry, a woman had approached for prayer. As I placed my hand on her shoulder, she collapsed, began crawling on the floor, and manifested what she claimed to be a Vodou serpent spirit known as Damballah. That moment marked the beginning of my understanding that my calling would involve ministering to people with deep occult histories, though at the time, I did not yet have language for it.

Comparing these two events, separated by years, context, and circumstance, I sensed that what was happening was not something evil being transmitted, but something being exposed or disrupted. Still, I lacked a framework to explain it responsibly. Somewhere in the back of my mind, I wondered whether this was connected to spiritual authority or anointing, but I resisted forming conclusions without clarity.

That clarity came later, unexpectedly.

One day, someone sent me a video link. It showed a live radio broadcast in Haiti where a pastor and an occult practitioner had been invited to debate their beliefs. At the end of the program, the host asked them to shake hands. The occult practitioner hesitated immediately. The pastor extended his hand without hesitation. The host insisted. Reluctantly, the occult practitioner complied.

As their hands clasped, the occult practitioner's face contorted. He grimaced as if something were entering or leaving him. He tried to pull away, but the pastor held the handshake firmly. The reaction was unmistakable.

Watching this, I immediately remembered the young woman's description of her experience, the sensation of shock, burning, or sudden weakness. Without her testimony, I might have interpreted the video as a display of greater power. But because I understood the physical sensation she had described, I saw the moment differently. I was not witnessing dominance; I was witnessing exposure.

Later still, I spoke with a former occult practitioner who had since become an evangelist and was living in Queens, New York. He explained that practitioners often cultivate what they understand as a specific spiritual "vibration" to sustain their connection with spirits. According to him, the presence of a true believer can create a crushing pressure that destabilizes this cultivated field. He described it as a weight that makes it difficult to breathe or think clearly, as though the spiritual environment they depend on collapses in the presence of light.

Many former practitioners testify that physical contact, especially a handshake, may act as a point of exposure. What they call "energy" can feel exposed. The spirits they rely on may feel seen, uncovered, and vulnerable. They often describe their power as suddenly neutralized. Significantly, they note that this reaction does not occur with nominal or cultural Christians, but with believers who live in active, prayerful, consecrated relationship with God.

This realization helped me reframe the fear many believers experience. When a brother or sister feels sudden exhaustion, weakness, or a spiritual jolt during an encounter, it is not automatically a sign of evil. It may indicate a spiritual interaction, but it may also require prayerful, pastoral, emotional, and practical discernment. Physical sensations can arise from many sources, including anxiety, trauma, fatigue, emotional overwhelm, or medical concerns. For that reason, no responsible leader should rush to accusation. The question is not only *What happened?* but *How should this be interpreted with wisdom, humility, and care?* There are several ways this kind of experience may be understood.

Sometimes it may be the friction between consecration and compromise.

Scripture tells us that iron sharpens iron, but if one blade is rusted or resisting, sparks may fly. The Holy Spirit is a consuming fire. When His holiness encounters resistance, hidden sin, lukewarmness, or unresolved rebellion, the sensation can feel jarring. This is not a call to accusation, but to prayer.

At other times, the sensation may be the weight of compassion. Some people are not dark, but deeply broken. Like the woman who touched the hem of Jesus' garment, they are hemorrhaging spiritually. When a believer in deep covenantal relationship with God encounters such a person, virtue may pour out instinctively. The drain is not theft; it may be intercession in action.

There are also moments when the Holy Spirit activates discernment. A sudden check, discomfort, or recoil may signal that a person, despite religious language and ecclesiastical titles, is operating under a different spirit altogether. Discernment is not fear; it is information.

And sometimes, what we feel is resonance. A believer who has been delivered from a specific bondage may feel the familiar weight when encountering someone still trapped in it. The Spirit may be alerting us to shared warfare, calling us to stand in the gap.

The danger arises when these experiences are interpreted outside of discipleship and covenantal theology. In this age of *Engineered Spirituality*, many believers are being formed not by pastors and Scripture alone, but by fragmented influences drawn from the world. Concepts borrowed from other spiritual systems, such as *prana*, *qi*, and life force, are absorbed without discernment. What should be understood as spiritual atmosphere becomes reframed as "energy management." Fear replaces faith, and accusation replaces inquiry.

Without the renewal of the mind, spiritual experiences become spiritual toxins. Even when the Holy Spirit is speaking, guiding, or teaching, conflicting voices can distort interpretation. What could have been clarified through prayer, fruit-testing, and pastoral conversation becomes suspicion. What could have led to intercession becomes accusation.

This is how ecclesiastical accusation takes root, not through overt heresy, but through misinterpreted experience, un-discipled perception, and fear allowed to speak louder than the Spirit of Truth.

This dynamic mirrors the Gospels themselves. Jesus was accused not because He harmed people, but because His presence disturbed them. Conviction was misnamed as threat. Exposure was reframed as violation. The accusation revealed more about the accusers than about Him. The same pattern now replays within the Church.

When experience is not discipled, it seeks explanation. When explanation lacks Scripture, it borrows from fear. And when fear governs interpretation, accusation follows naturally. This is how holiness is mistaken for harm, and why faithful leaders are quietly questioned for the very clarity they carry.

Accusation does not remain internal for long. What begins as misinterpreted experience or unexamined fear inevitably seeks expression. Once suspicion finds language, especially language clothed in spiritual authority, it gains momentum, recruits agreement, and reshapes atmosphere. In the Age of Ecclesiastical Accusation, fear first learns to interpret sensation as threat, then learns to speak that threat into existence. The next battlefield, therefore, is not merely perception but speech itself. To understand how accusation multiplies, why communities fracture, and how authority is either preserved or corrupted, we must now examine the instrument through which fear most often operates: the tongue.

CHAPTER 9

IMPROVISED PROPHECY AND THE MARKETPLACE OF FEAR

What earlier chapters introduced pastorally must now be examined through the misuse of prophetic speech. I use the phrase *improvised prophecy* to describe prophetic language that is not rooted in genuine revelation from God, but assembled in real time through emotional reading, spiritual performance, predictable human suffering, and the pressure to appear accurate. It sounds inspired. It may even feel precise. But its power often comes from recognizing common wounds rather than receiving a true word from the Lord.

I use the phrase *marketplace of fear* to describe the environment where pain becomes profitable, and anxiety becomes a doorway to influence. In this marketplace, sickness, financial pressure, marital conflict, delayed hope, legal trouble, infertility, and family crisis become spiritual entry points. The wounded person is made to feel seen, but then pressured to respond through money, loyalty, urgency, or obedience to the voice speaking. Fear becomes the atmosphere. Prophecy becomes the product. The desperate become the audience.

This does not mean prophecy itself is false.

Scripture affirms that God speaks, warns, comforts, corrects, and reveals. The problem is not prophecy; the problem is prophetic language detached from truth, accountability, humility, and love. God still speaks, but the voice of God never needs manipulation, payment, fear, or emotional pressure to prove its authority. When prophecy becomes improvised, it no longer serves the people of God. It performs for them. And when fear becomes a marketplace, spiritual speech is no longer used to shepherd the wounded, but to manage them.

Scripture never treats speech as neutral. From the opening lines of Genesis to the closing vision of Revelation, words are presented as carriers of authority, intention, and consequence. Creation itself unfolds through utterance. "And God said" becomes the governing rhythm of Genesis, establishing light, order, and boundary through speech rather than force (Genesis 1:3–31; Psalm 33:6, 9). Human speech, made in the image of a speaking God, is therefore derivative rather than incidental. To speak, biblically, is to act.

The fall corrupts language before it corrupts behavior. Adam's first recorded words after sin are evasive and accusatory, redirecting responsibility away from himself (Genesis 3:10–13). Speech fractures before obedience collapses. Throughout Scripture, divided hearts are consistently exposed through distorted language. David describes a people who speak "with flattering lips and a double heart" (Psalm 12:2), while Isaiah links injustice directly to lying tongues and murmuring speech (Isaiah 59:2–4). Jesus later confirms this pattern, teaching that "out of the abundance of the heart the mouth speaks," and that every careless word will be brought into judgment (Matthew 12:34–37; Luke 6:45). The tongue does not create corruption; it reveals it.

James provides the New Testament's most concentrated theology of speech. He describes the tongue as fire, a rudder, and a spring, small in size yet disproportionate in influence (James 3:3–12). Fire spreads beyond its origin. A rudder directs an entire vessel. A spring cannot produce both fresh and bitter water without contradiction. These metaphors are not rhetorical exaggerations; they are theological diagnostics. James teaches that spiritual direction is often determined not by intention, but by language. A community's spiritual health can be measured not only by its doctrine, but by its speech.

The tongue also functions covenantally. In Scripture, blessing and curse are not emotional reactions but covenant acts. God tells Israel, "According to your words I will do to you" (Numbers 14:28). James later warns that blessing God while cursing people made in His image represents a covenant contradiction (James 3:9–10). This explains why Scripture treats slander and false witness as serious sin. To destroy a person's name unjustly is to assault what God has established (Exodus 20:16). Language is not merely relational; it carries moral and spiritual consequence.

Accusation therefore carries spiritual weight. Satan is defined not first by violence, but by speech. He is named "the accuser of our brethren," accusing day and night (Revelation 12:10). His power operates through narrative, reframing identity, distorting motive, and planting suspicion. When believers adopt accusatory language, even unintentionally, they begin echoing the grammar of the adversary. Paul counters this directly by commanding that "no corrupt communication proceed out of your mouth, but only what is good for edifying" (Ephesians 4:29). Speech either builds or dismantles; there is no neutral category.

At the center of this theology stands Christ Himself. Jesus is not merely a speaker of truth; He is "the Word made flesh" (John 1:1–14). In Him, speech is inseparable from love, authority from sacrifice, and correction from redemption. When confronted with sin, He exposes without humiliating and restores without accusing (John 8:10–11). His words heal, restore, and raise the dead. To submit the tongue to Christ is to allow His Spirit to govern not only belief, but expression.

When the Church recovers a biblical theology of the tongue, spiritual authority regains clarity and weight. Prayer deepens. Worship steadies. Community becomes safer. But when speech is careless, accusatory, or malicious, even correct doctrine loses power. The tongue becomes either an altar of blessing or a platform of destruction.

This is where the theology of speech must move from principle to practice, because the same tongue that blesses in worship can also become a tool of control when it is detached from love.

It is precisely here that a dangerous confusion has taken root in many churches. Sorcery is often discussed as though it belongs exclusively to occult systems, while the destructive misuse of speech is minimized or excused. Yet Scripture warns that the tongue can set the entire course of life on fire. When words are used to manipulate, intimidate, or destroy a person's name or peace, they mirror sorcery itself, using invisible influence to produce visible damage. This form of power is subtle, socially acceptable, and deeply destructive.

That danger becomes even more serious when spiritual language is used to claim divine authority over another person's fear, pain, or decision.

Public accusation without proof constitutes spiritual violence. It wounds through language while hiding behind religious vocabulary. When humiliation is baptized as discernment, speech forfeits its capacity to heal. Truth becomes an instrument of control rather than a means of restoration.

Scripture therefore insists that speech must edify. To edify is to build carefully, intentionally, and patiently. Words are meant to function as material for building, not wrecking tools. They correct with compassion, warn with wisdom, and restore with gentleness. Any word that tears down rather than builds, no matter how accurate it sounds, betrays the Spirit of grace.

A necessary clarification must be made. This discussion does not condemn all strong language, nor does it excuse all harsh speech as prophetic. Scripture permits neither extreme. God sometimes authorizes language that confronts hardened authority and exposes systemic deception. Such speech is rare, accountable, and costly to the speaker. It is never casual, never whispered, and never self-serving.

Ezekiel spoke graphically because Israel had grown numb. Elijah confronted false authority publicly because God answered with fire. Paul rebuked false gospels openly because eternal truth was at stake. Jesus reserved His severest words for leaders who abused power, while extending mercy to sinners seeking repentance. In every case, the speech aimed at repentance, not the destruction of reputation.

To discern truth from abuse, language must be tested. Does it target hardened authority or vulnerable individuals? Is it direct and accountable, or circulated indirectly? Does it produce repentance or merely shame? Does it cost the speaker or consolidate influence? Language that fails these tests may sound biblical, but it does not bear the Spirit of Christ.

Evil speaking, slander, whispering, and ridicule are not minor faults. Beneath them lies the desire to manage perception. This is why they mirror sorcery. Sorcery uses ritual; gossip uses words. Both seek influence through manipulation.

Healing begins when the Church reclaims speech as a channel of grace. Words must pass through the filter of love: do they heal or harm, restore or fracture, clarify or confuse? True authority does not slander in order to be heard. Often the greatest deliverance needed is not from external darkness, but from the spiritual damage inflicted by careless language within the community of faith.

The tongue reveals a sobering truth: spiritual power never remains dormant. What is practiced through speech becomes a posture of the heart. Words train the soul toward either submission or control, trust or manipulation. When language blesses, it aligns with God's life-giving order. When it accuses, dominates, or distorts, it rehearses a counterfeit authority.

Once speech is treated as spiritual power, it does not remain limited to ordinary conversation. It begins seeking a platform, an audience, and a moment of confirmation.

When Prophetic Language Becomes Performance

This misuse of speech becomes especially dangerous when it enters prophetic language, because prophecy carries the expectation of divine authority. Power pursued apart from truth does not remain confined to intention or expression. It seeks validation. It searches for confirmation. What begins as careless speech soon demands reinforcement, first through interpretation, then through declaration. At that point, language no longer describes reality; it attempts to govern it. Scripture is no longer carefully discerned but rapidly reconstructed and applied to immediate crises, producing psychological momentum that temporarily reduces anxiety, restores a sense of control, and offers meaning in chaos.

This is how ecclesiastical accusations often begin, not in hatred, not in open rebellion, but in a mixture of spiritual performance, emotional vulnerability, and unchecked authority. I write this section with discipline, because even while exposing the pattern, I must resist the temptation to cross my own red line. The danger is real: a person can name deception and still become ensnared by the very spirit that fuels it.

The pattern becomes clearer when it is seen not only as a theological concern, but as something that unfolds in real lives, real churches, and real moments of vulnerability.

What I describe here is not theory. I have watched it unfold among people I know, in churches I have visited, and across movements I have observed closely. It appears most often in charismatic Christian environments, spaces that sincerely desire the supernatural, believe in prophecy, and hunger for visible evidence of God's power. The problem is not prophecy. The problem arises when prophetic language becomes improvised, detached from accountability, and repurposed for influence, money, or recognition.

I use the phrase *improvised prophecy* deliberately. It refers to prophetic speech that is not rooted in divine revelation but assembled in real time by reading the emotional temperature of a room, the cultural moment, or the predictable pain of human life. It sounds spiritual. It feels precise. But it is often generic, transferable, and strategically designed to land somewhere, anywhere, among a vulnerable audience.

The person practicing *improvised prophecy* often targets what I have come to call selective consumers of truth: comfort-driven believers, affirmation-dependent hearers, and prosperity-oriented listeners. These are not wicked people. Many are sincere, tired, fearful, or desperate. They carry real pain, unresolved crises, and long-standing prayers. *Improvised prophecy* does not create their wounds; it exploits them.

The Method of Improvised Prophecy

The method is simple and effective. A leader looks into a camera or scans a crowd and declares, "God is showing me a father with a sick child who is waiting for an organ." Another may say, "I see a mother whose son is in jail, and you are going to court tomorrow at nine in the morning. Call now for prayer." Another declares, "You are going through a divorce you did not want, but God says you will find joy again." Another says, "You are planning to buy a home, and I see blessings coming down upon you." Another announces, "You have been praying for a baby, and God has given you a beautiful baby girl." Still another says, "You just learned that you have cancer, but God is about to heal you."

Most of these statements do not require supernatural insight. They are statistically safe. In any large audience, several people will fit the description. The prophecy lands not because God spoke, but because life is full of suffering, longing, illness, fractured relationships, legal trouble, financial pressure, and delayed hope. The prophet appears accurate because human pain is predictable.

Then the second layer of manipulation begins. Once a person recognizes themselves inside the declaration, they feel seen. Relief mixes with fear. Hope rises. Urgency follows. The invitation is extended. Call the number on the screen. Come forward. Sow a seed. Release your faith. What was presented as divine compassion becomes a transaction. The moment is framed as a doorway, and the listener is pressured to pay before the door closes.

I remember a friend of mine, Zef, who was going through a deeply personal crisis at home. One evening, he watched a Christian television program, and the prophet on screen described what he felt was happening inside his household. It pierced him. He called the number immediately. Before any prayer was offered, he was told that a donation of one thousand dollars was required. When he explained his financial situation, the amount was negotiated down to six hundred dollars. Even that was beyond his reach. The conversation ended. No prayer followed. No counsel followed. Only the taste of shame and spiritual disappointment remained.

This is not prophecy. It is commerce. It is not intercession. It is negotiation. And the residue it leaves behind is not healing, but confusion, because the person was invited to believe they were seen by God and then treated as a customer who could not afford compassion.

Improvised prophecy rarely remains subtle. It escalates. It grows bolder. It reaches into more private territory. "God told me you struggle with potency issues." "God showed me your spouse cheated on you." "You are hesitating to give the money you saved for an emergency, and you are blocking your own blessing." Each declaration deepens emotional dependency while maintaining just enough ambiguity to avoid accountability. The person is pulled into fear and then offered relief through obedience to the voice speaking.

The damage does not end with the person who was manipulated. Eventually, the abuse of prophetic language forces other leaders to respond, and that response can either restore order or widen the conflict.

When Correction Becomes Another Performance

In time, pastors and leaders who witness this feel obligated to address it. Some correct it carefully. Others confront it publicly. The manipulation is named. The theft is exposed. But correction, when it becomes reactive rather than redemptive, can also ignite the very cycle it seeks to stop. Prophets respond defensively. Counter-accusations follow. Sermons answer sermons. Videos circulate. Platforms become courtrooms without judges. Before long, the Church is no longer discerning spirits; it is trading accusations. The original concern, protecting the vulnerable, gets buried beneath reputational warfare.

This is the trap. *Improvised prophecy* gives birth to improvised correction. Manipulation provokes outrage. Outrage becomes denunciation. Denunciation invites retaliation. What began as a sincere attempt to protect the flock evolves into an ecosystem of suspicion, labeling, and spiritual conflict conducted through microphones and screens.

Discipline is required here, because not every lie must be fought publicly, and not every deception requires a counter-performance. Correction without wisdom can reproduce the very spirit it claims to oppose. The goal is not to win arguments, expose personalities, or dominate narratives. The goal is to guard the flock, restore discernment, and refuse participation in systems that thrive on fear, spectacle, and emotional extraction.

This is why the discussion must end where accusation often begins: not with falsehood alone, but with truth handled without patience, process, or pastoral restraint.

Ecclesiastical accusations often begin not because truth is absent, but because restraint is missing. *Improvised prophecy* is dangerous, but improvised judgment is equally dangerous. When leaders operate without accountability, when audiences are trained to crave affirmation, and when correction becomes an emotional reaction rather than a pastoral process, the Church becomes fertile ground for accusation to multiply. The war begins quietly, emotionally, and convincingly, long before accusations ever start flying.

CHAPTER 10

COLLATERAL DAMAGE

When the Wounded Are Caught in the Crossfire

If there is war, there is always collateral damage. No conflict—spiritual or otherwise—remains contained to those who initiate it. In ecclesiastical warfare, the casualties are rarely the loudest voices or the most visible leaders. They are the quiet ones: wounded believers, recovering souls, and fragile hearts who come searching for healing and instead encounter confusion, suspicion, and fear. These are the people least equipped to defend themselves against spiritual noise, yet they bear the heaviest cost.

One member of my congregation became such a casualty—one among many living under the unseen consequences of ecclesiastical accusation. She joined GREMC in 2017 after years of deep spiritual trauma. A former Vodou practitioner, she had encountered Christ and was earnestly seeking restoration. Before arriving at our ministry, she had tried several others, including some online ministries, and had studied widely on her own in an effort not to fall prey to leaders without a genuine calling to help. Her caution was not rebellion. It was survival. She was trying to protect herself after years of spiritual manipulation.

But her wounds were layered. Alongside her history of occult entanglement, she carried emotional scars dating back to early childhood—wounds formed as young as six and later compounded by sexual violation as a young woman. These were not distant memories. They shaped how she trusted, how she listened, how she processed authority, and how she interpreted spiritual language. Her healing required more than deliverance alone. It required safety, patience, and wise pastoral care.

I share this story with care and permission. She testified publicly about her healing and named these experiences herself. Today she is restored. But her journey exposes the cost of unchecked accusation within the Church—a cost most often paid by those already wounded.

As she began opening up within the safety of our community, a thought came to my mind. I knew of a woman, widely respected and influential, who pastors a large church in the United States. This pastor had shared her testimony publicly thousands of times—how she was raped and molested as a teenager, how the gospel rescued her, and how God restored her life. Her story had become a source of hope for countless women. I had witnessed how her teaching helped survivors find language for their pain, context for their healing, and courage for their future.

Believing this could serve as a bridge rather than a burden, I encouraged Ma to listen to some of that pastor's sermons online. I intended it as pastoral care, not as an endorsement of an entire ministry. I hoped it might help her feel less alone and help her see that redemption is possible even after devastating violation.

A few days later, she returned to me—not angry, not dramatic, but firmly resolved. She told me she would not watch the sermons. When I asked why, she said the pastor was allegedly part of the Illuminati. She had found internet links, videos, and commentary that "proved" it—material she had encountered months before she ever joined our church. To her, the accusation was enough. The sermons were no longer safe. The testimony was no longer trustworthy. The message of healing had become suspect.

In that moment, I felt the weight of what the Age of Ecclesiastical Accusation produces. This was not a theological disagreement. It was not discernment grounded in Scripture or personal encounter. It was accusation absorbed, internalized, and weaponized against healing. A wounded woman, finally beginning to trust again, had been trained to distrust almost everything before it even had a chance to bless her.

Accusation does not remain theoretical. It does not stay online. It does not confine itself to comment sections and podcasts. It enters the sanctuary, the counseling room, the living room, and the inner world of the believer. It teaches people that suspicion is wisdom and distance is safety. It trains wounded souls to believe that nearly every visible servant of God is compromised, secretly dangerous, or spiritually corrupt. In doing so, it isolates the very people who need the Church the most.

For survivors of spiritual abuse, former occult practitioners, and believers carrying trauma, trust is already fragile. When accusation becomes the dominant lens, healing becomes difficult. Every testimony is questioned. Every leader is suspect. Every story of redemption is filtered through fear. The believer no longer asks, "Is this bearing fruit?" and "What secret evil might be hiding beneath this?" This is not discernment. It is paralysis.

Another story revealed the same pattern in a different way. A second cousin from my father's side reached out after more than fifty years of silence. We had grown up in the same community in Port-au-Prince, but contact was lost when his mother moved away. He reached out from Philadelphia, and we began to reconnect. Because we share the same lineage—our grandfather was the most feared Vodou priest in that community, and his mother was devoted to Vodou for many years—I wanted to understand his faith journey.

To my surprise, he told me his mother abandoned Vodou on her deathbed and that he himself had embraced Christianity and experienced freedom from generational oppression. Yet a concern rose in me, and I asked a simple question: what church are you attending? He could not name one.

He knew many pastors by name. He followed numerous online prophets. He consumed sermons and teachings from across the digital world. But he had no congregation, no shepherd, no covenant community, and no consistent discipleship. His Christianity had been assembled according to preference rather than rooted in fellowship. When I pressed further, he admitted the reason. Everything felt confusing, conflicting, and exhausting. Too many voices preached different versions of the gospel while accusing one another. The noise overwhelmed him. Disengagement felt safer than commitment.

This, too, is collateral damage. Ecclesiastical accusation often presents itself as protection, but it rarely protects the vulnerable. It burdens them. It shifts their focus from Christ to constant scrutiny, from healing to vigilance, from hope to suspicion. The irony is painful: in trying to avoid deception, many are robbed of nourishment.

I do not write this to defend any particular leader or ministry. That is not the point. The issue is not whether every accusation is true or false in every case. The issue is what accusation does when it becomes a culture rather than a tool. Scripture leaves room for discernment, correction, and even rebuke, but it never commands believers to live in constant suspicion, nor does it present fear as a mark of maturity.

When accusation becomes habitual, it fractures the Body and wounds the very people Christ came to heal. Former practitioners need patience, not paranoia. Survivors need safety, not scandal. New believers need shepherding, not endless alerts. Ma's story ended in healing because she remained in a community that emphasized restoration over rumor, Scripture over speculation, and Christ over conspiracy. Many are not so fortunate. Many drift from church to church, video to video, sermon to sermon—never settling, never trusting, never healing—because accusation has convinced them that safety lies in isolation.

This is the collateral damage of ecclesiastical war. When leaders attack one another publicly, when accusations spread without restraint, and when discernment is replaced by suspicion, the casualties are not only reputations. They are souls. They are wounded women who need to hear that God redeems pain. They are believers who want to heal but are taught to fear.

Accusation may feel powerful, righteous, even necessary in the moment. But when it silences healing voices and isolates the vulnerable, it reveals its fruit. Whatever its vocabulary, it is not building the Church. It is bleeding the Church.

A NECESSARY PAUSE

What has unfolded so far in this book has been intentional, not accidental. I have not been cataloging church failures or reacting to isolated conflicts, nor have I treated division as something abnormal or purely destructive. Scripture itself tells us otherwise. In 1 Corinthians 11:19, Paul acknowledges that divisions and disruptions are inevitable—not because God delights in disorder, but because such moments reveal what is genuine. Conflict, when exposed to truth, sifts the real from the counterfeit. Those who remain grounded, faithful, and submitted under pressure are often the ones who carry God's approval. In this sense, struggle within the Church is not evidence of abandonment; it is often the environment in which authenticity is revealed.

What I have been tracing is not chaos, but a pattern—one that Scripture, history, and lived ministry repeatedly confirm. From the Edenic age onward, the same distortion appears again and again: power grasped without trust, authority exercised without obedience, and knowledge pursued apart from submission to God. The form changes across generations, but the mechanism remains strikingly consistent.

Chapter by chapter, I have moved deliberately. I began with perception, because before behavior collapses, vision narrows, and fear reshapes how reality is interpreted. When perception is distorted, discernment weakens long before action follows. I then turned to language, because what is feared eventually demands a voice. The tongue was examined not as a moral accessory, but as a spiritual instrument—capable of shaping atmosphere, forming allegiance, and exerting control. From there, I confronted power itself: how authority, once detached from truth, seeks reinforcement through improvised prophecy, counterfeit leadership, and fear-based systems. When authority destabilizes, accusation follows. And when accusation takes root, the vulnerable carry the cost.

These are not isolated failures or personality clashes. What emerges is a connected system. Improvised prophecy, word-sorcery, unauthorized authority, and ecclesiastical accusation are not separate phenomena; they are interrelated expressions of the same disorder. When truth is bypassed, authority becomes unstable. When authority is unstable, language turns coercive. When language becomes coercive, accusation multiplies. And when accusation multiplies, spaces meant for healing quietly become unsafe for those who arrive wounded.

Throughout this work, restraint has been exercised deliberately. I have told the truth carefully, because careless exposure can wound as deeply as deception itself. When testimonies, failures, or encounters have been shared, only what was necessary has been named—enough to reveal the pattern without turning people into objects. That restraint is not stylistic caution; it is theological conviction. Discernment without love becomes violence, and revelation without responsibility becomes another form of harm.

I do not write as a distant observer. I write as someone who has stood inside these tensions, made mistakes, learned painfully, and watched real people bear the consequences when spiritual power is mishandled. Yet I have resisted turning this work into a memoir, because the focus is not my story. The focus is the pattern—and the people most at risk when that pattern goes unnamed.

What has been uncovered so far is preparatory, not performative.

The pace has been intentionally slowed so the architecture could be seen clearly, its ancient roots traced back to Eden, and its consequences understood without panic or spectacle. Power pursued apart from truth never remains contained to those who seek it; it always spills outward, demanding payment from others. Having traced that progression carefully to this point, the reader is now equipped to confront the danger at its center—not abstractly, but honestly—before stepping into the lived realities that follow.

CHAPTER 11

WHEN POWER IS SOUGHT WITHOUT TRUTH

From the beginning, humanity has sought power, the capacity to influence outcomes, secure safety, shape destiny, and make meaning of uncertainty. This desire is not inherently corrupt. It first appears in legitimate forms: leadership, courage, wisdom, protection, and service. Yet when the pursuit of power detaches from truth, patience, and submission to God, it becomes restless and dangerous. What begins as responsibility subtly mutates into control. What starts as leadership hardens into domination. This transition rarely announces itself. It advances quietly, justified by urgency, fear, and perceived necessity.

When Power Becomes Control

When authority cannot be established through character or obedience, shortcuts become attractive. Across many societies, people have often turned to rituals, oracles, divination, sacrifices, and spiritual consultations not because they lacked intelligence, but because they lacked restraint. When human effort felt insufficient, unseen power felt necessary. In those moments, impatience replaced trust, and method replaced relationship. Power was pursued without waiting for God to form the heart capable of carrying it.

Sorcery, therefore, is not a modern invention. Egyptians invoked deities for military victory. Babylonians consulted omens before war. Greeks traveled to Delphi seeking divine insight. Roman augury, European folk magic, indigenous protection rites, Aztec sacrifices, and Haitian ancestral engagements all reveal a repeated human temptation: influence without submission and authority without covenant. Though the symbols differed, the transaction remained similar. Power was sought apart from obedience, and control was preferred over trust.

What has changed is not the hunger, but the accessibility. Sorcery no longer hides exclusively in forests or private ceremonies. It circulates openly through entertainment, digital platforms, and spiritualized language framed as healing, empowerment, or ancestral connection. Even within Christian spaces, divided loyalty can quietly emerge. God is trusted publicly, while private sources of power are retained "just in case." This posture rarely begins in rebellion. It almost always begins in fear.

I have spoken with individuals who do not view witchcraft as darkness, but as necessity. One woman described using occult practices to force her in-laws out of her home. She expressed no guilt, only relief. This is the deception of sorcery. Rebellion is reframed as justice. Manipulation is justified as wisdom. Control is baptized as survival.

Sorcery unfolds gradually. What begins as verbal influence matures into spiritual manipulation. When Saul rejected obedience, Samuel did not accuse him of emotional weakness. He named the issue precisely: "rebellion is as the sin of witchcraft" (1 Samuel 15:23). The problem was not ritual alone, but authority detached from submission. Once power separates from obedience, technique replaces relationship. Sorcery promises results without righteousness and power without transformation. It offers freedom without surrender, yet always delivers bondage. Control feels efficient when obedience feels costly.

Sorcery as Counterfeit Covenant

At its core, sorcery functions as a counterfeit covenant. It offers protection or leverage, but demands ownership in return. What begins as assistance becomes possession. Peace erodes. Love gives way to fear. The heart is trained to trust technique rather than the father. Occult power never gives without taking more in return. It steals identity and leaves an emptiness no ritual can fill. Over time, what begins as a private decision can become a generational burden that affects homes, marriages, and even churches.

Those who engage in sorcery often experience an initial sense of mastery. They believe they can manipulate life itself. Yet dark power never serves; it demands service. It disguises itself as ancestral wisdom, cultural continuity, or spiritual depth to gain entry. I have met many who summoned spirits for success only to become prisoners of what they invited. Their will was exchanged for influence, and freedom was traded for fear. They were promised liberation, yet lived enslaved.

One of the earliest signs of bondage is the absence of peace. Peace cannot dwell where fear governs. The practitioner lives in constant anxiety, wondering whether protection will last or whether offense has been given to the spirits. Years ago, I visited a woman who had abandoned her faith for Vodou. As I prepared to leave, she whispered that she would need to cleanse her home because my presence had disturbed her energy. What she called energy, I understood as a spiritual collision between the presence of the Holy Spirit and the spirits she continued to serve. Though surrounded by ritual, she lived without rest.

Love cannot coexist with the spirit of control. In sorcery, affection becomes transactional and kindness becomes currency. I have seen gentle souls turn vengeful under its weight. Compassion withers because love and domination cannot occupy the same space. Only Christ restores the capacity for selfless love. When someone begins to leave sorcery, loneliness is often the first battle. Deliverance without discipleship can feel like abandonment. Freedom requires belonging.

Fear becomes the permanent atmosphere of occult life. Practitioners fear exposure, retaliation, and loss of control. Some even come to fear God Himself, mistaking holiness for hostility. Fear often outlives the ritual. It becomes a psychological habit. Deliverance may begin in the spirit, but healing continues in the mind.

Deliverance, Healing, and Discernment

Many who leave sorcery live under crushing guilt, questioning whether God truly forgives them. This guilt is one of the enemy's strongest chains. Redemption, however, is complete. Emotional instability may follow prolonged spiritual manipulation, and wise leaders recognize when spiritual care must be partnered with mental health support. This is not compromise. It is wisdom.

Sorcery's power lies not only in ritual, but in fear. A curse thrives where faith is weak; faith disarms fear.

False accusations often wound more deeply than sorcery itself. I have seen families damaged by reckless prophetic labeling. The Church must respond with discernment, not hysteria.

Sorcery does not spread through blood as though biology itself were cursed; it spreads through atmosphere, fear, language, practice, and agreement. Fear becomes language. Love becomes conditional. I once counseled a man who divorced his wife after a false accusation. Her humility eventually exposed the lie. A true sorcerer seeks control or revenge, not reconciliation. When accusation enters a home, it becomes the loudest voice at the table.

Where fear dominates, peace disappears. Worship becomes watchfulness. Deliverance becomes performance. Any ministry sustained by fear already serves darkness. Not every struggle is demonic, and not every wound is purely psychological. Discernment must walk with compassion. Deliverance and therapy can work together toward freedom.

True deliverance begins with trust. God restores before He exposes. My father's story remains an anchor of hope, raised in ritual, delivered by Christ, and freed by grace from a lineage of bondage. Heritage is not stronger than redemption. I hold no power of my own; I am a vessel. Faith and professional wisdom can work together. The greatest challenge is rarely manifestation, but roots. Some were initiated deliberately. Others were unaware.

Power without truth always leaves someone wounded, because control can never produce peace. Because the pursuit of power without truth leaves such varied scars, the restorer must be able to see past the symptoms to the roots. This requires a vital pastoral distinction: knowing when you are sitting across from a willful initiate or a soul simply unaware of the shadows they have inherited.

DISTINGUISHING BETWEEN THE INITIATED AND THE UNAWARE

When discernment is absent, misdiagnosis becomes inevitable. Leaders who approach deliverance or freedom from spiritual bondage without preparation, patience, compassion, or calling can wound those who come seeking help. At the same time, pastors who carry responsibilities beyond their formation can become exhausted and uncertain. When discernment falters, both shepherd and flock suffer. What should function as refuge can become a place of confusion. These outcomes rarely arise from malice. They usually arise from misunderstanding what people are carrying when they enter the Church.

Spiritual Residue and Wounded Perception

Over time, I have come to understand that what I describe as spiritual residue can also be described, in psychological language, as conditioned belief systems and fear-based responses. These are patterns formed through trauma, ritual exposure, or prolonged survival environments that remain active even after belief shifts. This distinction matters. Some individuals emerging from occult contexts report seeing entities, hearing voices or sounds, or sensing presences others cannot perceive. Spiritualist frameworks may interpret these experiences as gifts, while psychology may understand them as hypervigilance, dissociative responses, or trauma-linked perceptions. Confusing these categories can cause harm.

People shaped by violence or ritualized fear, especially in childhood, often develop nervous systems trained for survival rather than discernment. When churches elevate such individuals as gifted or condemn them as dangerous, both responses fail. One glorifies trauma. The other criminalizes it. Neither heals.

Restoration requires patience and a layered approach. Prayer grounded in Scripture calms the inner world. Structured routines and safe community weaken fear patterns. Yet pastoral care must not function in isolation. Collaboration with mental health professionals allows healing to become sustainable. Prayer, community, and professional care together form wisdom.

I once encountered someone who said quietly, "I can hear when people are badmouthing me." I neither affirmed nor confronted the statement publicly. What I recognized was not a gift or a threat, but a person in need of safety. Years later, the context emerged. During childhood, rituals had been performed over her without consent. Fear had been ritualized. With time, truth, and a new environment, the experiences faded without spectacle.

Another case involved someone close to our family. She described seeing transparent figures and speaking during sleep. Her interpretations were spiritual, shaped by family history. I neither validated the experience as a gift nor labeled her possessed. Instead, I guided her through prayer, Scripture-based meditation, dignity, community involvement, and time. Within three years, the experiences ceased. Healing arrived quietly.

Willful Covenant and Inherited Residue

Not all bondage begins the same way. Some enter knowingly through covenants and oaths. Others enter unknowingly through culture, desperation, or inherited exposure. What unites them is bondage, not always rebellion. What distinguishes them is the path taken.

One woman entered witchcraft seeking protection and retaliation, later confessing remorse and an inability to stop. Her bondage was sustained by environment, fear, and repeated agreement, not merely by original intent. Healing required separation, patience, and continued presence, not condemnation.

Sorcery often disguises itself as opportunity. Contracts entered for success can become systems of control. What is worn as ornament can become altar. When individuals carrying such entanglements enter church spaces, response must be restrained. Public exposure creates harm. Wisdom protects dignity.

A story within my wife's family illustrates this reality. A single mother sought survival for her children. Through ritual engagement, prosperity followed. Yet covenant deepened into initiation. Protection rituals performed in love became inheritance without consent. Illness briefly drew her toward Christ, yet unresolved fear pulled her back. Her children grew within divided spiritual environments, carrying residue they did not choose.

This raises a pastoral question. When such a person enters the Church, is she treated as a threat or as a wounded mother? Accusation begins with misunderstanding. Restoration begins with compassion strong enough to hold truth.

In a world where unrecognized forms of sorcery multiply through the language of manifestation, revenge, self-alignment, and hidden control, the Church must learn to distinguish between the initiated and the unaware.

Not every person who carries this attitude belongs to a sect, practices formal rituals, or identifies with witchcraft. Yet when a person develops a settled desire to get even by hoping others will fall, suffer, be humiliated, or be harmed, the heart has entered the territory of sorcery. The issue is not only affiliation; it is agreement. A person may never enter a secret society and still cultivate a spirit of revenge that seeks invisible harm against another human being.

Both the initiated and the unaware need grace. Both need truth. Both need time. Both need shepherds who understand the difference between formal occult covenant and an unrecognized posture of spiritual retaliation.

True authority does not begin with accusation. It begins with understanding. True deliverance does not start with confrontation. It begins with compassion capable of holding truth without crushing the soul.

To distinguish rightly between the initiated and the unaware is not an academic exercise; it is a pastoral necessity. Without this discernment, response becomes reactive and authority becomes reckless. Understanding who stands before us must precede any decision about what to do. Only when the Church learns to recognize the difference between willful covenant and inherited residue, between rebellion and survival, can it respond without harming those already wounded. This distinction prepares the ground for wisdom rather than haste, compassion rather than suspicion.

With that clarity established, the question now becomes not whether sorcery and spiritual bondage are real, but how the Church is called to respond biblically, culturally, and pastorally, without fear, spectacle, or abandonment of grace.

CHAPTER 12

RESPONDING TO SORCERY

Biblical, Cultural, and Pastoral Frameworks

When pastors or individuals with specific vocations encounter people whose histories include sorcery, known across cultures by many names, such as witchcraft, divination, shamanism, Vodou, Obeah, Santería, Ifá, Brujería, Palo, spiritualism, ancestral invocation, energy manipulation, and even so-called "angelic" systems like Solomonic magic, Enochian magic, or theurgy, the first response is often emotional. Some panic. Others confront recklessly. Still others dismiss these practices as cultural expression or harmless spirituality. These reactions are understandable, but they often reveal fear or unfamiliarity rather than discernment.

Moving beyond reaction requires clarity. Beneath the varied names, symbols, and cultural expressions lies a shared pattern: the attempt to access, invoke, command, or negotiate with spiritual powers in order to influence outcomes, control people, secure protection, or cause harm. What changes from culture to culture is the vocabulary; what remains constant is the orientation. Sorcery is not defined by aesthetics, but by allegiance, power pursued without submission and influence sought apart from covenant.

Recognizing this pattern places the Church at a crossroads. The Kingdom of God demands more than fear, denial, or impulsive confrontation. Christ never denied the reality of darkness, nor did He sensationalize it.

He neither minimized its presence nor allowed fear to dictate His actions. Instead, He spoke truth with calm authority and restored dignity where bondage had stripped it away. That posture remains the model. The Church is called to acknowledge spiritual realities without hysteria, confront darkness without arrogance, and seek restoration without abandoning compassion.

Authority Rooted in Compassion: The Biblical and Pastoral Response

Throughout the Gospels, Jesus encountered those under the influence of demonic or occult powers. He never humiliated them, never turned their suffering into public display, and never treated their bondage as spectacle. When He encountered the man possessed by a legion of demons, He did not interrogate him before the crowd or dramatize the deliverance. He addressed the spirits directly, restored the man, and left him clothed and in his right mind. Deliverance culminated in dignity. Restoration, not performance, was the goal.

The same pattern appears when Jesus confronted the woman caught in adultery. He exposed the hypocrisy of her accusers before addressing her sin. Mercy preceded correction. Dignity was restored before instruction was given. Deliverance and forgiveness were never separated from honor. Scripture consistently reveals this principle: freedom that does not restore dignity is incomplete.

The apostles followed this pattern. In Philippi, Paul cast a spirit of divination out of a slave girl, not to shame her, but to free her from exploitation. Her masters were outraged, not because she was healed, but because their profit collapsed. This moment exposes a crucial truth: genuine deliverance not only frees individuals; it confronts systems that benefit from bondage. Wherever the Gospel liberates, structures of control are disturbed.

Authority, therefore, is not noise. It is peace anchored in holiness. Demons fear authority, not volume. Authority flows from intimacy with

God, not from performance. Before leading others into freedom, leaders must examine their own alignment: clean hands, surrendered motives, and lives submitted to the Spirit. Without that grounding, power becomes spectacle and ministry becomes dangerous. True authority is quiet, steady, and unmistakable.

Compassion is not weakness; it is strength under control. When individuals confess past involvement in occult practices, the Church is not called to expose or shame them, but to walk patiently with them toward freedom. Once chains break, assurance must follow. Fear isolates; compassion restores. Deliverance without love becomes another form of violence. Deliverance shaped by love becomes the beginning of healing.

The Holy Spirit remains the true Deliverer. Human effort cannot convict the heart or cleanse the soul. Forced confession, rushed repentance, or pressured process replaces freedom with fear. Conviction belongs to the Spirit, and His voice does not humiliate; it illuminates. Transformation occurs when truth meets grace, not coercion. Deliverance driven by human impatience wounds; deliverance led by the Spirit heals.

From Deliverance to Discipleship: When Grace Interrupts Lineage

In pastoral practice, restraint is essential. Listening precedes prayer. Understanding precedes declaration. Many forms of bondage lose power when a person is finally heard. Teaching grounded in Scripture often dismantles deception before any formal renunciation occurs. Deliverance prayers, when necessary, must be calm rather than chaotic. Renunciation is not performance; it is covenantal realignment. And freedom, once received, must be protected through community, formation, and discipleship. Isolation remains the enemy's preferred terrain.

Cultural wisdom is equally vital. In Caribbean, African, and diaspora contexts, spiritual realities are often expressed through symbols, dreams, and ancestral language. These expressions must be interpreted with both cultural understanding and biblical truth. The goal is not to erase culture, but to redeem it, to confront what destroys while affirming what is noble. Christ redeems culture from within.

True deliverance bears fruit quietly. Peace replaces panic. Love displaces suspicion. Obedience grows where fear once ruled. The greatest evidence of freedom is not volume, but stability. Many churches today require healing not from demons, but from fear-based ministry that distorts God's character and wounds His people. The Gospel is not a courtroom of accusation; it is a house of restoration.

Yet there are moments, rare, sovereign, and unmistakable, when God intervenes beyond every pastoral strategy or theological framework. These moments are not engineered. They are interruptions of grace. What occurred in the lives of my father and Marie Michel did not unfold through method, persuasion, or process. It was not learned. It was not rehearsed. It was an invasion.

Both were born into bloodlines marked by sorcery. Ritual surrounded their earliest days. Spiritual covenants were spoken over them before they could choose allegiance. Darkness entered through inheritance, not curiosity. And yet, what no human intervention could undo, God interrupted without negotiation. Grace did not imitate deliverance; it invaded bondage.

What follows is not offered for spectacle. It is offered as witness. It is meant to sober, not impress. It reminds us that what the enemy claims through lineage, God reclaims through mercy. These are not stories of people who escaped darkness by strength. They are testimonies of darkness that could not survive truth.

Here, the framework yields to encounter. Instruction gives way to witness. Theology meets flesh and blood. The movement ahead does not argue; it testifies.

How These Testimonies Should Be Read

The testimonies that follow are not offered as spectacle, proof of doctrine, or universal templates for every spiritual experience. They are witnesses. They help show how fear, bondage, inheritance, and deliverance can take shape in real lives. No testimony replaces Scripture. No personal account carries the authority of the Word of God. Each testimony must be read through Scripture, pastoral discernment, and spiritual restraint.

Some testimonies referenced in this work were publicly available at the time of writing. Their later removal, editing, or change in availability does not erase the pastoral and theological patterns they helped illuminate. Public testimony is not treated here as final authority, but as lived witness that must be weighed carefully.

My engagement with testimonies from current and former Haitian Vodou practitioners did not begin as a literary project. It emerged from pastoral necessity. Over time, people entering my congregation carried forms of distress that ordinary language could not fully explain: persistent fear, fractured identity, intrusive dreams, spiritual confusion, and symptoms often associated with possession or prior ritual exposure. These were not abstract questions. They entered pastoral spaces seeking relief, clarity, and restoration.

For that reason, precision became necessary. General words such as "bondage," "darkness," or "spiritual attack" were not always enough. Some wounds had been shaped by years of ritual exposure, fear-based allegiance, family obligation, or spiritual coercion. To care well, we had to name patterns without sensationalizing them and distinguish testimony from doctrine, experience from interpretation, and spiritual bondage from human suffering.

These testimonies also help clarify the central concern of *The Age of Ecclesiastical Accusation*. They reveal how captivity forms and persists, not only within overt occult systems, but within human perception itself. Vodou, as experienced by those who lived inside its structures, provides a visible example of how fear, authority, allegiance, and silence can become normalized. This book argues that similar mechanisms can later reappear within ecclesiastical environments, stripped of ritual language, yet driven by accusation, distorted perception, and unexamined authority. The purpose is not to exoticize darkness, but to expose patterns of control the Church itself can unknowingly reproduce.

This examination also requires cultural honesty. Haitian Vodou spirituality has often been interpreted through external lenses, and Haitians have too often been spoken about rather than listened to. By engaging testimonies from those who lived inside Vodou's ritual and spiritual structures, this work allows Haitian voices to describe what they experienced from within. Precision matters because history is shaped by who is allowed to define reality. These narratives show how belief systems operated at ground level, how authority was mediated, how fear was normalized, and how allegiance was sustained in everyday life, not as theory, but as survival.

Theological responsibility also requires attention to fruit. Many spiritual systems promise protection, prosperity, power, or insight. But theology cannot rest on promises alone; it must examine what those promises produce. Do they produce life, peace, and wholeness, or do they generate dependency, anxiety, fragmentation, and fear? This question is central to the larger argument of this book, which confronts any system, religious or spiritual, that claims authority while producing internal collapse.

As testimonies accumulated, consistent patterns appeared across individuals who had no contact with one another: hypervigilance, intrusive dreams, fear of retaliation, difficulty trusting authority, and the persistent belief that harm could be enacted through spiritual means long after ritual involvement had ceased. These recurring markers required careful pastoral discernment. They helped distinguish spiritual language from trauma-shaped perception and showed how ritualized fear can condition the mind over time. This insight directly informs the book's concern with accusation, not merely as speech, but as an internalized way of interpreting reality, authority, and the self.

Cultural restraint is essential here. Haitian identity is sometimes defended through silence when Vodou is questioned, as though examination itself were rejection of heritage. Yet cultural honor does not require denial. Precision allows distinction between ancestral memory and spiritual captivity, between communal resilience and ritualized fear. Without careful language, critique becomes accusation and defense becomes blindness.

These testimonies distinguish between the parts of culture that sustained survival and the wounds created by spiritual obligations that were later mistaken for identity.

There is also an ethical dimension. Many testimonies describe initiation not as informed choice, but as pressure: economic desperation, family obligation, fear of consequence, or inherited vows made without consent. When harm is named vaguely, responsibility disappears. When power remains undefined, abuse hides behind tradition. Precision becomes a moral necessity, clarifying who benefited, who bore the cost, and who carried the burden long after rituals ended.

A generational concern also shaped this work. Surface-level explanations manage symptoms; they do not interrupt cycles. Many former practitioners describe patterns repeating across generations: dreams, illnesses, relational fractures, and persistent fear long after overt participation ceased. Precision allows continuity to be traced, not to assign blame, but to understand inheritance. Only what is clearly named can be confronted, healed, and prevented from reproducing itself in those who never consented to receive it.

Importantly, testimonies from several members of my congregation independently echoed accounts already available on public platforms. These individuals had no shared script, no contact with one another, and no incentive to align their narratives. Many shared their experiences privately and reluctantly, in pastoral settings rather than public forums. When placed alongside public accounts, their testimonies converged with striking consistency. This convergence does not establish doctrine, but it does create an ethical obligation to take these accounts seriously as converging witness rather than rumor or spectacle.

Within *The Age of Ecclesiastical Accusation*, the focus on my father, Marie Michel, and Bachon is therefore deliberate rather than exhaustive. This is not a matter of exclusion, but of discernment. While numerous private testimonies were recorded and preserved for future publication in *The Gods Inside My Brain* and *L'Importance de Comprendre la Possession Démoniaque*, this book required narratives capable of carrying theological, psychological, and cultural weight without fragmenting attention. These three accounts function as guiding witnesses, each representing a distinct entry point into the same larger pattern of captivity and accusation: inheritance, manifestation, and internalization.

My father's story establishes origin, showing an inherited spiritual system where belief precedes consent and identity is shaped long before agency is exercised. Marie Michel's testimony exposes scale, showing how private allegiance can produce public consequence and reshape social environments through fear and silence. Bachon's account offers proximity, placing us inside lived experience where captivity is not announced but assembled quietly, incrementally, until perception itself becomes confinement.

With this framework in place, the narratives that follow are not presented as isolated stories, but as guiding witnesses. They illuminate how the same mechanisms operating within overt occult systems, distorted perception, isolation, internalized authority, and fear, can later be reproduced within ecclesiastical life when accusation replaces truth. This is why these narratives belong here.

The movement that follows does not begin with theory, but with inheritance: my father's life, where ancestral spiritual systems were not chosen but received, and where identity was shaped long before he had the language to name what was happening.

CHAPTER 13

THE INHERITANCE OF SHADOWS

In the narratives that follow, theology does not stand above testimony as judge, nor does testimony compete with theology for authority. Theology provides language where experience was once silent; testimony gives flesh where doctrine risks abstraction. Nothing is offered for spectacle. Nothing is shaped to satisfy curiosity. These are witnesses, human lives bearing the imprint of spiritual formation, captivity, disruption, and mercy. They are presented slowly because speed distorts perception, and haste turns weight into noise.

These stories do not replace biblical revelation.

They illuminate how ancient spiritual dynamics continue to move quietly through real human lives long before language exists to explain what is happening. Read for what is assumed as normal. Notice how fear organizes behavior without announcing itself. Observe how authority operates without explanation, how silence becomes instruction, and how loyalty is formed long before belief is examined.

What unfolds here is not a case study assembled for illustration, nor a story selected for dramatic effect. It is the story that shaped my earliest understanding of how spiritual systems are inherited long before they are chosen, and how identity can be formed inside covenants a child never consented to make. Before theological categories were available to me, before spiritual language clarified experience, I lived near the consequences of this reality. This is why the narrative begins here.

Formation Before Choice

My father did not encounter Vodou as an outsider, a skeptic, a curious observer, or a tourist in search of something exotic. He was born into it. The world that greeted his first breath was already ordered by ritual, fear, obligation, and unseen authority. Spiritual allegiance was not introduced later through experimentation or rebellion; it was assumed as part of belonging itself. Long before identity could be named, it had already been shaped. Long before belief could be examined, allegiance had already been assigned.

This distinction matters. Much of what the Church struggles to understand about spiritual captivity comes from collapsing different paths into bondage into a single category. Some people pursue power. Others are surrounded by it. Some seek influence. Others inherit its consequences. My father's life belongs to the latter. His story does not begin with desire, but with environment; not with curiosity, but with atmosphere; not with rebellion, but with formation.

In the spiritual systems that governed his childhood, protection was inseparable from fear, obedience from survival, and authority from silence. These realities were not taught through formal instruction. They were absorbed through daily life, through what was warned against, what was never questioned, and what was quietly enforced. The sacred and the dangerous lived side by side, woven into ordinary routines. There was no clear boundary between the spiritual and the practical, between ritual and necessity. To live was already to participate.

This is why his story cannot be reduced to a single moment of conversion or a dramatic confrontation. What Christ confronted in his life was not merely a practice, but an inherited order. What grace disrupted was not only belief, but a system that had shaped perception, loyalty, and fear across generations. His deliverance was not simply from spirits, but from an identity formed under covenantal pressure long before he could name it.

Inheritance Without Consent

My father did not search for light. He was born into darkness before he could walk, before he could reason, before resistance was possible. His childhood was shaped by rituals he did not choose and covenants he did not understand. Spirits were not introduced to him as danger, but as inheritance. Power was not something to be questioned; it was something assumed, accepted as part of life's order.

There was no moment in his early years when he stood outside that world and evaluated it. Darkness was not an option; it was an atmosphere. Identity, protection, meaning, and survival were all interpreted through the same spiritual system. What many encounter later through curiosity, experimentation, or crisis, he inherited through blood.

There was no conscious consent, only immersion.

And yet, when grace came, it did not come by invitation.

There was no altar prepared. No ritual reversed by another ritual. No deliverance strategy executed with precision. Grace entered unannounced, unnegotiated, and irreversible.

In a single moment, light confronted what generations of darkness had normalized. Chains recognized a higher authority without being named. Allegiance shifted without ceremony, bargaining, or resistance.

What changed my father was not fear of judgment, fascination with power, or persuasion by argument. It was encounter, not an emotional surge, not a ritual confrontation, but a sovereign interruption. Truth met surrender at the moment resistance collapsed.

Here, theology steps back and allows testimony to speak, because what followed cannot be explained by technique, only by grace.

The Ritualized World He Inherited

In the Haiti of my father's childhood, Vodou was not taught through historical narratives of African ancestry, philosophical reflections on liberation, or symbolic interpretations of resistance. It was absorbed through atmosphere, repetition, silence, obligation, and ritual expectation. Entry points were created quietly, allowing contact, interaction, replication, and eventually possession. Children did not choose participation; participation chose them.

Some families pass down land. Others pass down recipes, stories, or customs. In my father's family, spirits were inherited, names never chosen, rituals never explained, pacts no one dared to question. Often there was no ceremony to mark transmission, no warning that agreements forged long before birth were still active. The spirits were simply there, present in silence, in unexplained illness, in offerings no one discussed, and in fear that lingered even during celebration.

This inheritance shaped worldview before language could define it. It trained reverence toward what inspired fear and obedience toward what could not be questioned. For many, including my father, it meant living bound to forces that demanded loyalty, deepened suspicion, fractured community, and offered little freedom in return.

Interruption and a Rerouted Inheritance

Born in July 1920, my father's path appeared predetermined. His own father, Constant Demosthene, was a Vodou priest, respected, feared, and deeply immersed in ancestral practices. The future had already been mapped. My father was nicknamed Baron, after the Vodou spirit associated with death and funerals. His inheritance was named before he could choose otherwise. One night altered everything.

It was around three in the morning. He had finished assisting his father and returned to the small, doorless dwelling where he slept. He was not praying. He was not seeking deliverance. He was preparing to rest. An inner voice spoke, clear, calm, unmistakable: "Jodi a, ou se yon lòt moun." Today, you are a different person.

The voice did not dominate his will. It restored it. It carried no threat, no secrecy, no coercion. When he awoke at daybreak, something had reordered him. He remained himself, fully conscious, fully present, yet freed from the authority that had governed his life. His family recognized the change before he spoke. The spirits were gone.

He was expelled immediately from the ancestral compound to prevent what they believed was contamination. From that rupture, a new path opened. He attended school for the first time. He later planted churches near the very areas once governed by fear. What had been inherited was interrupted. What had been claimed was reclaimed.

I often pause in awe when I consider that rerouting. Had grace not intervened, my inheritance would have followed the same path. Instead, I was raised under a different authority, one marked by service rather than sorcery, by calling rather than covenantal fear.

Why This Story Belongs in *The Age of Ecclesiastical Accusation*

My father's story is not preserved here for shock, nostalgia, or dramatic contrast. It belongs in this book because it exposes the preconditions that make accusation possible long before accusation ever speaks. Before words are weaponized, perception has already been shaped. Before judgment is pronounced, allegiance has already been assigned. Before condemnation becomes public, fear has already organized identity in private.

What my father inherited was not merely ritual practice, but a worldview in which unseen authority governed meaning, loyalty, and consequence. In such an environment, discernment never develops. Submission replaces understanding. Silence becomes survival. These are the precise conditions under which accusation later thrives.

His deliverance did more than sever spiritual bonds. It restored perception. It returned agency where fear had dictated obedience. It disrupted an inherited logic in which power spoke first and truth followed only if it did not threaten survival. In this sense, his life is not simply about ancestral bondage; it is about the recovery of discernment itself.

Where inheritance replaces truth, accusation eventually follows, whether clothed in ancestral ritual or religious language. Where grace restores perception, accusation loses its authority.

The circumstances change, but the pattern remains. Bondage forms quietly. Grace interrupts without negotiation. From inheritance to interruption, from shadow to restored sight, this testimony prepares us to recognize the same architecture in another life, another scale, and another expression.

CHAPTER 14

MARIE MICHEL

From Blood-Stained Vodou Priestess and
Sanpwèl Queen to a Life Redeemed by Grace

The expanded title is not an exercise in sensationalism. It is a spiritual map, one that reveals both the depth of Marie Michel's former bondage and the magnitude of the grace that freed her. As a shepherd, I want the reader to see clearly who God rescued, because only by facing the depth of the darkness can we rightly measure the height of His mercy.

Her name is now defined by freedom, but her former identity was constructed deliberately, stone by stone, through spiritual titles that carried real authority and real consequence.

Vodou Priestess. This was not a casual or cultural affiliation. It was a formal spiritual office. As an established priestess, a *manbo*, she presided over rituals, served as a conduit for ancestral spirits, the *lwa*, and exercised recognized authority within a structured religious system. She was not peripheral. She was central.

Sorcerer. This title describes her function. Marie Michel was not merely initiated; she was active. She deployed spiritual power intentionally, using ritual force to control outcomes, enforce vengeance, and manipulate lives. This was not symbolic spirituality. It was operational power, feared because it worked.

Blood-Stained. This is the most severe designation. It points not to ordinary transgression, but to covenantal entanglement. Blood sacrifices sealed allegiance to the entities she served. In the spiritual realm, blood is not metaphorical; it is transactional. It establishes ownership, obligation, and debt. This title marks the weight of what had to be broken.

Sanpwèl Queen, here her influence extends beyond the local shrine. The *Sanpwèl* is associated with a clandestine, high-level occult society operating through secrecy and fear. To be identified as a "Queen" signified leadership, governance, and reach within networks deliberately hidden from public view.

Shapeshifter. This title exposes the supernatural core of her spiritual function. Known in Creole as a *lougarou*, it described an ability to transcend physical limitation, operating beyond the visible body to access spiritual dimensions for destructive purposes. This detail matters. It reveals that the forces claiming her were not symbolic, psychological, or merely cultural. They were profoundly non-human.

And yet every one of these titles is canceled by the final phrase: Redeemed by Grace. Her freedom was not achieved through counter-ritual, personal resolve, or spiritual negotiation. It came solely through the undeserved, relentless intervention of Jesus Christ.

By naming the gravity of her former identity, we are not glorifying darkness. We are magnifying the God who breaks chains others cannot see, let alone sever. Her life stands as testimony that no depth of entanglement places a soul beyond His reach.

Before grace found her, Marie Michel was no ordinary woman. In her community she was both feared and revered, a *seasoned* Vodou priestess and shapeshifter, widely known as a *lougarou*. Stories followed her presence. People whispered that she could leave her body, traverse distances instantly, appear and vanish at will. She was said to command invisible forces, summon spirits, and impose judgment or favor through unseen means.

Within Haiti's shadowed spiritual landscape, she stood as a living threshold between the human and the supernatural. Her presence generated awe, fear, and silence. Through her reputed abilities, she summoned both human souls and spiritual entities, the former to be bound or judged, the latter to function as emissaries within the unseen realm.

She was a blood-stained practitioner of ritual, convinced she had mastered Vodou's mysteries, its ancestral systems, hierarchies, and inherited power. Yet over time, something shifted. What she called mastery became mutation. Shadows inherited through lineage surfaced as personal and generational torment. Fear became the currency of authority. Power slowly revealed itself as captivity.

Beneath her influence lay ancestral debts she could neither fully perceive nor repay. What promised control delivered confinement. What appeared as wisdom collapsed into torment.

Her descent into Vodou, and her eventual renunciation of its power, has been chronicled across years of testimonies and sermons. These accounts do more than recount events; they expose the mechanisms of spiritual entanglement and the moments where divine interruption shattered them. Her story warns of the hidden cost embedded within cultural and spiritual allegiances, forces that imprison not by force alone, but by gradual consent.

At the center of her journey is the reality of soul capture: an invisible snare that draws individuals deeper into spiritual contracts long before they recognize their bondage. Such forces do not merely invite participation. They entangle. They weave obligation, fear, and loyalty into chains that tighten quietly over time.

Yet her story does not end in descent. It moves toward exposure, confrontation, and redemption. Her battle was not only against external spirits seeking possession, but against inherited belief systems and ancestral loyalties that once defined her identity. To break free meant risking everything, status, belonging, protection, and the illusion of control.

Her testimony endures because it reveals both the architecture of spiritual captivity and the triumph of divine mercy. No darkness proved too deep for grace to enter. No bondage proved stronger than God's authority to liberate.

How I Approach Marie Michel's Narrative within the Age of Ecclesiastical Accusation

I did not approach Marie Michel's testimony out of fascination, spectacle, or spiritual curiosity. I approached it with restraint and theological intent, fully aware that we are living in what this book names *The Age of Ecclesiastical Accusation*, a climate where testimonies are weaponized, suspicion masquerades as discernment, and fear is baptized as vigilance.

In such an age, narratives emerging from spiritual darkness are rarely received with patience. They are interrogated before they are heard, dissected before they are understood, and judged before they are shepherded.

My engagement with her story is therefore not reactive, but corrective. It resists a culture that rushes to indict rather than discern, to expose rather than restore. Her testimony is examined here not to provoke fear, but to model how the Church can listen responsibly when listening itself has become endangered.

Within this accusatory climate, testimonies are often treated as evidence against the individual rather than as witness to the grace of God. Scripture, however, presents testimony as revelation, not prosecution. I therefore approached her narrative as a means of establishing spiritual and moral clarity, not constructing a case against her past.

In a digitally saturated world marked by outrage and spiritual fatigue, believers easily forget the Church's primary vocation: to restore identity, form meaning, and anchor ethics in Christ rather than fear. Information overload erodes memory. Suspicion replaces wisdom. Accusation flourishes where discernment grows thin.

Studying her testimony also disrupts accusatory reflexes. In this age, motivation is assumed rather than explored. Intent is assigned rather than discerned. By examining the structure, pacing, vocabulary, and internal logic of her narrative, I sought to understand how her worldview was formed, why she acted as she did, and where divine intervention ruptured that formation. Redemption cannot be understood where motivation is ignored. Accusation thrives in the absence of context.

Her story also illuminates behavioral and psychological patterns often misread within the Church. Individuals emerging from occult, ritualized, or spiritually violent systems frequently carry conditioning shaped by fear, hierarchy, and survival. In an accusatory culture, such patterns are mislabeled as pride, deception, or rebellion. Careful analysis allows leaders to distinguish residue from intent, trauma from moral failure. Without that distinction, accusation becomes inevitable.

Memory and cognition matter as well. Inconsistencies in testimony are often treated as proof of falsehood rather than signs of human processing under extreme spiritual conditions. I observed how her clarity developed over time, how recall stabilized, and how coherence emerged gradually. Accusation demands perfection. Redemption works through integration.

Cultural context is equally essential. Her testimony opens a window into ancient spiritual systems still active in modern societies, realities often discussed abstractly but rarely understood experientially. When such realities surface through lived narrative, fear frequently overrides compassion. By situating her story within its communal and cultural framework, I aim to cultivate empathy rather than suspicion.

I paid close attention to her language and delivery, aware that in an accusatory age, tone is scrutinized more harshly than truth. Her speech retained traces of fear-based and power-oriented language alongside emerging relational and restorative patterns. Importantly, she did not universalize her experience, exaggerate urgency, or rely on theatrical intensity. Emotion was present, but governed.

Her nonverbal communication reinforced this coherence. There was no attempt to control the audience through fear, no performance-driven dramatization. In a culture that equates volume with authority and intensity with authenticity, such restraint is often misread, but it is a mark of internal stability, not deception.

Context mattered as well. She spoke in environments ranging from intimate gatherings to large auditoriums, often under emotional pressure and minimal aesthetic support. On one occasion, she shared space with a former Vodou priest turned evangelist whose life later ended violently under occult circumstances. Even then, her composure remained consistent.

Her testimony demonstrated emotional regulation, cognitive clarity, and detailed fluency in occult hierarchies and ritual systems, evidence of deep involvement rather than superficial association. In an accusatory culture, such knowledge becomes grounds for suspicion. Here, it is treated as part of what redemption redeems.

Her story also aligns with patterns echoed by former occult practitioners across Africa, the Caribbean, and the United States. Identity reconstruction, ethical reorientation, and spiritual disentanglement recur across these narratives. Her testimony is not anomalous. It is illustrative.

Finally, I frame her narrative against the misuse of legal logic within ecclesiastical life. In law, testimony is weighed carefully to establish understanding before judgment. In the Church, legal language is often adopted without legal discipline. Verdict precedes listening. Accusation replaces discernment.

By approaching her testimony with methodological care, I model a different posture, one that refuses premature judgment. The reader is invited into that same posture. Marie Michel's testimony is not presented to provoke fear or reinforce suspicion, but to expose the spiritual cost of an accusatory culture.

In *The Age of Ecclesiastical Accusation*, the greatest danger is not darkness being exposed, but light being misused. This testimony asks whether we will listen as prosecutors, or as shepherds entrusted with restoration.

Marie Michel's Story: A Testimony Entered into the Record

Marie Michel, known by different surnames across her life, from Saint-Fleur to Jean-Philippe, and later Pelissier through her marriage to Frenel Pelissier, was drawn into the intricate world of Vodou. But her initiation was not clean, voluntary, or desired. From the beginning, her relationship with Vodou carried resistance. It was shaped by the disturbing conduct of her father, whose actions cast a long shadow over her imagination and conscience. He did not introduce Vodou to her as heritage. He introduced it as fear.

For Marie, Vodou was never a harmless inheritance. It felt like secrecy, coercion, manipulation, an atmosphere where the unseen was used to govern the seen. Even as a child, she regarded it with suspicion. Yet the forces around her were not merely cultural; they were familial, communal, and spiritual. She attempted distance, but distance was not permitted. The tension between rejection and reluctant involvement became the first spine of her journey: pulled toward what she feared, pressed into what she distrusted, and forced to confront the very practices she instinctively resisted.

In Haiti, where mountains rise into the sky and the sea presses against the land, ancestral traditions are not merely remembered; they shape daily life. In Marie's family, those traditions reached beyond custom into devotion. The spirits of the ancestors were treated as active powers, believed to influence the living, reward loyalty, and punish refusal. These practices were woven into her upbringing so thoroughly that escape felt impossible. Beneath the surface of what appeared ordinary lay a darkness that would eventually entangle her in ways she could not foresee.

Her father dominated her life through fear. The air in that house did not feel neutral or safe; it felt claimed. His reputation extended beyond the household, striking terror in the surrounding community. He was known for his mastery of what was described as the sinister art of "zombification." To outsiders, it was a dark myth whispered in fear. To Marie, it was proximity. It was atmosphere. It was knowledge learned too early.

Those subjected to his practices were reduced to a near-death state, their bodies alive, yet emptied of will. Autonomy collapsed. Identity thinned. They walked and breathed, but the sense of self had been stripped away. What remained was a fragile existence suspended between life and burial, functioning at the barest level of human presence. Marie witnessed these realities not as rumor or folklore, but as lived exposure.

Despite advances in medical science, the nature of her father's methods remained obscured. His process combined Vodou ritual with toxic substances, producing effects that resisted scientific explanation. The boundary between the natural and the supernatural blurred, not in theory but in practice. His work thrived in secrecy, beyond record, beyond accountability, occupying the space where chemistry and curse could no longer be cleanly separated.

Cruelty was not incidental to his authority; it was the means by which it was enforced. He did not merely harm these individuals, he claimed dominion over them. Their stolen essence, whether understood as mind, will, or soul, remained under his control even before burial. Some lingered within the confines of the home, silent witnesses to Marie's childhood, their emptied presence a constant reminder of what power could do to a person.

This environment shaped Marie's earliest years. Fear was not an emotion she entered and exited; it became the structure of daily life. Uncertainty was constant. Before she possessed language for power or submission, she understood their weight. Her father's actions settled into her inner world like a cold draft through a foundation, imprinting her understanding of survival long before she could name the danger. She learned early that to be seen by him was to risk being emptied, that survival often meant making oneself small enough to pass unnoticed.

From Innocence to Initiation: Marie Michel's Early Years

Marie's first initiation did not begin in a public ceremony. It began inside her childhood home, where spiritual devotion saturated the atmosphere and shaped her earliest categories of reality. Her father, a devoted practitioner, cultivated a house steeped in ritual and mystery. Born in Hinche, a commune in Haiti's Centre department, Marie occupied the position of the seventh-born among her siblings, a birth order marked not by celebration, but by tragedy.

Her early years were haunted by repeated, untimely deaths. One sibling after another was lost, leaving Marie described as the sole surviving child of her mother's exhausting birthing history. Survival, in that context, did not feel accidental. It was interpreted as covenant. Her father believed he had entered into an agreement with ancestral spirits to preserve her life. Through ritual and supplication, he consecrated her from birth to the path of Vodou service, marking her not merely as a child, but as an offering.

In that framing, her destiny was sealed before consent was possible. She was defined by decree, by her father's intention and by a spiritual covenant he claimed had been accepted. In Hinche, where spiritual reputations carried real weight, her father was both revered and feared. Within that crucible of devotion, dread, and obligation, Marie's journey into Vodou began not as a choice, but as an ordinance.

As a child, she resisted. She did not trust the spirits her father served. She believed their presence brought harm rather than blessing to her family. But defiance carried consequences. She fell gravely ill, seized by a mysterious malady that appeared intent on ending her life. Under the pressure of looming death, her mother pleaded with her father to intervene, an appeal born of desperation, not faith.

Her father responded with ritual. He placed a written charm beneath her pillow and petitioned the spirits for mercy. Then came the turn that would shape Marie's imagination for years to come: the same spirits believed to have caused her illness were also credited with relenting. Her condition improved. She emerged from the brink. From that moment forward, her recovery was interpreted as a bond, an unseen claim established through sickness and survival.

Her illness became more than a medical crisis. It became an initiation. She stood at a crossroads where fear and protection wore the same face, and where the spirits were framed as both tormentors and healers. By receiving their "aid" through ritual compliance, her recovery was treated as submission, her survival as consecration. Pain and healing fused into a spiritual rite that did more than restore her body; it bound her identity to the ancestral order her father served.

Marie entered elementary school at the typical age for Haitian children, those formative years devoted to reading, writing, and arithmetic, while remaining immersed in a cultural world where spiritual tradition was not background, but atmosphere.

The Dream by the River

One night, Marie experienced a dream she would later identify as pivotal. In it, she found herself immersed in a calm, moonlit river. The scene was peaceful, almost inviting. As she lingered in the water, a crimson scarf drifted toward her on the current, deliberate in its movement, as though sent.

She shared the dream with her father. It stirred something in him that exceeded curiosity. It registered as recognition.

Days later, the dream bled into action. In the depth of night, her father woke her abruptly. His voice carried urgency without explanation. He instructed her to leave her shoes behind so their movement would make no sound. Barefoot, she followed him into the darkness, the familiar path dissolving into silence.

As they approached the family's land near the river, disorientation overtook her. Her senses dulled. Her vision dimmed. Consciousness slipped away without warning.

When awareness returned, the landscape was both familiar and altered, recognizable, yet charged with a weight she could not name. It was the same place, but not the same reality. She stood at a threshold where the visible world felt permeated by something unseen, something active.

Crossing Into the Invisible Realm

In that space, Marie described encountering beings whose appearance was both captivating and unsettling. Their features were pale and luminous under the moon, resembling persons with albinism, yet carrying a spectral quality that seemed to exceed ordinary human categories. Their presence felt detached from race, gender, and culture, an image of otherness, ambiguity, and power. Whether interpreted literally or symbolically, the encounter functioned as an announcement: she had crossed into a realm where the spiritual and physical intertwined, and where her understanding of life, and her role within it, would be reshaped.

Her father returned home before dawn, slipping back into his bed as if nothing had occurred. By morning, Marie's absence triggered panic. Her mother searched. The household searched. The community searched. Her father feigned ignorance, adopting the posture of a concerned parent as the search intensified.

Desperation drove Marie's mother to broader appeal. She enlisted the community and turned to local radio, broadcasting descriptions and pleas, her age, her features, when she was last seen, urging anyone with information to come forward. The community responded with the solidarity of a tight-knit people, multiplying efforts, spreading word, and searching everywhere.

Days turned into weeks. Then her father claimed he had sought guidance from the spirits and that they had revealed Marie was dead. A memorial was arranged. The community gathered. Mourning settled like dust over the streets. They grieved a child vanished without a trace, resigned to the cruelty of unanswered disappearance.

But Marie's story, as later told, did not end at the memorial.

Beneath the river where she had been taken, she described an initiation unfolding, quiet, secretive, and profound, while her life above continued to be counted as lost. In that hidden place, she was drawn deeper into the rites of Vodou. Unlike many who first passed through the traditional *kanzo* rite, a grueling passage often described as death and rebirth, she reported bypassing that stage entirely. Instead, she was propelled directly into what she later described as a higher, more secretive tier of occult training. In her telling, this leap was not random. It signaled a unique positioning within the hierarchy, an early indication that her role would be unusually deep, unusually formed, and unusually dangerous.

The realm she described felt submerged, as though she had entered a world beneath the ocean's surface. There, she underwent training guided by the same pale, otherworldly beings. Under their tutelage, she was instructed in esoteric knowledge, ritual structures, and spiritual operations she would later recount with unsettling fluency.

She described being shown a bottle, a vessel containing a mysterious liquid, presented as a means of transcending ordinary human limitation. In her vocabulary, the liquid enabled travel beyond normal boundaries of distance and form, producing transformations she described as explicitly non-human. Whatever language one applies, the function within her testimony remained consistent: she believed she was being trained to move across realms, to shift states, and to operate beyond ordinary physical restriction.

As she absorbed this knowledge, her perception of reality expanded. She later described it as a world where thought and movement, desire and displacement, were tightly linked. The experience reshaped her inner map of what was possible, and clarified what had claimed her.

The Return and the First Witness

When she later spoke of returning, Marie described instruction rather than escape. She was told to close her eyes and extend her arms, a posture of surrender rather than effort. Then, without transition, everything shifted.

She opened her eyes on the shore of the same river where her father had left her months earlier. The return did not feel sequential. Distance collapsed. Time folded. The movement defied ordinary travel, registering instead as displacement.

Dizziness overtook her again. She lost consciousness. When she awoke, she found herself on a road in Maïssade, a familiar route leading back toward Hinche, approximately eighteen kilometers away. The span of distance bore no relationship to the passage of time. Moments compressed into what felt like a single instant. Consciousness slipped again.

When she awoke once more, she stood in front of her home.

In her account, the experience extended beyond movement. The boundary between thought and environment blurred. Reality felt responsive, as though external space bent to internal command. Whatever the mechanism, spiritual, occult, or psychological, the experience conveyed one unambiguous conviction: she believed herself to be operating under a power not native to ordinary human life.

The first person to see her reacted with terror. Convinced she was an apparition returned from the dead, he accused her of being a ghost sent to torment him and fled in panic. Marie later recalled laughter, not playful, but disoriented, the response of a child standing inside an impossible moment.

Her testimony then records consequence. The man who saw her was struck blind. News spread rapidly. Neighbors came, one by one, drawn by fear and awe, compelled to see whether the impossible stood before them. What had been mourned as death now confronted them as presence.

The *Ason* and Her Initiation

In the midst of that hidden training, beneath the surface of ordinary life, Marie reported receiving an artifact: an *ason*, an ornate gourd rattle adorned with beads and small bells. Within Vodou, the *ason* carries profound significance, functioning as a ceremonial instrument associated with authority and communication with the *lwa*.

She said she was instructed to keep it in her school bag. Its sound, she was told, would function as a signal, a summons, announcing the presence of unseen visitors awaiting her return from school. Invisible to others, audible only to her, the *ason* became a private marker of affiliation: a reminder that she was no longer merely observing a spiritual world. She had been claimed by it.

The Awakening of Shape-Shifting Power

Marie explained that during her underwater initiation, she encountered her abilities with a mixture of awe and curiosity. She believed the liquid given to her endowed her with the capacity to become a shape-shifter, an entity capable of transcending ordinary physical limitation. In her testimony, this transformation manifested as fire emerging from her mouth, anus, and vagina, each described as carrying distinct symbolic meaning.

The fire from her mouth signified the ability to transcend physical barriers, allowing entry into and exit from dwellings without doors or windows. It represented freedom of movement across spiritual and material thresholds, a capacity to navigate unseen realms without obstruction. For her, this marked the beginning of a new identity, one shaped by power, mystery, and altered belonging.

She described a fiery manifestation upon the roof as a protective ward, casting light across the surrounding area. It functioned as a safeguard, repelling other spiritual forces and asserting dominance over contested space. In her telling, it was both defense and declaration.

The flame she described as emanating from her vagina carried a different significance. It functioned as a signal to others within the same clandestine network, women, priestesses, and practitioners embedded in the spiritual fabric of the community. This manifestation announced the presence of a new initiate, summoning recognition and communion. Through it, she believed she was being woven into a collective identity shared by those who walked hidden paths within the spiritual hierarchy.

The Path of Power and Recruitment

In this way, the celestial fires that manifested upon Marie's transformed form came to function as symbols of mastery within the arcane order she now inhabited. They were not merely signs of ability, but markers of advancement, guiding her through the labyrinthine corridors of the Vodou tradition and illuminating what she understood as a path toward spiritual transcendence.

Marie's journey did not remain confined to private transformation. It extended outward. She assumed the role of recruiter, tasked with expanding the reach of ancestral entities into the lives of those closest to her, unsuspecting schoolmates and friends. Her identity remained concealed beneath a veil of secrecy. Among her peers, she moved quietly, like an emissary operating in plain sight, weaving subtle threads of influence that drew others into the ancient tradition without their full awareness.

Unaware of the depth of her involvement or the forces directing her actions, classmates and friends found themselves caught in a web of intrigue and fascination. They were drawn by the allure of mystery and the promise of hidden knowledge. Through persuasive presence and careful attention to personal desires, Marie guided them gradually into initiation, presenting the path as ancestral "heritage" rather than spiritual submission.

As she watched her peers yield to the promise of transcendence offered by the ancestral entities, her sense of purpose deepened. Recruitment became confirmation. Expansion became validation. Even as she balanced secrecy and exposure, she remained vigilant, guarding the traditions she believed had been entrusted to her by unseen powers that now ordered her steps.

In fulfilling the relentless demands of these spirits, Marie entered a dangerous rhythm of sacrifice and supplication. The methods prescribed to her increasingly bent toward coercion and control. Within Hinche, whispers of her actions spread quickly, casting fear and suspicion across a childhood already surrendered to unseen authority. Power, once granted, demanded obedience. And obedience came at the cost of restraint.

The Video Chronicles of Transformation

In a later s*eason* of her life, Marie meticulously documented her journey through a series of recorded testimonies. In these video chronicles, she described her transformation following initiation into what she identified as an esoteric spiritual realm. Each account unfolded with precision, offering viewers an intimate window into her evolving consciousness.

She described traversing the depths of awareness until the boundaries of self-dissolved. According to her testimony, she entered into communion not with a single entity, but with multiple malevolent spirits, merging her essence with theirs. This union, as she narrated it, erased distinction, between thought and presence, between inner and outer reality. Her individuality blurred as her consciousness expanded into what she perceived as a unified field of spiritual existence.

Within that expanded state, she spoke of a profound sense of interconnectedness, as though her being resonated in alignment with a vast, unseen order. Yet even as she articulated transcendence, the seeds of loss were already present.

The Loss of Empathy and Descent into Darkness

Amid the exhilaration of spiritual elevation, a quieter transformation unfolded. The same union that granted her access to power also diminished her capacity for human empathy. As the spirits entwined themselves with her identity, they eroded emotional connection. Compassion thinned. Detachment took root.

What began as pursuit of enlightenment gradually estranged her from ordinary human feeling. The spirits she once perceived as external influences became integrated facets of her inner life. Enlightenment and alienation advanced together, binding her in a paradox she could not yet recognize.

This descent began at an age when most children remain sheltered within innocence. Before adolescence, Marie became a conduit for multiple vengeful entities, spirits associated with illness, chaos, and misfortune. Drawn to her availability, they found in her a vessel through which their influence could move outward into the community.

Though young in years, she carried a weight that exceeded childhood capacity. Their presence distorted perception and eroded moral clarity. Over time, their whispered influence reshaped her sense of right and wrong until she functioned as an instrument of their intent. Darkness did not arrive suddenly; it tightened gradually, coiling itself around every facet of her developing identity.

Within her testimony, Marie later served as a guide through this system, mapping its structure with unsettling clarity. She delineated its logic, its hierarchy, and its cost, leaving little room for ambiguity.

The Path of Power and Consequence

Whether interpreted as ancestral inheritance or as demonic manipulation, Marie Michel's account functions as a call to discernment. Through her experiences, she exposes both the promised "virtues" and the hidden violence embedded within this spiritual economy.

By this stage, she had left her parents' home. Still a teenager, she operated independently, recruiting and initiating two classmates into Vodou practice. Together, the three adolescents, guided by ancestral entities, exercised their abilities with tangible effect across the community.

Reactions were mixed. Some sought them out for prosperity or vengeance. Others recoiled in fear. Their activities disrupted existing power balances, introducing instability and tension within social and spiritual structures that had long governed community life.

Each consultation demanded ritual. Some were familiar, others increasingly ominous. Animal sacrifice, invocation of ancestral entities, and ceremonial chanting became common. Tarot readings preceded action, determining ritual direction. For those seeking retaliation, "spiritual arrestation" was employed, using human essence or spirits to restrain or afflict a target. Marie explained that gender polarity was often exploited: female spirits sent against men, male entities against women. In the most extreme cases, rituals escalated toward human death, justified as spiritual necessity or ancestral command. These practices exposed the destructive trajectory of power exercised without moral boundary.

Reflecting later as a Christian evangelist, Marie identified the underlying principle as soul capture, not human invention, but inherited knowledge transmitted through the Vodou pantheon. The cost of such knowledge was bondage. Her testimony stands as revelation and warning, exposing the convergence of power, spirituality, and human agency within the system she once served.

Soul Capture: The Tale of Familial Turmoil in the Shrine of Marie Michel

Marie later recounted the case of a woman who came to her shrine seeking healing for her son. The boy suffered from a mysterious illness believed to be the result of a Vodou attack orchestrated by his uncle, his mother's brother. The attack stemmed from resentment within a shared household and community.

The uncle's bitterness was rooted in cultural and linguistic tension. Speaking primarily Creole, he felt humiliated when the boy addressed him in French, a symbol, to him, of social disparity and disrespect. That resentment festered until it manifested as spiritual aggression directed at the child.

Unaware of her brother's actions, the boy's mother sought Marie's help, desperate to save her son. Trusting her family, she entered the shrine blind to the source of harm. Her desperation entangled her in a web of manipulation that compounded suffering rather than resolved it.

Marie, feared and revered, stood at the center of this conflict. Navigating resentment, family fracture, and spiritual demand, she confronted the volatile intersection of personal grievance and ritual power.

Under pressure from the uncle, Marie summoned a spirit that prescribed a ritual to detach the boy's soul from his body. This act, associated with advanced Vodou practice, left the child suspended between realms.

Two manifestations followed: the physical body, asleep in the healing room, and the soul form, described as a luminous, holographic presence, bound to a post in the altar room. At the moment of detachment, the boy experienced himself bound, witnessing his own separation in a disorienting dream-state.

At noon, believed to amplify ritual potency, Marie prepared to strike the soul form three times, head, heart, and right abdomen. As the knife was raised, a cry pierced the silence: "Jesus, save me." The knife fell. The ritual collapsed.

Rushing to the healing room, Marie found the boy still asleep, yet engaged in intense inner dialogue. When he awoke, he requested immediate transport to a Protestant church, where he renounced Vodou. At that moment, the soul form vanished from the shrine.

The mother emerged devastated, financially ruined by ritual costs and spiritually disillusioned. Instead of healing, she inherited debt and loss.

As Marie and other practitioners later acknowledged, attempting to harm someone under what they termed Divine Immunity carried severe consequences. Accounts from ex-practitioners, including Emmanuel Etienne, the late Bachon, and Anold, confirmed this reality. In one account, Anold attempted to retrieve a corpse for sorcery and was confronted by a radiant being guarding the grave. Mistaking the figure for rival priests, he advanced, only to be struck by a sword that shattered his upper front teeth. The grave was sealed. Access denied.

These testimonies reinforced a shared conclusion: attacking those under divine protection invited catastrophic consequence. Marie knew this. And so the boy was released.

Frozen in Place: Divine Immunity and the Shapeshifter's Limits

In modern storytelling, the shapeshifter has become a familiar figure, often explored through themes of fractured identity, imitation, and transformation without consequence. Contemporary series such as *Fringe* present shapeshifting through unsettling yet controlled imagery: bodies shedding skin, faces reforming, identities exchanged with clinical precision. Though the visuals echo ancient folklore, the narratives ultimately reframe these transformations as engineered phenomena, products of advanced science, parallel realities, or biological manipulation. The viewer is disturbed, but also reassured. The horror remains fictional, contained, explainable.

What *Fringe* repeatedly exposes, however, is that imitation is not the same as humanity. Its shapeshifters replicate appearance flawlessly, yet something essential is a*lways* absent, empathy, conscience, moral restraint. Transformation becomes an act of replacement rather than growth. The unease does not arise from change itself, but from what disappears in the process.

In this account, shapeshifting does not remain metaphor. For Marie Michel, transformation was neither symbolic nor cinematic. It was lived reality, rooted in Vodou's esoteric systems and sustained through ritual, covenant, and prolonged engagement with unseen forces. Where modern fiction explains transformation through science or fantasy, Marie's abilities emerged through spiritual authorization.

Her metamorphosis involved literal movement beyond the visible body: the shifting of presence, the summoning of entities, and the extension of influence into physical space. She entered environments unseen, altered perception, and imposed fear or favor upon human lives. These capacities placed her among the most feared and respected practitioners of her time. Her power was not theoretical. It produced consequences. People adjusted their behavior around her name because her influence was tangible, and costly.

Yet even at the height of her mastery, her authority carried an unspoken limit. It could manipulate access and form, but it could not generate peace, permanence, or freedom. Control masked dependency. Authority concealed bondage. Transformation without truth reshaped the surface while leaving the deeper fracture untouched. What appeared as dominance was, in reality, conditional.

That illusion collapsed the night she attempted to abduct a child shielded by divine immunity.

By every occult calculation she understood, the operation should have succeeded. Assisted by a specific entity, Marie entered the family's cement-block home without resistance, passed through physical barriers, and lifted the child into her arms. Until that moment, nothing opposed her. But as she moved to exit, something shifted. The power that enabled her entry now refused her departure.

At the threshold of the gate, her movement ceased.

Her spells did not weaken gradually; they stopped entirely. Her psychic reach met silence. The unseen pathways she relied upon collapsed without warning. Divine immunity, the spiritual covering Jesus provides that renders a person inaccessible to malevolent intrusion, stood before her as an absolute boundary. It did not counterattack. It did not negotiate. It simply nullified her presence.

Frozen in place, Marie confronted a reality she had never encountered: not all power operates by the same rules. What she had assumed to be universal dominance revealed itself as conditional authority. Her abilities could summon entities, shift presence, and instill fear, but they could not penetrate a life sealed by divine will. The realization exposed something more unsettling than defeat, vulnerability.

At that same moment, the child's mother, awakened by an inexplicable prompting, stepped into the backyard and found Marie immobilized near the gate, holding her son. Without fear, she reclaimed the child and spoke with unexpected authority, declaring divine power and redemption into the stillness of the night. Marie stood unable to move or resist, exposed before a sovereignty she could neither challenge nor comprehend.

This encounter did more than interrupt a ritual; it reframed Marie's entire spiritual framework. The entities she trusted proved powerless. Her mastery dissolved at the boundary of divine authority. For the first time, she confronted a power that did not rely on secrecy, transformation, or fear, but rested on alignment with a higher sovereignty, one that rendered every counterfeit authority ineffective.

Marie would later wrestle with a question that haunted her: why were some immune while others were not? That distinction lingered. The experience left her frozen, both outwardly and inwardly, forced to confront the limits of her craft, the ethics of her power, and the existence of an order that could not be subverted. What began in confidence became the moment her certainty fractured, planting the first seed of doubt about the path she had chosen and the forces she had trusted to guide her.

The Abilities of a Hybrid Being

Marie Michel's existence as a hybrid being placed her in a category modern audiences instinctively recognize, even if they struggle to name it. Like the mythic hybrids of *Pan's Labyrinth*, whose power flows from crossing the boundary between the human and the otherworldly, Marie operated in a space where realms overlapped rather than opposed one another. Her condition also echoes the unsettling premise of *Splice*, where hybridity grants extraordinary capacity while violating natural order.

Marie's abilities were not imagined or symbolic. They emerged from deep spiritual entanglement that allowed her to function with rare fluency in both physical and spiritual domains. She moved between realms with an ease unavailable to most Vodou practitioners.

Despite the tensions surrounding her hybridity, there existed an undeniable collaboration between the entities she served and the systems that recognized her value. Traditional practitioners remained wary of her engagement with forces beyond the ancestral framework. The ancient beings she channeled were indifferent to human concerns. Yet both accepted her as an indispensable asset.

This hybrid identity became both strength and undoing. It elevated her influence while drawing her toward moments of reckoning. One such moment, the failed abduction of a divinely protected child, forced her to confront the limits of her reach and the presence of authority beyond her control.

A Living Enigma: The Depth of Marie Michel's Powers

Marie Michel's story embodies the unsettling complexity of spiritual hybridity. Her dual alignment with the Vodou pantheon and ancient non-human intelligences placed her beyond the reach of ordinary practitioners, marking her as a figure of rare capacity and deep contradiction. This hybridity did not merely expand her abilities; it exposed her to ethical tension, spiritual risk, and existential conflict.

It is reasonable to conclude that Marie operated beyond the spirits she served and even beyond entities commonly labeled as demonic. Her command of spiritual and physical domains, coupled with an intuitive grasp of transcendence, positioned her in a category of her own. By her testimony, her movements aligned with principles modern science associates with quantum theory, non-locality, permeability, and simultaneous presence. For Marie, these were not borrowed metaphors. They formed the architecture of lived experience.

While contemporary culture approaches transcendence through fiction and speculation, Marie embodied it daily. Her capacity to bypass physical barriers, manipulate unseen forces, and navigate hidden thresholds reflected a depth of engagement rivaling scientific imagination, without the safety of fiction's distance. She moved through layered realities, altering outcomes with a fluency that mirrors the hypothetical abilities attributed to interdimensional beings, yet without abstraction.

Her story demands a reevaluation of spirituality, transcendence, and unseen influence. In her former life, Marie Michel was not merely a practitioner executing learned rituals. She was a living convergence of power and peril, embodying both the reach and the danger inherent in engagement with forces beyond human comprehension.

Marie Michel's Lifestyle: Wealth, Fear, and Shadows

Marie Michel lived suspended between wealth and deprivation, fear and authority, ancient tradition and modern greed. She earned substantial sums from clients seeking domination, revenge, healing, or protection. Her clientele ranged from villagers to foreigners who traveled long distances, drawn by her reputation.

Yet her wealth was never fully hers. Payments were divided with the entities she served, demanded as compensation for allegiance and continued power. She operated within a rigid framework dictated by these forces, leaving little space for autonomy. Her thinking aligned almost mechanically with prescribed tradition. Innovation was absent. Questioning was forbidden.

Despite her earnings, Marie lived in poverty. Her life remained static, frozen in habit. She resided in a small, deteriorating hut, surrounded by isolation and dread. The community, aware of her powers since childhood, kept its distance, balancing fear with reluctant respect.

Her home stood at the end of a winding dirt road, marked by symbols and traps designed to repel intrusion. Iron artifacts representing Ogou guarded the gate, with human bones buried beneath as sentinels. Weeds overtook the land. What once may have been fertile now served as warning.

Beyond the Veil: Unraveling Remedies for Marie Michel's Hybrid Identity

Marie Michel's story exceeds the reach of conventional frameworks. Her identity, human, yet spiritually hybridized, resists classification by science, law, medicine, or technology. Rooted in ancestral covenant and reinforced through esoteric engagement, her condition exposes the limits of modern systems designed to address only the visible.

This inquiry does not seek immediate resolution. It asks whether contemporary structures can engage realities they neither recognize nor regulate without inflicting further harm. Marie's existence reveals a gap between institutional capacity and spiritual causation.

Scientific methods rely on measurement. Legal systems require jurisdiction. Technology addresses material processes. None can diagnose covenantal bondage or metaphysical intrusion. Marie's life therefore demands an approach that acknowledges the unseen shaping human agency.

Before examining her eventual abandonment of Vodou and her reluctant turn toward Christianity, it is necessary to ask whether any alternative path existed. Could she have been restored without rupture? Healed without dismantling the architecture that sustained her power? Or would every intervention have treated symptoms while preserving the core?

These questions expose the inadequacy of reductionist remedies. Marie's case insists that some harm originates beyond visible mechanisms and therefore requires discernment rather than denial, humility rather than containment, and compassion that does not confuse tolerance with healing.

It is necessary to pause and inhabit the atmosphere that surrounded Marie Michel's activities, the disruption, the suffocating uncertainty, and the collective psychological weight borne by families under her shadow. Fear did not announce itself loudly. It settled quietly, altering behavior before language could name it. Streets emptied early. Children clung to their parents. Sleep thinned, fractured by the cries of animals in the night. The community waited for permission to breathe that never came.

Marie's name was rarely spoken, yet it pressed constantly against daily life, shaping movement, speech, and vigilance.

Her testimony concerning her role as a *Sanpwèl* Queen resists full exposure. Even in restraint, it speaks of nocturnal abductions and operations too dark to recount without compounding harm. Terror did not depend on spectacle. It multiplied in the space between certainty and possibility.

Over time, Marie organized a clandestine network of shapeshifters, men and women bound by shared abilities and obligations. This network functioned as an invisible apparatus, destabilizing neighborhoods and villages alike. Their presence fractured rest, invaded dreams, and eroded safety.

Those without higher spiritual covering, including lower-ranking practitioners, were especially vulnerable. Parents awoke to trembling children unable to articulate what had reached them.

I remember this fear as a child. One night, I saw my father crouched in darkness, gripping sea salt, waiting for a cat he suspected was not an animal at all. Even when no intruder appeared, fear returned nightly, immune to reassurance.

This silence nourished Marie's authority. Her influence expanded because victims could not name or confront its source. Endurance replaced resistance.

When divine protection is referenced here, it does not describe ritual safeguards or esoteric defenses. Marie's network operated across boundaries of culture and belief. Only one group remained beyond her reach: those living under the authority of Christ. Marie and former priest Emmanuel Etienne referred to them simply as *moun sa yo*, "these people."

Their immunity did not originate in lineage, hierarchy, or technique. It rested in righteousness and faith. According to Marie's testimony, it was the only force capable of resisting her network completely. In acknowledging that boundary, she unknowingly identified the limit of her authority, a limit that would ultimately collapse her power and lead to the confrontation that followed.

The Divine Clash: Chains Broken, Demon Fled, and Ancestral Spirits Shattered as God Comes for Marie Michel's Soul

Marie herself bore a heavy burden. Beneath the veneer of power, she was ensnared by forces far greater than her own will. Rituals consumed her days. Nights were haunted by spirits she could neither escape nor govern. Existence became a cycle of servitude to entities that fed on fear. Yet before the final collapse of her foundation, a dark chapter unfolded, one that would reveal the reach of her influence with terrifying clarity.

It began with a neighbor's tragedy. A man's wife had suffered repeated miscarriages, each ending abruptly, each without medical explanation. Grief settled into the couple's face, and Marie noticed it. She chose to intervene, not out of mercy, but to settle a vendetta against a woman who was the most unlikely of suspects.

Marie approached the husband, steady and cold. "It is your mother," she said.

The man froze. His mother was frail and elderly, living in his home because she could no longer care for herself. She had *always* been his refuge, his source of unconditional love. To him, Marie's accusation was unthinkable.

But Marie did not soften. She branded the older woman a shapeshifter, a high-ranking member of her own nocturnal network. This was no divine revelation. It was a calculated strike. The older woman had once defied Marie, refusing to honor a deal. Now Marie exacted repayment by turning a son against his mother, using heartbreak as the blade.

Torn between devotion and desperation, the man demanded proof. He set a condition he believed would be impossible: a thunderclap at precisely noon under a cloudless sky. If the heavens spoke in broad daylight, without storm or wind, he would accept the truth.

Marie accepted without hesitation. She retreated to her shrine and performed a grueling ritual to her deity, Holorum, an intense ceremony of offerings and chants, designed to compel the supernatural to answer on command.

As the clock drew near noon, a suffocating silence settled over the household. The man stared at the horizon, caught between hope for his mother's innocence and dread of the alternative. Then the hour struck, and the impossible happened. A deafening crack of thunder shattered the stillness, reverberating over the roof. The sky remained a perfect blue, no rain, no wind, yet the sound was unmistakable.

The man stood frozen. The precision of the sign met his demand, and in that instant, his world collapsed. The woman who had given him life became, in his mind, the architect of his wife's suffering. He broke down, crushed by a revelation he did not know how to carry.

Marie watched with detached satisfaction. This was more than victory. It was demonstration. She had destroyed an enemy and tightened her grip on the community's imagination, cementing a dominance that reached beyond fear and into belief itself.

But triumph proved to be a prelude.

Not long after, the atmosphere shifted. It began like an ordinary afternoon at the shrine, followers calling her Manman, herbs heavy in the air, ritual familiarity holding the room together. Then a strange stillness took hold.

The quiet deepened so profoundly that even the spirits seemed to withdraw.

Without warning, a group of men and women entered the shrine. Uninvited. Unannounced. Dressed plainly, carrying only worn Bibles, they bore no resemblance to her usual petitioners. They brought no offerings. They did not hesitate. Most striking of all was the absence of fear in their eyes.

They moved with an unwavering confidence that rattled Marie and her partner. It stripped the room of dominance. It exposed, suddenly, the vulnerability of the forces she served. And it forced her to confront a higher authority, one that did not negotiate with her network and did not bend to her rituals.

The Spread of Scandal and the Arrival of the Missionaries

News spread quickly through Hinche. Whispers traveled from market stalls to street corners, from private kitchens to the town square. The story, already unsettling, collided with a scheduled open-air evangelization led by Protestant missionaries from out of town. Known for bold preaching and direct outreach, they arrived with a mission of renewal.

When they heard of the couple's ordeal, they visited the man's home to pray and offer support. In a modest living room still marked by grief, they listened as the man poured out the story, his wife's miscarriages, the despair that had overtaken the household, and Marie Michel's sudden claim.

When the missionaries asked for proof, he described the events in detail. He told them of Marie's accusation, the condition he had demanded, and the thunder, no storm, no clouds, only the sound, exact and impossible.

The missionaries exchanged glances, shock giving way to resolve.

"And this woman," one missionary asked, leaning forward, "Marie Michel, where is she now?"

The man lowered his voice, as if afraid she might hear. He pointed toward a neighboring yard. "She's right there," he said. "She was the one who exposed my mother."

Marie Michel, tending her yard just beyond the gathering, sensed the conversation before she understood its words. Her spiritual alertness stirred. She moved closer. The voices sharpened. And then she realized, with certainty, that they were speaking about her.

From her vantage point, she overheard everything. She listened as the man recounted her role, her methods, her knowledge. She stiffened as the missionaries debated her involvement. Their tone shifted from curiosity to purpose. When one of them said, "We must pay her a visit," Marie felt something she had not felt in years: unease.

She had seen their kind before, fearless, unwavering, shielded by an authority she could not manipulate.

Marie retreated to her shrine, her mind racing. The planned visit hovered like a storm cloud. For the first time in years, she felt exposed. She began to prepare, summoning courage, gathering what strength she believed remained in her network. Yet beneath preparation, doubt had already taken root. She could feel their authority, not in noise, but in weight.

As the hours passed, anticipation tightened. Marie knew this would not be ordinary. It would be confrontation. It would challenge what she had built, what she had believed, and the power she had treated as final.

Marie, Sheila, and Jonise Prepare for Confrontation

Marie paced the dim interior of the shrine, nerves taut, mind replaying the overheard words. The missionaries' declaration, that they would come, uninvited, through the gate, pressed on her like a threat she could not dismiss.

She summoned her two closest confidants, Sheila and Jonise, and told them what she had heard. Both women listened in silence at first, disbelief shifting into indignation.

"They plan to come here," Marie said, voice low, charged. "They said they will walk through the gate, uninvited, and enter the shrine."

Sheila slammed her hand on the table. "If they dare step here without your permission, they'll face consequences," she snapped. "We're not responsible for what happens if they enter this place."

Jonise nodded, expression dark. "They don't know what they're walking into," she said. "The shrine is guarded. It's their risk."

Marie held her composure, but turmoil rose beneath it. Sheila and Jonise spoke with confidence, yet Marie's apprehension kept growing. Something about this group unsettled her. Still, she forced strength into her voice.

"They don't understand what they're dealing with," she said. "This shrine is not a place they can simply walk into. The spirits will not tolerate disrespect."

Sheila leaned forward, eyes blazing. "Then let them come," she said. "We'll let the spirits handle it. They won't make it past the gate."

Marie nodded, but her thoughts raced. The audacity of the missionaries was unprecedented. Their fearlessness hinted at a power she did not fully understand.

They spoke strategy in hushed tones. Marie outlined measures. Sheila and Jonise pledged loyalty. Threats were rehearsed as if speaking them could secure outcomes.

"If they come," Sheila said, "we'll let them experience the full power of this place. They'll regret ever thinking they could enter."

Marie agreed, though her unease did not lift. "Let them come," she said finally. "But if they cross the threshold, they'll face consequences. The spirits will see to that."

And so they waited, the shrine, once a place of control, now feeling like a stage set for a confrontation already written in the unseen.

A Bold Entrance

Without hesitation, the Christian group, women and men, entered Marie Michel's yard. The air thickened with tension, the kind that warns of collision. They ignored the customary spiritual toll of thirty-seven gourdes that visitors were expected to pay to appease guarding spirits. They walked forward with unwavering intent, voices raised in hymns that carried through the yard.

They stopped at the shrine entrance, where Sheila stood as gatekeeper, posture firm, eyes defiant. A woman among the missionaries stepped forward, serene, resolute, and said, "We've come to see Marie Michel."

Sheila answered sharply, with menace. "Marie Michel is here, but you won't be able to see her. Any attempt to step inside this shrine will be your last. You won't leave here alive."

A man near the center of the group spoke without hesitation. "In Jesus' name," he declared, "we will enter."

The boldness of the name struck like a direct challenge. For Sheila and Jonise, it was insult, an assault on the spirits protecting the shrine.

Inside, Marie sat on her ceremonial chair and scoffed when she heard it. "Jesus?" she said with a smirk. "I'd love to see how Jesus looks. Let Him come if He dares."

Her confidence leaned on years of dominance and a network that had always answered her call. Yet as the hymns grew louder, something in the atmosphere shifted. It felt as though a force was pressing back against the invisible protections surrounding the shrine.

Marie continued to smile, but unease flickered beneath it. The name of Jesus had been spoken with a weight she had not encountered before. The clash was no longer theoretical. It was present. It was deciding.

The Confrontation

One missionary stepped forward and knocked firmly on the weathered wooden door where Marie had barricaded herself. From behind it, her voice rang out, sharp and guarded: "Who is it?"

A calm, authoritative voice replied, "We are the Christian missionaries who came with a message. We'd like to know if you received it."

Marie answered curtly, hoping to defuse the moment. "Yes, I received it."

She assumed that would end the exchange. But another voice responded, "Great. Now that you've received it, open the door. We want to talk to you. If you received it, then we are now brothers and sisters in Christ."

Marie bristled and refused. The tension tightened. A third voice declared, "If you don't open this door, we will break it down."

Fury surged. Marie flung the door open. "What do you want?" she demanded.

But before she could say more, they stepped in, boldly crossing into her shrine without invitation.

Marie moved to reassert dominance. She turned toward a chair suspended mid-air, a display she attributed to her mastery of dark arts. With a commanding gesture, she ordered it to lower. It descended instantly. She sat. With another gesture, it rose again, lifting her above the room. From that elevated position, she looked down on the missionaries, trying to reclaim the old fear.

She reached for a small glass bottle. Its contents glowed faintly, a potion she claimed could capture a soul instantly. She raised it, prepared to use it against the intruders.

Before she could act, one missionary stepped forward and spoke with unwavering conviction: "What you're doing is nothing. We are here to destroy your demons and their powers in the name of Jesus."

Prayer erupted. Hymns rose. Declarations filled the room. The atmosphere shifted. And Marie, still on the suspended chair, felt something unfamiliar: heat. It began as warmth, then intensified, burning from within.

The bottle trembled in her hand. The glow inside flickered, as though losing potency. Her confidence faltered as the sensation spread. She tried to command the chair higher, to distance herself. It did not respond. The hymns grew louder, striking her like waves. And she realized, with rising fear, that the forces she relied on were retreating.

For the first time, Marie Michel was powerless in her own shrine, confronted not by rival practitioners, but by a divine authority she had never anticipated. Heat. Fire. Prayer. And the beginning of a transformation she never imagined.

Marie stormed out, drenched in sweat, frustration erupting into motion. Outside, she found Sheila pacing. The two agreed: the next stage would require traps.

They prepared deadly snares throughout the yard, poisonous objects buried in the ground, invisible spiritual mechanisms designed to kill anyone who stepped on them. They worked deliberately, confident in their dark resolve.

Then, an eerie silence descended from the shrine, as the missionaries continued in worship. Time felt suspended. Marie stopped, senses sharpened. Was this victory, or something worse?

Out of that silence, a burst of "Alleluia" erupted with such force it reverberated through the yard. To Marie, it sounded like the onset of trance or possession by a *lwa*. In her tradition, such moments required immediate salutation, alcohol poured, spirits acknowledged.

Believing her network had finally arrived, Marie surged with triumph. She grabbed a bottle of alcohol and moved toward the shrine.

But as she approached, the voices inside shifted, sharp, declarative, precise.

"You've placed traps outside to kill us," one of them said.

Marie froze.

Pride pushed her forward, but dread pulled at her instincts. The group shouted in unison, "If you touch us, you'll be burned!"

The warning halted her. The authority in their words was unlike anything she had encountered. For the first time, doubt landed hard.

Still, she clung to Holorum. Holorum had *always* proclaimed himself creator of heaven and earth, boasting Christians would burn while Vodou priests would ascend. That belief kept her defiance alive.

A Miraculous Intervention

The missionaries began to leave. A woman led them, steady, determined. To Marie's astonishment, the woman bent down and unearthed every trap with her bare hands. The toxins, designed for instant death, were rendered powerless in her touch. She moved without hesitation, worship still on her lips.

Marie and Sheila watched in disbelief. The sight shook them. For the first time, Marie questioned the strength of the spirits she served, not privately, but in the open air of reality.

After the missionaries departed, Marie and Sheila regrouped. Two options emerged: summon Holorum, or consult a seven-headed snake spirit. They chose Holorum.

Rituals were performed. Holorum appeared, but his presence was different. Less commanding. Disturbed.

He began with apology. "What has happened here," he said, "has shaken even me."

Marie felt her stomach drop.

Holorum continued: "I have decided to leave. I can no longer withstand what they've done. Their power, this divine force, is beyond anything we can counter. If I could act, I would. But even I am powerless against this."

For the first time, Marie saw her trusted deity defeated and despondent. His departure was the ultimate betrayal. The one entity she believed would stand with her had confessed limitation and abandoned her. The confession did more than wound her, it shattered the architecture of her confidence.

Marie was devastated. Her spirits had fled. Rituals had failed. Now Holorum had deserted her. The missionaries' victory did not merely disrupt her practices; it fractured her identity. In that aftermath, she stood facing an uncertain future, alone, exposed, and unable to return to the certainty that had once governed her life.

And yet, even in despair, the first seed of transformation had been planted.

The Invocation of Manman Jumeaux

In the aftermath of Holorum's departure, Marie Michel, desperate for guidance and reinforcements, turned to another powerful entity within her spiritual arsenal: Manman Jumeaux, "the Mother of Twins." Deeply revered within Haitian Vodou, this spirit occupied a unique position in Marie's network. Known for her association with duality and balance, Manman Jumeaux was often summoned in moments of crisis, believed to bridge realms and restore equilibrium where rupture had occurred.

Marie performed the required rituals with urgency, hoping this spirit would provide an alternative path, some counterforce capable of matching what had devastated her shrine. But when Manman Jumeaux manifested, the verdict was the same as Holorum's. The power carried by the Christian group, she declared, lay beyond the reach of any Vodou deity.

This pronouncement marked the collapse of Marie's spiritual framework. The presumed omnipotence of her network, the source of her confidence, dominance, and identity, began to unravel. As both Holorum and Manman Jumeaux faltered, their limitations were exposed. In a rare admission of weakness, the spirits acknowledged their inability to withstand the authority confronting them. The force Marie had served revealed itself as conditional, fragile when measured against the power of the Holy Spirit.

With Manman Jumeaux's final oracle still hanging in the air, Marie Michel stood in the center of her yard, her shoulders slumped as though bearing the weight of the world itself. Her posture spoke before she did, head bowed, eyes fixed on the ground, avoiding light, avoiding life. Deep lines carved her forehead, etched by worry and despair. The corners of her mouth sagged into a frown that seemed permanent.

Her eyes, once sharp with cunning and command, had dulled. They appeared glassy, lifeless, holding back tears that refused to fall. There was an emptiness in her gaze, a hollow stillness that reflected a soul trapped inside grief too large to escape. When she finally lifted her eyes toward the horizon, the sadness there felt almost tangible, as though sorrow itself had weight.

Even her movements carried exhaustion. Each step required effort. Each gesture felt delayed, burdened, as if she were carrying an invisible load that drained her strength. Her presence radiated melancholy, forming a quiet barrier between herself and the world, a woman consumed by an inward collapse.

Sheila watched her with a mixture of sympathy and fear. She understood the source of Marie's devastation. It was not the missionaries who had invaded the shrine; that assault had been bold, but not unprecedented. What truly shattered Marie was abandonment. The ancestral pantheon, the spirits she had served with loyalty and fear, had deserted her.

With Holorum gone and the pantheon silent, Marie felt betrayed beyond anything she had imagined. The ground no longer felt sacred beneath her feet. Rituals once rich with response now echoed hollow. The spirits that had shaped her life evaporated without explanation, leaving her exposed.

Yet even in despair, defiance remained. Sheila saw it flicker behind Marie's weary eyes. Though defeated, Marie was not ready to surrender.

"I may be down," she muttered, her voice low but firm, "but I am not dead. As long as I have weapons in my arsenal, the fight will continue."

To Marie, this was not an ending, only a setback. Her spirits were gone, but her knowledge remained. Her rituals, her cunning, her memory of power still burned. The fire had dimmed, but it had not gone out.

Her defiance was not aimed solely at the Christians. It was directed at the silence left behind, at the betrayal of Holorum, at the unseen authority that had stripped her bare.

The Battle Ahead

Even as her world collapsed, Marie resolved to press forward. She would find new allies. She would seek deeper rituals. She would reclaim the dominance she believed was her birthright. The struggle was no longer about control, it was about survival.

Yet amid the ruins of her spiritual empire, a question lingered. How long could she fight forces greater than herself? How long could resistance hold against surrender?

Her armor had cracked. Seeds of transformation had been planted, though she could not yet see them.

She replayed the events relentlessly. A small group of Christians, once dismissed as nuisance, had become an overwhelming force. Their precision and spiritual authority struck her network like lightning, severing connections she had trusted since childhood. Her shrine, once impenetrable, had become a battlefield.

One word echoed in her mind: *Vilokan.*

Vilokan, the ancestral realm of initiation, the source of her portion. It was from *Vilokan* that she received the capacity to transform bodies, capture souls, command entities. If her spirits had failed her now, *Vilokan* would be her fallback. The wellspring. The last remaining source of legitimacy and power.

The Trial of the Absent Pantheon

Marie's resolve hardened into declaration. *Vilokan* had given her the tools to reshape reality itself. If she could summon that authority again, she could reverse the collapse, not just of this conflict, but of her legacy.

She summoned Sheila and Jonise and outlined a plan: a ritual so severe it would force her reputation to recover. Yet even as Marie spoke, doubt flickered in Sheila's eyes.

When the missionaries invited Marie to accept their faith, she refused outright. Submission to the God who had humiliated her was unthinkable. Defiant but wounded, she withdrew to plan retaliation.

Together, Marie and Sheila decided to summon a spiritual default judgment. They would put their own allies on trial, Holorum, Tibichet, Tipice, and the thirty-three other spirits Marie had served. Why had they failed to appear? Why had they abandoned her?

They purchased fresh candles and waited for the Solar Zenith, noon, when the sun stands directly overhead, erasing shadows and exposing deception. At this hour, heaven and earth were believed to align vertically.

Under the blistering midday sun, they began the ritual. Invocations were chanted. The path to the invisible was opened.

Nothing answered.

A suffocating silence filled the shrine. None of the *lwa* appeared. Sheila broke first. "This is the final betrayal," she said.

The air grew heavy, not with presence, but exhaustion. The Noonday Demon seemed to replace the ancestors, bringing weariness instead of justice.

Petitioners gathered, the sick, the desperate, those bound by contracts, watching in mounting dread. They had come to witness the chief *lwa* at his zenith. Instead, they faced an empty sky.

No mounting occurred. No violent spasms. No trance. No rolling eyes fixed on the unseen. The temperature did not drop. The air did not thicken. The veil did not part.

Marie searched for signs. There were none. No tobacco. No perfume. No sulfur. No earth.

No voices. No xenoglossy. No double speech. No alien cadence tearing through the heat. Only wind.

In that silence, the ritual became a funeral.

Murmurs spread. The spirits had vacated. One by one, the crowd dispersed, leaving Marie Michel alone, standing beneath the merciless noon sun, abandoned, exposed, and stripped of authority.

The silence of the Solar Zenith was not a temporary failure. It was a permanent eviction.

Desperate to understand the "the failure to appear" that had shattered her authority, Marie Michel sought out three of her most trusted *ougan* colleagues, renowned Vodou priests whose mastery of the mysteries rivaled her own. She brought them into the quiet of her shrine and demanded interpretation. She needed to know why the chief *lwa* had remained deaf to her summons, and why the vertical bridge of the noon sun had sealed itself shut.

Each priest withdrew into his own ritual space, consulting ancestral oracles and employing the *ason*. One by one, they returned bearing the same chilling verdict. The spirits had not merely failed to appear. They had vacated the realm entirely.

"The trial is over, Marie," the eldest *ougan* whispered, his voice weighted with finality. "They have left. They will not return. And more than that, they cannot return."

He gestured toward the *vèvè* traced across the floor, symbols that had once functioned as keys to Holorum and Tibichet. Now they were nothing more than chalk dust. The sacred objects that once vibrated with possession lay cold and inert. To the priests, the signs were unmistakable: the metaphysical weight had lifted. The symbols were hollow.

While this pronouncement delivered a devastating blow to Marie's pride, the world beyond her darkened shrine began to breathe.

As Marie sat in the shadows with Sheila and Jonise, confronting the absolute silence of their pantheon, an unexpected calm spread through the neighborhood like a cool tide. For years, residents had lived under spiritual siege, their nights fractured by drums and guttural, stentorophonic cries echoing from Marie's compound. Now, for the first time in memory, they slept.

The air that had long felt heavy under the reign of the Noonday Demon finally cleared.

Those who had lived in terror found a new center of gravity. The Haitian Christian missionaries, who had stood their ground when the *lwa* fled, became anchors of stability. One by one, neighbors turned toward Jesus, trading contracts and rituals for freedom and rest. As the community moved toward light, Marie remained behind, a petitioner whose gods had not only lost the trial, but vanished from the court altogether.

The silence of the spirits was not merely emotional. It was economic.

The Vanishing Wealth: The Custodians of the Shadow Treasury

Marie Michel and Sheila were not merely practitioners; they were custodians of the pantheon's treasury. Over decades, they had amassed a sprawling fortune by commodifying desperation and vengeance. Their income flowed from an exacting economy of spiritual services, exorbitant fees for healing, protection rackets against spirits they themselves controlled, and dark contracts for retribution and death.

Their most lucrative operation was spiritual debt collection. Clients pledged homes, vehicles, furniture, clothing, entire lives, as collateral. These blood contracts ensured that once a prayer was answered, everything else would be seized.

The money never touched a bank. It was spiritualized, bound to the shrine's power and stored in bottles, buckets, and terracotta vessels tucked into soot-stained corners. To an outsider, it looked like ritual clutter. In truth, it was a hoard sealed in sweat and blood, representing decades of human desperation.

When their reputation collapsed, Marie and Sheila viewed this hidden capital as their final lifeline, the war chest that might buy escape or restore influence.

Then the unthinkable occurred.

The wealth vanished without theft.

Just as xenoglossy faded, just as stentorophonic voices fell silent, just as violent mountings ceased, the currency evaporated. Haitian gourdes. American dollars. Gone. As if the money itself had been an extension of the spirits' presence, unable to exist without the power that birthed it.

Marie and Sheila were left destitute.

The transition was brutal. With no spirits to protect or provide, the vertical bridge was gone. Clients disappeared. Former allies turned away. Hunger, an unfamiliar companion, returned.

The woman who had once commanded thirty-three spirits now begged for food.

As Marie walked the same streets where neighbors now slept peacefully under a new faith, she moved like a ghost. The midday sun, once her instrument of judgment, now illuminated her desperation. She was a fallen queen, stripped of voice, gods, and bread.

The collapse was no longer quiet. It was total.

And in the lengthening shadows of afternoon, the seeds of transformation were sown in bitter soil.

The Audacity of Sheila

While Marie withdrew into reflection, Sheila reacted with predatory rage.

Sheila had *always* been the more ruthless, relishing debt, cruelty, and domination. To her, the loss of wealth and the silence of the *lwa* were insults to be answered with force.

Driven by recklessness, she descended into ancient caves rumored to house the Living Entity, the primordial "boss" of their spiritual network. This was not a spirit to be summoned, but a physical being said to dwell in the deep earth.

Sheila did not bow. She issued an ultimatum.

"Restore our wealth and power," she demanded, "or I will defect to the Christians."

The entity laughed.

"Go ahead."

Sheila returned humiliated but defiant. That night, she ate greedily, red beans, rice, stew, refusing despair. But as the final bite passed her lips, her body failed. The food lodged in her throat. In moments, she collapsed. Her life extinguished as abruptly as a candle in a draft.

Her death was hidden in secrecy. There was no public mourning. No sympathy awaited her. Even her parents remained distant, fear outweighing grief.

Under cover of night, she was buried quickly, without ceremony. The woman who once commanded terror returned to the earth unloved and unmissed.

For Marie, this loss was crushing. Authority. Wealth. Enforcer. Gone.

As the sun sank behind the hills, the unthinkable took root. The missionaries' offer, once an insult, no longer felt like surrender. Under isolation and fear, the path toward light began to feel like survival.

The Homecoming: A Journey of Rejection and Revelation

With Sheila buried and their dominion in ruins, Marie and Jonise fled. They returned to families long abandoned, hoping for refuge.

When Marie stood before her parents' home, there was no reunion, only terror. Her mother trembled and spoke words that froze the air: "It is true that I gave birth to you, but now, you are my mother."

It was an inversion of order, fear replacing kinship.

Marie stood in garments made of brown sugar sacks, the uniform of her bondage. Stripped of spirits and power, she asked for one thing: a dress.

Her mother refused. In Marie's world, objects were conduits. Fearing spiritual linkage, she went to the market and purchased a new dress, virgin cloth, untouched by blood or history.

Marie was clothed.

But she was not welcomed.

Seated in the oppressive quiet of her childhood home, Marie laid bare the wreckage of her life. She recounted the hollow silence of the Solar Zenith, the betrayal of the spirits who had fled their trial, and the overwhelming, radiant, force of the Christian missionaries who had laid siege to her sanctuary. Finally, she revealed the choice that felt like the ultimate heresy: her decision to abandon Vodou and accept the faith of her rivals.

Her father's reaction erupted into pure hostility. As a feared *ougan* himself, he was the architect of Marie's destiny. It was he who had performed the rituals to dedicate her to the ancestral spirits when she was still a child.

To him, Marie was not merely a daughter, she was a sacred vessel of their lineage. Her conversion was a sacrilegious insult to the bloodline, a betrayal of an ancestral inheritance no one in their family had ever dared to challenge, let alone abandon.

Marie's mother, though quieter, was no less resolute. Where the father saw wounded pride, the mother saw breached safety. To her, Marie had become a spiritual lightning rod for the wrath of the abandoned *lwa*. Harboring a daughter who had turned her back on the pantheon was an invitation for calamity to strike the entire household, and perhaps the community around it.

In the end, the fear of the spirits proved stronger than the call of blood. The verdict was final: Marie could not stay. Her mother would not allow her daughter to sleep even one night under that roof. Instead, she arranged for Marie to be exiled again, this time to the home of a Christian acquaintance in a neighboring town. It was strategic. It pushed Marie into the arms of the very "enemy" she had chosen, and it ensured that if the spirits struck, they would strike far from the family hearth.

The Scarf of the *Ougan*

As Marie settled into her new life, the heavy silence of familial rejection was replaced by the quiet hum of Christian teaching. But a year into this budding peace, the darkness of her heritage delivered a final, lethal, blow.

Back at the family home, a domestic dispute escalated into what can only be described as a supernatural execution. Marie's father, the high priest, the pillar of local Vodou tradition, became consumed by a toxic mixture of rage and resentment. He accused his wife, Marie's mother, of enabling their daughter's "heresy." To the neighborhood, he was no longer simply a grieving husband. He was a failing master of spirits searching for a scapegoat.

Then, with chilling precision, he produced a scarf.

To an outsider, it would have looked like a mundane accessory. But to those who understood his craft, it was a charged vessel, loaded with ancestral energy. Neighbors watched in horror as he shook the fabric over his wife. The effect was immediate. Marie's mother, a Vodou practitioner, collapsed and died where she stood, only thirty-six years old.

In that realm of stentorophonic manifestations and spiritualized transactions, the scarf functioned as a conduit for killing force. It revealed how fragile the balance truly was: between spiritual power and total destruction.

With her mother's sudden death, and her father's cold, absolute refusal to acknowledge her existence, Marie Michel became an orphan in every sense. Her father viewed her conversion as a permanent stain on the lineage, a betrayal that rendered her dead to him long before her mother ever fell.

Yet this total rejection cleared space for a radical adoption. Where her biological family had offered contracts, sugar-sack servitude, and a death-dealing scarf, Mrs. Jeanette offered sanctuary, pure compassion.

Mrs. Jeanette was a woman of unwavering faith. She looked beyond the terrifying reputation of the "Lead Priestess" and saw a soul in need of redemption. She did not fear the links or the shadows Marie might carry. She offered Marie a place on the same sleeping mats as her own children, an act of maternal love that told the whole community Marie was no longer a threat.

In the warmth of this home, Marie was no longer custodian of a Shadow Treasury, no longer defendant in a spiritual trial. She was, for the first time, a daughter by choice, rather than a vessel by blood.

The Illumination of Grace

Through Mrs. Jeanette's unconditional love, Marie encountered a relationship that defied every law she had ever known. This life was not built on leverage, fear, or hierarchy. It was built on grace, quiet, steady, and unforced. The refuge became more than a bed. It became a sanctuary for healing, a space where Marie could finally imagine an existence outside the suffocating shadow of ancestral spirits.

Mrs. Jeanette's home became fertile soil for transformation. The contrast was absolute: where blood had handed her a death-dealing scarf, a stranger offered her a seat at the table. Even in the deepest hollows of brokenness, Marie discovered that kindness carries a light the Noonday Demon cannot extinguish.

Under Mrs. Jeanette's guidance, the former lead priestess surrendered fully to her new faith. She became a constant presence in the local church, immersing herself in prayer meetings and Bible studies with the intensity she had once carried into the shrine.

The turning point came when Marie stood before the congregation to deliver her testimony. She publicly renounced *Vilokan* traditions and every member of the ancestral pantheon she had served. This was not merely a change of heart. It was a formal declaration of war. Her words sent a seismic shock through the community, and, as she believed, through the spiritual realm itself.

And Marie soon learned: the veil does not tear without resistance.

Her former life was a labyrinth of covenants, blood pacts, spiritual marriages, legalistic bonds. They were not metaphors. They were contracts, metaphysical and enforced, binding her soul to a network of malevolent claim.

The Spiritual Most Wanted

By defecting, Marie was no longer regarded as a runaway. She was reclassified as a traitor of the highest order. She became the primary target on what she called the "Spiritual Most Wanted", a hierarchy's list designed for two purposes: to silence her before she exposed the inner machinery of darkness, and to terrify any other high-ranking practitioner tempted to defect.

The potions and ritual elixirs she had consumed over decades were not symbolic. In her interpretation, they functioned as biological wetware, liquid programming that re-mapped her nervous system, optimizing her physiology into a conduit for the *lwa*. For years she had lived in what she described as "superhuman mode," senses sharpened, body tuned to the frequency of spirits.

Now that optimization became torture.

Without the handshake of the spirits to regulate the flow, the imprints within her system began to misfire. Her heightened receptors turned against her. Past covenants became points of pain. Ritual history became systemic failure, as the abandoned spirits sought to override her internal "operating system" and reclaim their vessel.

The warfare did not remain confined to Marie. True to predatory nature, the spirits targeted her new links, Mrs. Jeanette, her children, the church. Fear was weaponized in an attempt to isolate her, casting her as a perceived curse upon anyone who loved her.

At times, these forces manipulated her allies, causing those who had extended help to revolt against her without warning. Confusion and dread were used to turn support into rejection. In church, reception fractured. Some saw a soul redeemed. Others saw a relic of darkness. They avoided her in the pews; whispers formed a barrier you could feel.

And still, hope persisted.

Despite hunger, despite the lack of proper clothing that exposed her destitution, Marie endured spiritual trials that functioned as refinement. Each battle forced her to see the entities she once served as they truly were: ancient promises woven into manipulation and lies.

Each survived attack stripped away fear and replaced it with resilient boldness. Her journey became humility in the flesh. For the first time, she lived dependent on others. That dependence hurt, but it became soil where a new identity could grow.

Amid rejection, she clung to an internal promise: redemption was real. The default judgment she once sought was finally being rendered, not through her power, but through the enduring light of a faith the shadows could not extinguish.

As the struggle deepened, the warfare shifted again, moving from metaphysical pressure to direct physiological siege. The spirits she had once commanded attempted to turn her own body into a prison, using the old programming as proof of lingering claim.

Among the many challenges Marie faced, sleepwalking emerged as a distressing manifestation of conflict. It was not presented as a mundane medical condition, but as rhythmic nocturnal puppetry. At night her body would rise and move as though commanded by an unseen force, drawing her toward danger, toward thresholds, toward the edges of places she had fled.

These episodes unsettled the household. It was as though the Noonday Demon had traded the sun's glare for the night's shadows, attempting to use unconsciousness to bypass conscious faith. The scene became a living symbol of the lingering wetware within her: a ghost in the machine trying to re-establish connection to the old network.

Perhaps the most strategic torment was her sudden, unexplained loss of voice. Whenever Marie attempted to recount her experiences or expose the inner workings of the ancestral pantheon, she would be struck with aphasia, a temporary but total inability to speak. It was as if an invisible hand clamped down on her vocal cords, targeting testimony itself.

Marie described profound cognitive dissonance. Her mind remained clear. Her thoughts remained intact. Yet the bridge between intellect and voice was severed. This was an attempt by the "Spiritual Most Wanted" hierarchy to maintain stronghold by silencing truth. If she could not speak the names of former captors, she could not dismantle their power over others.

Still, Marie persisted.

Hunger gnawed. Peers betrayed. Night wandering returned. Aphasia suffocated. Yet she understood these afflictions not as defeat, but as clearing, final draining of a system that had been occupied for decades. Each weakness reminded her the battle was too great for her strength. She was forced to rely entirely on the power that had silenced the shrine at noon.

The forces that sought to silence her ultimately failed. Her resilience became a beacon to those still bound, proving that while spirits may manipulate the body, they cannot touch a soul reclaimed. Out of despair, Marie emerged not only as survivor, but as living testimony: redemption's light is more enduring than the most sophisticated shadows.

The Journey to Divine Immunity

Marie's deliverance was not immediate. It was a process, expelling demons that clung, breaking covenants that bound, unlearning lies she had believed for years. It was painful. It was exhausting. Yet each step drew her closer to freedom.

Through this process, Marie received divine immunity. This was not only freedom from the forces that once controlled her, but a new kind of authority, power to expose darkness, to speak boldly of the Gospel of Jesus Christ, and to stand as a living testimony of redeeming love. This divine immunity became both shield and empowerment for those who walk by faith.

Marie Michel's transformation was not only for her salvation. It prepared her to lead others out. She became a beacon for those still trapped in Vodou and ancestral worship. Her deliverance and redemption inspired many to seek freedom in Christ.

And though she could not fully comprehend the scope of her journey during the trials, by the time she emerged it became clear: God had been shaping her for a purpose far greater than herself. Her story became proclamation, victory, resilience, and boundless grace.

The Final Marriage: Overwriting Demonic Claims with Human Love

Marie Michel grew up where love was an unrecognizable language. Her childhood was barren, no warmth of affection. Her father regarded tenderness as weakness. Her mother remained an emotional ghost. In that void, bitterness took root. Her heart calcified. By the time she became lead priestess, she had built walls high enough to keep the world out, surrounding herself only with those who reinforced darkness.

Then, in the storms of transition, an unexpected presence appeared: a man in her church named Fenel. His affection was genuine, untainted by "Spiritual Most Wanted" labels or terror of her past. To Marie, it was incomprehensible. She had been optimized for fear and power, not for being valued.

The church elders were rightly cautious. They warned Fenel that Marie was on a divine mission to expose the dark world. "If you hinder her purpose, walk away now," they cautioned. But Fenel did not retreat. He sought a divine handshake through prayer. To the community's surprise, the answer was affirmative.

Supported by his family, who pooled resources to lift Marie out of stark poverty, Fenel married her within months. The union signaled a new beginning, a woman who had never known a home without contracts now stepping into covenant.

But tranquility was immediately tested.

After the first night of their honeymoon, Fenel entered a nightly battle. In dreams, a massive, menacing snake appeared, asserting a prior claim over

Marie. The oppression was so heavy that Fenel repeatedly found himself physically pushed off the bed, waking shaken on the floor.

When he told her, Marie disclosed the chilling truth. "When I was a priestess, I was married to several demons in the form of snakes. These were powerful entities tied to blood covenants. They do not let go easily."

Armed with that knowledge, Fenel did not retreat. He recognized the old programming attempting to override the new legal covenant of marriage. That night, they knelt to pray, and Fenel asserted divine and legal authority: "Lord, You instituted marriage between a man and a woman, not between a woman and a demon. I claim my rightful place."

In the dream that followed, the serpent returned to strike. But this time Fenel wielded a machete, gleaming with divine, iridescent light. In a decisive struggle, he cut the serpent into pieces.

When he awoke, the atmosphere had shifted. The oppressive weight, the lingering signal of old spiritual marriages, had vanished. It was a final break from entities that had claimed Marie's body for decades. The victory sealed their bond, revealing that a husband's legal right, backed by divine authority, could dismantle even ancient contracts.

And in the spiritual landscape of Marie Michel's journey, we witness a clash between entrenched darkness and the supreme authority of the Creator. To understand that authority, we must look above every hierarchy, earthly and spiritual, toward El Gibhor.

The Mighty God: El Gibhor

This is the "Mighty God" of Isaiah 9:6. Unlike dark principalities that rule through fear and coercion, El Gibhor exercises a power so absolute, so complete, that He can afford to be gentle. He does not need to shout to be obeyed. His presence establishes jurisdiction.

The Intervention: He is the Divine Restorer. Where other entities sought to use Marie as a vessel, to drain her, weaponize her, discard her, El

Gibhor came to dwell within her. His mission was not to renovate the surface, but to rebuild her hardened architecture from the inside out, replacing the cold mechanics of the *lwa* with the warmth and governance of the Holy Spirit.

The Victory: El Gibhor is the One who took the "Spiritual Most Wanted" list, the record of debts, accusations, and legal claims, and nailed it to the cross. He did not enter a skirmish with dark rulers; He disarmed them. He stripped them of presumed authority and turned what they guarded most carefully into footstools beneath His throne.

Marie Michel's testimony, therefore, was far more than a conversion story. It was a forensic deconstruction of a kingdom. Because she had operated at high levels of the dark hierarchy, her cognitive faculties, consciousness, perception, judgment, memory, became instruments of the enemy's undoing.

In the spiritual realm, her mind functioned like a breach in a system that survives by secrecy. When her internal archives were brought into the light of El Gibhor, she did not merely "share her story." She exposed infrastructure. She revealed hidden pathways. She destabilized the operating system that had held her, and so many others, in bondage.

Her testimony was raw, unfiltered, and surgically precise. Under the protection of El Gibhor, she did not speak of "darkness" in vague terms. She named names. She identified stations. She described methods that had remained hidden for generations.

The Ritual Mechanics: She exposed the composition of elixirs, those "quantum potions", and explained how they were used to bind physiology to a specific entity. By naming the ingredients of the bond, she handed others keys to dismantle the locks the enemy had placed on their lives.

The Network of Influence: She pulled back the curtain on how false prophets and counterfeit "men of God" used ancestral links to produce improvised prophecies and manufactured miracles. This exposure threatened the livelihoods, and reputations, of those who profited from spiritual deception.

The Legal Loopholes: Guided by the wisdom of El Gibhor, she explained how spirits exploit vulnerabilities, unhealed trauma, buried resentment, secret blood pacts, as legal standing to occupy and oppress a life.

For these *reasons*, Marie Michel became a marked woman. The "Spiritual Most Wanted" list was no longer a metaphor; it began to manifest in the physical world. There were coordinated attempts on her life, planned by those whose power and secrets she had stripped away. Yet they found themselves fighting El Gibhor.

The Physical Strikes: Assassins were dispatched. "Accidents" were staged. Yet again and again, the Government on His shoulders acted like a kinetic shield. Weapons jammed. Plans leaked. Timing collapsed. Marie walked through the shadow of death untouched. El Gibhor stood as her Guardian, and the enemy's weapons could not prosper.

The Spiritual Blowback: Sorcerers attempted to strike her from a distance using the scaffolding of her old life. They sent snakes. They sent stentorophonic voices. They tried to reclaim her mind by reactivating prior claims. But because Fenel had already wielded the Divine Machete, and because Marie had undergone true repentance, there was no hook left for the enemy to grip. The old account had been closed by the hand of El Gibhor.

God did not merely protect Marie; He used her life to humiliate the opposition. As Colossians 2:15 declares, having disarmed the powers and authorities, He made a public spectacle of them, triumphing over them by the cross.

Marie's life became a living manifestation of that truth. Each time a false prophet tried to curse her and failed, it exposed their impotence. Each time she spoke a secret that was supposed to carry a death sentence, yet remained standing, she proved that "entities" in caves were nothing compared to the Living God.

The practitioners who once lived in terror of the shrine now saw its former queen living in peace, married to a man of faith, clothed in dignity. The spectacle was not Marie. The spectacle was the shattered illusion of the enemy's invincibility.

Marie's refusal to filter her testimony became one of her sharpest weapons. By refusing to be polite about darkness, she gave others permission to be free. Through the power of El Gibhor, she proved that deliverance is not the hiding of your past. It is the turning of the enemy's secrets into a roadmap for someone else's escape.

The absolute victory Marie found in El Gibhor was not merely a change of heart. It was a total replacement of dependency. She moved from a world governed by the cold mechanics of ritual and physical anchors into a jurisdiction where authority is established by a single Name.

Yet for many still caught in the crossfire of spiritual oppression, this shift, from the material to the spiritual, remains the hardest hurdle. They see the power Marie once wielded and the attacks she survived, and instinctively they look for a physical shield to mimic her protection. They reach for what they can see and touch, unaware that the enemy they are fighting is not repelled by matter, but by the sovereignty Marie now lives under.

To understand the true nature of her freedom, we must first dismantle the most common trap the oppressed fall into: the belief that an object can hold the line where only God can stand.

CHAPTER 15

WHEN THE SOUL MAKER RECLAIMS HIS OWN

As I move to the threshold of what comes next, my purpose shifts from recounting events to discerning meaning. Up to this point, her testimony has been allowed to speak largely for itself—its intensity, its contradictions, its unmistakable weight. Now, having examined its patterns, symbols, reactions, and aftermath with greater care, it becomes necessary to slow down and name what is actually being revealed. What follows is not an attempt to embellish her experience or to sensationalize her past, but to characterize her testimony within a broader spiritual framework—one that distinguishes between narrative, authority, transformation, and the governing laws of both darkness and the Kingdom of God.

What Marie Michel's Deliverance Reveals

Marie Michel's testimony cannot be reduced to a simple conversion story. It is a forensic deconstruction of a spiritual system, offered by someone who did not merely encounter darkness from the outside, but operated its internal machinery from the highest levels. She was not a peripheral participant. She was a priestess, a *manbo,* a queen within a shrine—functioning as a living interface between the physical world and the second heaven. Her conversion therefore represented more than personal repentance; it constituted a catastrophic breach in the architecture of the system she once upheld.

Her deliverance functioned as what might best be described as a high-level intelligence collapse. She carried operational knowledge—names, rituals, frequencies, and legal claims—that sustained generational bondage. When she exited the system, she did not leave quietly. She exposed the infrastructure that had relied on secrecy, fear, and myth to maintain authority. Her testimony stripped darkness of mystery by revealing it not as magic, but as mechanics—cold, transactional, and illegal.

What made her account uniquely disruptive was its precision. She described the occult not in poetic abstractions, but in functional terms. She revealed how elixirs bound physiology to spiritual entities, how amulets functioned not as protection but as mobile altars—hardware that stabilized possession and maintained constant access. By explaining the how, she dismantled the fear that depends on the unknown. Darkness thrives in ambiguity; exposure is its undoing.

Her story also stands as a living demonstration of legal disarmament. She did not merely claim that Christ is powerful; she revealed Him as Jurist. Through repentance and obedience, the legal standing of blood pacts, ancestral contracts, and ritual agreements was revoked. Once the hardware—the amulets, music, ritual objects, and physical anchors—was destroyed, the enemy lost jurisdiction. Authority did not shift because of confrontation, but because access was removed.

What followed was not silence, but retaliation. Attempts were made on her life through accidents and spiritual assault. Yet the most striking feature of her testimony is that she remained standing—married, clothed in dignity, and publicly declaring secrets that once carried a death sentence. Her survival became a public humiliation of the opposition. The queen of the shrine had found a higher throne.

This brings us to the ecclesiastical challenge her story exposes. In the current age of ecclesiastical accusation, the Church must confront an uncomfortable truth: most modern congregations are unprepared to receive a person like Marie Michel. Churches are structured for seekers, social belonging, and moral instruction—but not for high-value defectors from deeply embedded systems of darkness. When such individuals enter the Church, they do not arrive empty-handed. They bring histories, retaliation, and exposure with them.

Without discernment, congregations respond in one of two ways: exploitation or exile. Some elevate such testimonies prematurely, placing them on platforms before inner architecture has been fully dismantled. Others retreat in fear, distancing themselves under the guise of caution. Both responses fail. True integration requires neither spectacle nor suspicion, but governance—pastoral authority capable of bearing weight without transferring risk to the vulnerable.

Yet Marie Michel's story also reveals something profoundly corrective. Her initial integration into the Kingdom did not occur through a strategic operations center or a council of experts. It occurred through radical simplicity. A woman of faith opened her home, fed her at her table, clothed her with dignity, and took her to church. No risk assessment was conducted. No spiritual mapping was drawn. Instead, love re-humanized a soul that had been treated as infrastructure rather than personhood.

This simplicity was not naïveté. It was jurisdiction. Innocence became a shield not because it was unaware of danger, but because it operated under a different government. The shared table functioned as a covenant of peace that darkness could not penetrate. Where the occult required constant ritual maintenance, the Kingdom required only surrender and presence.

At the same time, Marie's deliverance revealed a critical truth that must be stated plainly: freedom does not coexist with dependency. Her victory was not merely internal. It required the destruction of physical objects—

amulets, ritual instruments, music, and images—that functioned as portals. The danger was never in the objects themselves, but in the authority assigned to them. When objects replace obedience, faith mutates into mechanics.

Scripture allows physical signs to point toward covenant, but never to substitute for relationship. The Ark of the Covenant did not compel God; it testified to His kingship. When Israel attempted to wield it as a weapon without obedience, its protection vanished. Likewise, power flowed from Christ through garments and handkerchiefs not because fabric carried authority, but because faith aligned with covenant. Objects only function rightly when they remain subordinate to relationship.

In occult systems, however, objects are not symbolic; they are infrastructural. They serve as anchors for disembodied entities that require physical access points to operate illegally in the material world. Marie's amulets were not charms—they were stabilizers. When she destroyed them, backlash followed because infrastructure was being dismantled. Deliverance is not emotional release; it is structural demolition.

This exposes the incompatibility of two temples. A person cannot serve as a dwelling place for the Holy Spirit while maintaining the hardware of a mobile altar. One system is sustained internally by grace; the other requires constant external maintenance. One produces adoption and freedom; the other containment and bondage. When the object falls, authority rises. When the portal closes, freedom begins.

Yet deliverance is not merely eviction—it is reclamation. God does not function as a cosmetic fixer, but as the original Architect reclaiming His own design. Darkness may manipulate trauma, bloodlines, and fear, but it does not understand the soul. It exploits what it did not create. God alone holds the title deed.

The Threshold: When Conflict Relocates to Perception

This is where Marie Michel's story intersects decisively with The Age of Ecclesiastical Accusation. Her deliverance made visible how control once enforced through ritual and objects does not simply vanish when those structures collapse. When the shrine is emptied and the hardware destroyed, conflict often migrates inward—from possession to perception, from ritual to memory, from external authority to internalized certainty. What no longer speaks through altars begins to speak through accusation, distortion, and the inner ear. Authority is no longer imposed through force, but through interpretation.

This is the quieter phase of captivity—the one most easily misnamed, mishandled, or spiritualized into silence. It is also the phase where ecclesiastical accusation thrives. When discernment collapses and perception becomes confined, individuals can be cornered internally long before a word is ever spoken publicly. Deliverance removes visible chains; discernment must guard the mind.

It is here—at the threshold where freedom has been declared but perception remains vulnerable—that another architecture of captivity must be examined. Not one built through shrines and rituals, but through familiarity, isolation, and internal negotiation. The next form of captivity does not arrive wearing ritual language; it arrives wearing familiarity. It does not begin with overt confrontation, but with quiet disorientation, subtle isolation, and a narrowing of reality until the individual can no longer recognize where freedom ended and confinement began. To understand this quieter architecture of captivity—the one built not by altars but by perception—we now turn to Bachon's testimony, where confinement is assembled step by step inside spaces that appear ordinary, recognizable, and safe.

INSIDE SPIRITUAL CAPTIVITY

Many people will recognize this territory. They have prayed, repented, renounced, and broken ties with darkness, yet still find themselves contending with accusation, distorted perception, or a quiet isolation they cannot fully explain. Freedom was real, but it did not unfold as cleanly or completely as they were led to expect. It is here that Bachon's testimony becomes a lamp, not to question deliverance, but to reveal how captivity can relocate, shifting from external control to internal confinement. His account helps us understand why deliverance may function as a threshold, and why discernment must address not only what was cast out, but what remains untested within.

Why Bachon Belongs in This Book

Over years of studying testimonies of former Vodou practitioners, I have learned that not every account belongs in this book, but Bachon's does, and for reasons that must be stated plainly. In 1998, he was invited to speak during a week of revival at Église Chrétienne Évangélique in Port-au-Prince, near Pélé. Before his conversion, he was widely known as a *malfektè*, an active practitioner of destructive works. After encountering Christ, he became an evangelist and exposed his former life with a precision that left little room for folklore, exaggeration, or myth.

I have intentionally avoided recording operational details, not out of denial, but out of responsibility. Testimony must never become instruction. Yet there was one dimension of Bachon's account that remained with me and demands careful attention. Beyond what he shared publicly, he lived for a time in my brother's home, my brother who is now the pastor of that same church. In that private setting, removed from platform and performance, Bachon shared additional testimonies with sobriety and restraint. It is that private disclosure, measured, undramatic, and diagnostic, that makes his account essential to the themes explored in this book.

Marie Michel's Method and the Logic of Capture

Marie Michel's method of essence, or soul capture, is only one among hundreds documented within occult systems. It is neither unique nor isolated. Through years of study, testimony analysis, and pastoral exposure, I have come to understand that while these methods vary in form, they often share the same internal logic. Darkness adapts its tools, but it repeats its structure.

One such account was shared by Bachon, now deceased, a colleague of my father. His testimony, which I studied closely, offered insight into a method he himself once practiced. Unlike indiscriminate attacks, this method was deliberately selective. It targeted what he described as "high value" individuals, genuine pastors, uncompromised men and women of God, and those whose spiritual integrity posed a threat to systems of darkness.

In the language of unseen conflict, targeting a high value spiritual leader is not merely an act of malice; it is a calculated attempt to weaken a larger spiritual community. To the occultist, a church is not merely a building, and a pastor is not merely a man. They function as a lighthouse and a guardian, anchoring and stabilizing a collective spiritual territory.

To dismantle such a fortress, the weaver of shadows follows a specific logic of spiritual structure. This logic seeks to generate a dream state not by accident, but by design. Creating this state is an act of theurgic engineering, a deliberate descent into what Bachon described as the "vast internal." This process is known within those systems as *dream baiting*.

According to his account, the operation often began in a dream state. The environment appeared familiar and convincingly normal. The dreamer might find himself in surroundings closely resembling real life, homes, streets, trees, pathways, or neighborhoods that felt recognizable and safe. There was nothing immediately frightening or overtly sinister. The realism of the setting was intentional, designed not to provoke fear but to lower discernment by bypassing the target's most primal defenses. In some instances, the target might even encounter deceased parents.

In Bachon's understanding of the nocturnal siege, the appearance of a deceased parent was rarely a visitation of the true spirit. Rather, it functioned as an occult strategy, an impersonation designed to exploit emotional trust and disarm vigilance at the deepest level.

Confinement Through Familiarity

Within this environment, the target would often experience disorientation. He might feel lost, attempting to find his way home, entering and exiting spaces without clear direction. Movement remained possible, but progress did not. Direction existed, but destination remained elusive.

In many cases, the dream gradually led into confined or descending areas, basements, tunnels, underground passages, sealed rooms, or spaces that narrowed with each step. At first, there was no visible threat. In other instances, a sense of pursuit emerged, as though someone or something was following just beyond sight. The pressure was subtle, persistent, and cumulative.

A defining feature of this method was psychological manipulation through familiarity. The dream environment often included people the target recognized, some living, some deceased, engaged in ordinary activity. These figures were not present to assist. Their function was normalization. Their presence reassured the target just long enough to guide him, gently and incrementally, toward a predetermined location.

The illusion of safety was essential. The objective was never immediate terror, but gradual containment.

The Threshold of Collapse

The goal, as Bachon explained, was to corner the target in a space from which escape was no longer possible. If the individual entered a confined area and could not exit, and did not awaken, what he described as "phase one" was complete. At that point, the physical body ceased functioning during sleep, while the essence became accessible for capture.

Not every encounter ended the same way. Some individuals realized they were dreaming and fought to awaken. Others attempted repeatedly to leave, only to find doors locked, paths blocked, or movement restricted. In certain dreams, pursuit never ceased. The target was constantly running, hiding, or fleeing without rest.

Those who awoke often did so with intense physical symptoms, racing heart, shortness of breath, exhaustion, or overwhelming fear. Others, according to the testimony, never woke at all. Their hearts failed under the strain experienced within the dream state. In such cases, if no one intervened physically to wake the person in time, the operation was considered successful.

Pastoral Restraint and Responsibility

Bachon emphasized that this method relied on timing, vulnerability, and isolation. The dream was not random. It was structured, staged, and intentional. At the same time, testimonies of this nature must be handled with great pastoral care.

They are not offered as universal explanations for dreams, illness, or sudden death. They are not predictive frameworks or diagnostic tools. Not every disturbing dream carries spiritual intent, and it would be irresponsible to interpret ordinary psychological, emotional, or medical experiences as occult activity.

Pastoral caution does not require dismissal. When testimonies are carefully checked across cultures and independent witnesses, similar patterns do emerge. These parallels do not establish doctrine or certainty, but they do suggest that deception often operates through repeatable structures, always limited, always restrained, and always subject to God's sovereignty.

For this reason, no leader has the authority to declare "soul capture," assign spiritual causes to death, or interpret dreams in isolation. Where natural explanations exist, they must be honored. Where uncertainty remains, restraint is wisdom. The purpose of sharing such accounts is not to magnify darkness, but to cultivate sobriety, discernment, and pastoral responsibility, grounding people in truth rather than fear.

Why This Matters in the Age of Ecclesiastical Accusation

Ultimately, the relevance of this account is not found in dream imagery or in the mechanics of the method itself. Its significance lies in the pattern it reveals: how confinement begins invisibly, how familiarity lowers discernment, and how isolation precedes collapse.

These same dynamics operate within ecclesiastical accusation. Long before a word is spoken publicly, a person can be cornered internally, cut off from shared reality, guided by distorted perception, and left alone with an unchallenged narrative. When accusation takes root, the Church does not require occult ritual to reproduce captivity. Silence, fear, and the refusal to test perception in the light of truth are sufficient.

This is why such testimonies belong here. They remind us that accusation is not merely something spoken; it is something constructed. If left unexamined, it can quietly imprison individuals and communities under the appearance of righteousness.

What makes this structure especially dangerous is that it often forms before it speaks. Captivity is assembled quietly, through familiarity, disorientation, and isolation, until perception itself accepts confinement as reality. Once that inward structure is complete, it rarely remains silent. What is built in perception inevitably seeks a voice.

It is to that voice, and to the battlefield of the inner ear, that we now turn.

CHAPTER 16

AUDITORY PERCEPTION IN SPIRITUAL CONFLICT

Bachon's testimony taught me something I did not understand at first, that captivity often forms long before it ever speaks. What he described was not an attack that began with words, but a slow narrowing of reality itself. Familiar places became disorienting. Ordinary environments lost their reference points. Isolation crept in quietly, until perception itself became enclosed. Only later did accusation find its voice.

That detail remained with me. Once this kind of internal structure is in place, it does not remain silent. What forms inwardly eventually seeks expression. And one of the most common places it surfaces is not in public confrontation, but in the inner ear. Accusation that has already taken root in perception begins to speak, not always audibly, not in ways others can hear, but with a force that feels external, authoritative, and deeply convincing to the person experiencing it. It was here that I realized the conversation had to move beyond visible systems of control and into the far subtler terrain of perceptual influence.

After walking with people who had left behind charms, rituals, and objects, I began to notice something unsettling. Freedom did not always unfold as expected. The hand was empty, the altar gone, the objects destroyed, yet something remained active. What could no longer be carried or worn seemed to find another route of access. This was when I began paying closer attention to auditory perception in spiritual conflict, not as a sensational category, but as one of the most overlooked adaptations of accusation.

The Phenomenon of Spiritual Auditory Perception

Over the past fifteen years of ministry, I have encountered a pattern I did not know how to name at first. Individuals would come to me convinced they had heard words spoken about them, statements, conversations, accusations, that no one else present had heard. These were not vague impressions. They were specific, personal, and certain.

What made this difficult was that these individuals were not unstable. They were not detached from reality. They were active in church life, coherent in conversation, responsible in leadership, and relationally engaged. Nothing about their behavior suggested psychosis or emotional collapse. And yet, they were utterly convinced that something had been said, about them, against them, or around them.

I could not reduce this to heightened spiritual sensitivity. It produced no peace, no clarity, no humility. At the same time, it did not fit neatly into psychological categories either. What persuaded me that I was dealing with a spiritual phenomenon was not theory, but repetition. The same pattern surfaced again and again among people with similar histories, past involvement in occult practices, prolonged exposure to spiritual oppression, or sustained contact with compromised spiritual environments.

What they perceived was almost never neutral. It was accusatory, undermining, destabilizing. The "voice," whether perceived internally or attributed to others, worked methodically to erode trust and isolate the individual. In several cases, the timing itself was striking, appearing during the same season, sometimes the same month, year after year. That recurrence was impossible to ignore.

At first, the experience might pass quickly. But over time, something shifted. What began as uncertainty hardened into conviction. The individual no longer wondered whether something had been said; they knew it had. Evidence no longer mattered. Context no longer helped. The certainty itself became final.

And once that threshold was crossed, the effect was no longer internal. It began reshaping interpretation, suspicion, and relationships.

The Erosion of Character and Shared Reality

Over time, I began noticing changes that troubled me even more than the perceptions themselves. What initially appeared as an isolated experience was often followed by subtle but persistent shifts in character.

Some individuals developed an inflated confidence in their own discernment. Others spoke with increasing certainty, as though personal perception had become final authority. Humility thinned. Accountability felt intrusive. Correction was no longer received as care, but interpreted as threat.

In some cases, moral boundaries eroded. In others, incompatible beliefs were held side by side without tension. Language hardened. Opinions were no longer offered; they were pronounced. Listening diminished. Discernment narrowed. The inner world became self-confirming.

When the phenomenon resurfaced, the conviction was unshakable. They had heard something. No reassurance could dislodge it. No context could soften it. In those moments, shared reality lost its authority. And once shared reality fractures, community does not rupture loudly. It thins, strains, and quietly withdraws.

The most concerning element was not the perception itself, but the authority it carried. It did not arrive as a question. It arrived as a verdict. And once accepted, it justified distance, suspicion, and accusation. Over time, I came to see that this was not merely an issue of perception. It was interacting with ego, identity, and unresolved spiritual vulnerability in a way that slowly corroded trust.

Pastoral Sobriety in the Age of Accusation

At this point, restraint is essential. What I am describing should not be rushed into the category of possession. In the cases I encountered, there was no loss of agency or overt control. But neither can this phenomenon be dismissed as benign.

What I observed was something more complex, a convergence of unresolved spiritual influence, identity distortion, and perceptual certainty that had escaped communal testing. It was not dramatic, but it was formative. And once accusation became internalized, it no longer required reinforcement.

The defining feature was certainty without verification. Perception no longer submitted itself to community; community was expected to submit to perception. Once that shift occurred, accusation sustained itself. The individual no longer needed an external voice, the echo was already inside.

This cannot be healed through confrontation alone, nor through affirmation alone. It requires the slow restoration of humility, shared reality, and trust. Perception must be examined, not enthroned.

Community must be entered again, not resisted. Accusation must be named, not as truth, but as influence.

Leadership carries an enormous burden here. Affirm too quickly, and false reality is validated. Confront too harshly, and leadership becomes the enemy. In the age of ecclesiastical accusation, the Church must relearn how to hold compassion and discernment together, how to care for people without surrendering shared truth.

What this chapter ultimately taught me is this: spiritual conflict in this age rarely announces itself loudly. It moves quietly, shaping interpretation long before it shapes behavior. Auditory perception becomes dangerous, not because it is dramatic, but because it carries untested authority.

When perception is examined rather than obeyed, accusation loses its power. And when community remains intact, even subtle forms of captivity can be dismantled without fear.

The stories of my father, Marie Michel, and Bachon reveal that spiritual captivity does not always begin with personal choice. Sometimes it begins through inheritance, coercion, fear, ritual exposure, or environments that shape perception long before a person has the language to understand what is happening. My father's story reveals how grace can interrupt an inherited spiritual order before it becomes the next generation's destiny. Marie Michel's story reveals how power without truth eventually becomes bondage, even when it appears to offer authority, wealth, protection, or spiritual mastery. Bachon's testimony reveals how captivity can move inward, shaping dreams, perception, isolation, and fear until a person becomes confined from within. Together, these stories show that accusation, fear, and distorted authority are not isolated events. They are patterns that form quietly, travel through systems, and can reappear even inside religious spaces unless Christ restores discernment, truth, dignity, and freedom.

For this reason, the next chapter turns deliberately away from exposure and toward healing, from deliverance into discipleship, where freedom is no longer sustained by vigilance alone, but by formation, truth, and love.

CHAPTER 17

HEALING AND RESTORATION

Throughout our journey into the life of Marie Michel, we have seen that deliverance is only the beginning of a much larger process: the work of restoration. We have spoken of hacked souls, divine encryption, and system overwrites, metaphors that help finite minds grasp the infinite power of a God who reclaims what the enemy attempted to steal.

After someone is delivered, they stand at the threshold of a new life. There is often a genuine season of relief and clarity, a quietness of mind, a lightness of spirit, a sense that something heavy has finally been lifted. Yet this moment also requires a shift in understanding. The person who has been delivered is not a machine, and the human mind is not a piece of hardware.

Though the work of deliverance may feel decisive, it does not unfold like a machine or a formula.
The "clean install" has taken place.
The "master key" has turned.
The intruder has been evicted.
But now it is time to set aside the language of technology and speak the language of family.

What follows is no longer about systems and protocols, but about belonging and care. It is no longer about access and restriction, but about relationship itself. We step away from the courtroom and the server room and into the Father's house, where the delivered person must not only be welcomed, but nurtured, protected, and taught how to live in freedom. "If the Son sets you free, you will be free indeed" (John 8:36).

Deliverance is mighty, but it is not the finish line. It is the doorway into a new life of learning, belonging, and becoming the intended vessel of purpose. We are liberated not merely to be free, but to be restored to our original mandate: to live in relationship with the Creator, to steward His creation, and to walk in the light of truth, freedom, and obedience.

Freedom from sorcery or spiritual bondage is like stepping out of a dark room into the morning light. At first, even good things can feel overwhelming. The eyes must adjust. The body must relearn safety. The soul must learn to live in what once felt unfamiliar. That adjustment is what discipleship provides. It gives the soul a protected place to grow.

We must be careful, however, with the timing of this process. Like a photograph exposed to light too early in the darkroom, premature exposure can disturb a person's formation in Christ. When someone is exposed, criticized, or scrutinized before healing and internal formation are complete, a profound distortion occurs. What should have matured in the safety of a nurturing community becomes overwhelmed by the pressure of premature expectation. Discipleship is the shield that ensures the soul matures in safety before it is asked to stand against the winds of the world.

Many experience the power of deliverance only to find themselves sliding back into the cold grip of fear or the suffocating fog of confusion. This tragic regression often occurs when there is no one to walk beside them, or when a spiritual leader fails to help the new believer understand the careful, sovereign nature of God's restoration process.

In a misguided haste to prove effectiveness, some leaders begin to improvise. They attempt to manufacture a healing that has not yet taken root in the deep soil of the soul. This improvisation is often driven by a hollow desire to display a "special anointing" or elevated calling, a need to appear powerful before learning how to be humble.

When God's timing is ignored in favor of human recognition, the result is a soul that is spiritually preterm, born into freedom, yet deprived of the nourishment required to survive it.

Without the steady hand of guidance, and without the patience to abide by God's schedule, the person who was just delivered may drift back toward the gravitational pull of the very patterns they once escaped. We must never forget that authentic restoration requires more than the dramatic, visible act of casting out. It requires the quiet, persistent, and largely invisible work of building up.

Jesus warned that when an unclean spirit leaves a person, it searches for rest and, finding none, returns to the house left "empty." Deliverance clears the house. Discipleship furnishes it. One without the other leaves the soul vulnerable.

When God frees someone from darkness, He does not merely remove demons, He restores dignity, purpose, and identity. Healing addresses the wounds left behind: guilt, shame, mistrust, and fear. Those who have lived under spiritual bondage often carry invisible scars that shape how they think, trust, and love. Their emotions may remain fragile, their self-worth distorted, and their worldview filtered through constant vigilance rather than grace.

That is why deliverance must always be followed by teaching, mentoring, and community. Freedom must be understood before it can be sustained. Liberation without learning is short-lived; understanding transforms freedom into lasting peace.

Restoration unfolds across multiple dimensions. Spiritually, the first task after deliverance is the reestablishment of intimacy with God. Many who lived under fear or ritual never knew Him as Father. They related to power, not presence. Their prayers were transactions rather than conversations. Through worship, Scripture, and quiet reflection, they begin to rest again in the Father's love. God is no longer perceived as a distant judge, but encountered as a gentle Redeemer. Identity shifts from servant to child.

Emotionally, deliverance frees the spirit, but the inner life must still be healed. Old patterns of shame, anger, and mistrust require patient restoration. I often encourage newly freed believers to practice intentional forgiveness toward those who harmed them, and toward themselves. The Holy Spirit, the Comforter, specializes in this work. He does not erase memory; He removes its poison.

Relationally, restoration draws people back into family and community. Sorcery isolates; Christ reunites. This rebuilding is often delicate, especially where accusation or fear once caused separation. As pastors and leaders, we must encourage reconciliation wherever possible. Deliverance that divides is incomplete; healing that restores is divine.

Functionally, restoration reaches fullness when the healed individual begins to serve. Those once bound become intercessors, teachers, and instruments of hope. Their scars become credentials of compassion. Deliverance that does not lead outward turns inward. Freedom deepens when it is poured out in love.

A healthy church understands itself as a hospital, not a courtroom. It treats the wounded without condemnation. It offers therapy for the soul through faithful teaching, prayer, fellowship, accountability, and discretion. Such a congregation replaces fear with truth, models forgiveness in both public and private life, protects confidentiality in pastoral care, and encourages testimony that transforms shame into gratitude rather than spectacle.

Every delivered soul also needs companionship. Mentorship lies at the heart of discipleship, a mature believer walking beside another with patience and wisdom. This is not control, but care. Not surveillance, but shared growth. The Church must recover this rhythm, gathering new believers into spaces where they are known, guided, and formed under the steady presence of spiritual elders.

Even after deliverance, many remain haunted by guilt, quietly asking, "Can God truly forgive me for what I did?" That question itself becomes a chain. Scripture answers without ambiguity: "There is now no condemnation for those who are in Christ Jesus" (Romans 8:1). Condemnation looks backward; grace looks forward. The blood of Jesus not only cleanses, it reinstates.

Pastors must proclaim grace boldly, especially for those emerging from occult backgrounds, because shame is one of the enemy's most persistent instruments of control.

Wholeness is not perfection; it is peace. It is living reconciled with God, with others, and with oneself. It is sleeping without fear, loving without suspicion, and serving without shame.

When healing is complete, the believer no longer identifies as a former sorcerer or a perpetual victim, but simply as a child of God.
That is the miracle of grace.
"He restores my soul" (Psalm 23:3).

If healing is the goal, then restorers must be formed. The Church cannot sustain freedom through isolated moments of prayer alone; it must raise people who know how to walk with the wounded responsibly.

RAISING RESTORERS

"And He gave some to be apostles, some prophets, some evangelists, some pastors and teachers, to equip the saints for the work of ministry" (Ephesians 4:11–12).

Every restored soul carries within it the potential to restore others. Those who have walked through deception, fear, accusation, or spiritual bondage possess a rare authority, not because they are flawless, but because they have encountered truth in the midst of survival. Their scars become sources of wisdom. Their testimony becomes instruction.

Yet zeal alone is not enough. To lead others safely toward freedom requires more than passion; it requires wisdom, maturity, and restraint. Deliverance and discernment demand steady hearts, not loud voices. The Church must therefore raise restorers who are both spiritually alive and emotionally grounded. Only then does revival become sustainable, when healed people rise not to perform, but to heal.

The Need for Wise and Mature Leadership

History is filled with well-meaning believers who caused harm in the name of deliverance because they lacked formation, humility, or discernment. Some confused emotional intensity with spiritual authority. Others mistook suspicion for revelation. Without maturity, deliverance becomes theater. Without love, discernment hardens into judgment.

Raising restorers means shaping men and women who are biblically anchored, emotionally stable, and spiritually humble, leaders who understand that authority flows from submission, not visibility. As Jesus taught, "Whoever wants to be great among you must be your servant" (Matthew 20:26). Deliverance leaders must never seek recognition. They must seek restoration.

The Character of a True Restorer

True deliverance ministers are not identified by titles, loudness, or dramatic displays of power, but by fruit. Integrity steadies their words. Compassion governs their actions. Self-control shapes their tone. They listen more than they speak. They give glory to God rather than drawing attention to themselves.

They know when to pray, when to teach, and when to wait. They understand that timing is as spiritual as authority. Above all, they remain accountable, never isolated, never beyond counsel. These qualities are not received instantly through an anointing; they are cultivated through prayer, mentoring, correction, and faithful service within the local church. A restorer's authority grows not through performance, but through proven faithfulness.

Understanding True Discernment

Discernment is not suspicion. It is spiritual clarity without fear, prejudice, or projection. Many mistake intuition or emotional reaction for discernment, but Scripture defines discernment as a gift of the Spirit that reveals both the problem and the path toward healing.

True discernment does not end at exposure. It moves deliberately toward restoration. Revelation without love becomes accusation. Exposure without wisdom becomes harm. As Proverbs teaches, "He who covers a transgression seeks love, but he who repeats a matter separates close friends" (Proverbs 17:9). Discernment exists not to humiliate sin, but to heal the sinner.

Training Restorers: A Pastoral Path

The Church must develop clear and intentional pathways for training leaders in deliverance and discernment. Spiritual formation is foundational, grounding leaders in salvation, grace, and identity in Christ while prioritizing character over charisma. They must learn to pray deeply, fast wisely, and study Scripture carefully.

Theological grounding follows. Leaders must be trained in biblical teachings on spiritual authority, warfare, the fruit of the Spirit, and the proper handling of dreams, impressions, and prophetic insight. They must learn to distinguish between revelation and emotional manipulation, between conviction and accusation.

Practical ministry training then completes the formation. Emerging restorers should observe seasoned ministers, learn to pray with calm authority, and understand how to maintain order and dignity during intense spiritual moments. Ethics must be emphasized: confidentiality, consent, boundaries, and post-deliverance care. Mentorship and accountability remain essential. Deliverance ministry is never a solo performance; it is a team assignment under divine order.

The Role of Emotional Intelligence

Emotional intelligence is as essential as spiritual anointing. Leaders who cannot regulate their emotions often confuse reaction for revelation. When fear or anger drives deliverance, the enemy gains ground, first through deception, then through disorder.

Emotionally intelligent restorers listen well and respond gently. They recognize that behind every manifestation is a wounded soul longing for peace. As Scripture reminds us, "A gentle answer turns away wrath, but a harsh word stirs up anger" (Proverbs 15:1). Calm leadership creates safe environments where the Holy Spirit can work deeply and without resistance.

Ethics and Boundaries in Deliverance Ministry

Power without ethics becomes abuse. History bears witness to the damage caused when spiritual authority crosses moral boundaries: public humiliation, coercion, breaches of confidentiality, and demands for unquestioned loyalty. Such practices grieve the Holy Spirit.

Every deliverance minister must operate within holy boundaries. Dignity must be honored, privacy protected, and trust preserved. The Spirit of Christ never humiliates. He restores.

The Relationship Between Teaching and Power

Power without teaching creates dependency. When believers view deliverance as a recurring event rather than an entry point into discipleship, they remain vulnerable. A true restorer uses power to open the door but relies on teaching to help the person walk through it.

This is the pattern of Jesus' ministry. He healed the sick and then said, "Go and sin no more" (John 5:14; 8:11). Miracles were invitations to maturity, not substitutes for formation. Deliverance initiates freedom; teaching preserves it. The Word must always follow the work.

Training in Cultural Sensitivity

In communities shaped by ancestral spirituality, such as Haiti, Africa, and the Caribbean, discernment must be paired with cultural understanding. Not everything mystical is demonic, and not every tradition is harmless. Restorers must learn to distinguish between cultural expression and spiritual bondage.

Drumming, dance, art, and communal rituals can be redeemed rather than rejected. The goal is not cultural erasure, but sanctification. When the Gospel honors heritage while liberating the heart, transformation becomes durable. Christ redeems culture from within, by breathing holiness into it, not by alienating it.

Building Teams of Restorers

Deliverance and discipleship thrive in teams. Each member contributes distinct gifts: prayer, teaching, counseling, worship, and administration. A healthy ministry rejects the "superhero" model that elevates one individual as the sole vessel of power.

Unity multiplies effectiveness; division multiplies confusion. A well-balanced deliverance ministry operates under pastoral oversight, sustained intercession, emotional care, sound teaching, and worship that guards the spiritual atmosphere. As Jesus said, "A house divided against itself cannot stand" (Matthew 12:25).

Raising the Next Generation of Restorers

The Church must invest intentionally in its young believers. Today's youth are immersed in horoscopes, manifestation rituals, energy language, and digital spirituality. They need education, not condemnation.

Youth retreats, workshops, and honest conversations about spiritual realities can equip them to discern truth from imitation. Imagine a generation of Haitian and Caribbean youth who understand both their ancestral history and the liberating authority of Christ, able to honor their heritage while breaking its spiritual chains. As Daniel writes, "Those who are wise will shine like the brightness of the heavens, and those who lead many to righteousness, like the stars forever and ever" (Daniel 12:3).

Practical Development for Emerging Leaders

Developing restorers requires both study and lived experience. Training should include guided reflection on Scripture, careful examination of fear-based ministry models, supervised ministry under mature oversight, and spaces for renewal through prayer retreats. Through these practices, emerging leaders learn to balance authority with patience, boldness with gentleness, and knowledge with compassion.

The Marks of a Mature Deliverance Leader

A mature restorer carries a peaceful presence and sound doctrine. Their theology aligns with Scripture, not superstition. Their empathy matches their authority. Their humility reflects their power. They reconcile relationships rather than fracture them. The fruit of their ministry is not fear, but fellowship.

Such leaders reflect the true image of Christ, the Deliverer who came not to destroy lives, but to save them. Their maturity is not measured by how loudly they command darkness to leave, but by how quietly they lead people into light.

Reflection and Prayer

Pause and reflect. How do you respond when you encounter spiritual bondage, through fear, pride, or compassion? Do you seek recognition for power, or joy in restoration? How might you help cultivate a culture of accountability, teaching, and care within your ministry?

Leadership is never an endpoint; it is a legacy. Those trained as restorers must eventually pass on what they have received. This journey continues as the Church learns to build a culture of light, where knowledge becomes practice, deliverance matures into discipleship, and freedom is sustained across generations.

BEYOND FEAR

"For you were once darkness, but now you are light in the Lord. Walk as children of light" (Ephesians 5:8).

Every generation must decide what kind of atmosphere it will live in: fear or faith, suspicion or love, darkness or light. Throughout this journey, we have witnessed how misunderstanding sorcery has divided families, wounded churches, and turned prophets into accusers. We have also seen how truth, compassion, and rightly exercised spiritual authority can heal, restore, and transform.

Yet knowledge alone is not enough. The greater challenge is cultural. We must build environments where fear no longer governs conversations about evil, and where love, stronger than suspicion, defines spiritual maturity. When the people of God walk in light, sorcery loses its influence. When leaders walk in humility, false prophecy loses its audience. When love governs community life, accusation finds no home. The world is not waiting for another spectacular deliverer; it is waiting for a compassionate, balanced, fearless Church.

Understanding Culture as a Spiritual Atmosphere

Culture is more than language, food, or custom. It is the invisible air a community breathes, the shared assumptions, emotional climate, and interpretive lens through which life is understood. This invisible air is the atmosphere.

In many communities shaped by slavery, colonization, trauma, or religious syncretism, fear has long been part of that atmosphere. Stories of curses, betrayal, hidden enemies, and spiritual retaliation are passed from one generation to the next. Though these narratives may teach vigilance, they often cultivate suspicion. When fear becomes normal, people live as if danger is inevitable and peace is naïve.

The Gospel does not come merely to change behavior; it comes to change atmosphere. It invites us to breathe new air, the air of the Kingdom, where freedom is normal and peace is possible. "For the kingdom of God is not eating and drinking, but righteousness and peace and joy in the Holy Spirit" (Romans 14:17). When a community learns to live in that atmosphere, sorcery cannot thrive. Fear dies when it can no longer find agreement.

What It Means to Build a Culture of Light

A culture of light is not simply the absence of evil; it is the presence of discernment, unity, and love. It is an environment where people no longer whisper about demons but speak openly about healing, where the question shifts from "Who did this?" to "How can this be restored?" Truth is tested in shared light rather than weaponized in private suspicion.

Such a culture is formed in three primary places: the pulpit, where truth is preached with balance and responsibility; the home, where faith replaces fear in daily language and practice; and the community, where believers model compassion rather than condemnation. A culture of light grows one conversation at a time, one prayer at a time, one act of forgiveness at a time.

Jesus said, "You are the light of the world. A city set on a hill cannot be hidden" (Matthew 5:14). Light becomes culture when it is consistently lived, not occasionally proclaimed.

The Church as a Lighthouse in the Storm

In an age marked by confusion, false prophecy, and fear-based spirituality, the Church must become a lighthouse, not a courtroom. A lighthouse does not chase storms; it shines steadily until the lost find their way home. That is the Church's calling when many are spiritually disoriented.

Our congregations must become places where those once bound by darkness can breathe again, where worship feels safe, teaching feels trustworthy, and love feels tangible. When someone walks through the doors, they should not feel suspected; they should feel seen. The atmosphere should quietly communicate, *You are home.* Every service, every pastoral decision, and every prayer meeting is an opportunity to rebuild God's house as a place of refuge rather than fear.

Transmitting Freedom to the Next Generation

One of the Church's most urgent responsibilities is ensuring that our children do not inherit our fears. In many Caribbean and African families, children grow up hearing stories of witches, curses, and spiritual enemies. Even after salvation, some parents unknowingly pass those fears down, baptizing anxiety in religious language and calling paranoia discernment.

We must teach our children that the power of Christ is greater than any curse. Faith must be demonstrated, not merely declared. This happens when stories of terror are replaced with testimonies of deliverance, when Scripture affirms victory rather than vulnerability, and when young people are invited into prayer, service, creativity, and worship. When they experience the Church as joyful, grounded, and fearless, they will not search for power elsewhere.

"Train up a child in the way he should go, and when he is old he will not depart from it" (Proverbs 22:6).

The Role of Education in Spiritual Transformation

Education remains one of the Church's strongest tools of deliverance. Ignorance has always been one of the enemy's most effective weapons. When believers learn to distinguish between culture, superstition, and biblical truth, manipulation loses its power.

Teaching must never be treated as secondary. Sermons, Bible studies, small groups, and community forums should address spiritual deception, how fear is cultivated, how truth is distorted, and how discernment is replaced with superstition. When believers understand why they believe what they believe, fear loses its grip. Knowledge does not merely inform; it liberates. "You shall know the truth, and the truth shall make you free" (John 8:32).

Confronting Fear-Based Religion

We must also acknowledge that many Christians have been wounded by fear-based religion, a faith shaped more by threat than love. They were taught that every setback was witchcraft, every illness an attack, every disagreement a conspiracy. Rarely were they taught how to rest in the finished work of Christ or to interpret life through the security of God's fatherhood.

Jesus did not die to make us paranoid; He died to make us free. When the Church preaches fear, it unknowingly partners with the darkness it claims to oppose. When it preaches peace, it multiplies God's presence. Power without peace becomes noise; peace with power becomes light.

Practical Pathways Toward a Culture of Light

Building a culture of light requires intention. Churches must teach biblical discernment rather than suspicion, encourage intercession rather than investigation, and protect the accused rather than amplifying fear. Pastoral care must be strengthened, ethical leadership enforced, and safe spaces created for honest questions and healing conversations.

When these rhythms take root, the spiritual atmosphere changes. People begin to breathe differently. Fear loses credibility. Love gains authority. This transformation is not cosmetic; it is generational.

The Theology of Light

Light is not merely a metaphor; it is the nature of God Himself. Wherever light enters, darkness loses its form. It cannot compete; it can only retreat. A church that walks in light does not need to chase shadows; the presence of Christ becomes its warfare.

"And the light shines in the darkness, and the darkness has not overcome it" (John 1:5). The mission of the Church is not to obsess over darkness, but to reflect the character of Christ. Every sermon, every song, and every act of kindness becomes a beam that makes fear less believable.

The Legacy of Freedom

Every revival leaves a legacy. The question is what kind. Will we be remembered as a generation that spread fear, or one that rebuilt faith? Will our churches be known for accusation or compassion? Will our children inherit trauma or testimony?

God calls us to leave behind more than buildings. He calls us to leave behind a way of life, a culture shaped by freedom, forgiveness, and truth. A Church that lives beyond fear produces leaders of integrity, families that forgive quickly, and communities that heal generational wounds. That is legacy. That is the victory of the Cross.

A Pastoral Closing Reflection

I have witnessed both the power of darkness and the quiet strength of light. I have seen families shattered by fear and restored by forgiveness, churches fractured by accusation and healed through repentance. I have learned that no amount of shouting can drive out darkness if love is absent. But when love becomes sincere, fear quietly departs.

The deepest work of deliverance is not only the casting out of demons; it is the casting out of fear. It is the replacement of superstition with truth, condemnation with grace, and shame with belonging. Wherever truth, compassion, and authority dwell together, the Holy Spirit finds a true home.

And yet, one question still lingers in the hearts of many sincere believers, a question that binds even the faithful in quiet anxiety: *Can witchcraft, enchantments, or spells truly harm a child of God?*

The answer, rooted in Scripture and confirmed through lived experience, is profoundly liberating. Understanding it closes the final door to fear and teaches believers how to walk in peace, not merely for a season, but for life. It is to that assurance, and to the unshakable security found in Christ alone, that we now turn.

CHAPTER 18

DIVINE IMMUNITY

Central to this discussion is a truth often misunderstood: the nature of divine protection. The covering of God is not fragile, nor does it depend on human strength, vigilance, or merit. It is secured by covenant, sealed by the Spirit, and anchored in the Word. To live under that covering does not mean a believer will never face spiritual opposition. It means such opposition can never ultimately prevail. Darkness may resist, threaten, or intimidate, but it cannot overthrow what God has established in Christ. To understand this is to step out of fear and into freedom, resting in the assurance that no power of darkness can cancel what God has purposed. The believer's security in Christ is not theoretical. It is structural.

From the beginning, God's intention for each life is already known to Him. Before birth, He sees destiny, assigns purpose, and governs timing. No witchcraft, enchantment, spell, or manipulation can overturn what God has decreed. Even when resistance appears, His sovereignty remains intact. Scripture repeatedly shows that God can use even hardened or wicked individuals to protect, deliver, and position those He has chosen. His authority is absolute. His protection is not negotiated. The futility of witchcraft against divine purpose is therefore more than comforting; it reveals the supremacy of God over every hidden system.

Through years of ministry and careful observation, I have come to recognize that witchcraft, enchantments, and spells tend to affect people according to their spiritual posture. The first group includes those who practice occult activity, knowingly or unknowingly, through rituals, consultations, hidden agreements, or spiritual transactions. In seeking control, power, protection, or insight, they open themselves to forces they cannot govern. The second group includes those who make morality their covering. These are men and women who rely on outward goodness, religious discipline, or personal righteousness while lacking true security in Christ. Their confidence rests in performance rather than grace, leaving them vulnerable to deception. The third group includes genuine believers whom God permits to grow in discernment. These individuals are not victims of darkness. They are students of revelation. God may allow them to perceive and understand spiritual operations so they can guide others toward freedom without fear.

Each group represents a different spiritual reality, but only one remains unshaken: the life hidden in Christ. This chapter is written for those who want to understand that difference, live with discernment rather than fear, and walk in the settled truth that no enchantment, spell, or unseen power can reverse what God has already blessed.

When God exposes the reality of witchcraft, He does not do so to terrify His people, but to educate them. One of the clearest biblical examples appears in the book of Numbers. Balaam, an experienced diviner, was hired by King Balak to manipulate Israel's destiny through spiritual means. Yet when Balaam opened his mouth to curse, blessing came forth instead. Scripture declares, "Surely there is no enchantment against Jacob, neither is there any divination against Israel" (Numbers 23:23). His failure reveals a timeless spiritual law: no curse can prevail where divine blessing governs.

As shown throughout this book, former occult practitioners from Haiti, Africa, and the West testify to the same reality: their enchantments could not reach a genuine believer anchored in Christ. Ignorance and fear can still torment the mind. Anxiety, panic, and obsessive concern about witchcraft can trouble even sincere Christians. Yet fear is not evidence of spiritual defeat. It is a sign that focus has shifted away from truth. When truth is restored, fear loses its authority.

This chapter clarifies how enchantments and spells function and why they cannot spiritually penetrate a believer who abides in Christ. To do so, we must first understand their nature, then consider the unseen structure through which spiritual systems operate.

The Meaning of Enchantments and Spells

Across Scripture and ancient tradition, enchantments and spells refer to deliberate attempts to influence people, events, or unseen forces through words, gestures, or ritual actions outside the will of God. They represent humanity's effort to manipulate spiritual power for personal desire, control, or harm. Scripture uses different terms, including sorcery, divination, charms, and magical arts, but they share one principle: unauthorized spiritual manipulation.

Enchantments: The Power of Spoken Influence

The word *enchantment* traces back to the Latin *incantare*, meaning "to sing or chant over." Ancient cultures believed repeated words could summon spirits or alter reality. In that setting, the voice became a tool of domination. Biblically, enchantments represent the spoken dimension of witchcraft, verbal formulas attempting to activate power without divine authority. Pharaoh's magicians attempted this against Moses. Balaam attempted it against Israel. Both failed because words separated from God's covenant carry no authority over those protected by it.

Spiritually, enchantments can also appear through manipulative speech. They may come through language designed to charm, intimidate, threaten, or control. Paul warned against smooth speech that deceives the hearts of the unsuspecting (Romans 16:18). The goal of such speech is not truth, but leverage.

Spells: The Act of Spiritual Manipulation

A spell extends beyond words into deliberate spiritual manipulation. It may involve symbols, actions, objects, offerings, sacrifices, or ritual gestures directed toward a desired outcome. Yet beneath every spell lies a deeper reality: the practitioner does not truly command the spirit invoked. He yields to it. In attempting to control unseen forces, he becomes an instrument of the very power he seeks to use.

Where enchantments persuade, spells attempt to bind. They function as spiritual contracts, seeking to attach a person's mind, spirit, or circumstances to an ungodly will. Their effectiveness does not rest only on the sorcerer's strength, but on fear, agreement, or spiritual access. Fear opens doors. Faith closes them. Scripture says, "Like a fluttering sparrow or a darting swallow, an undeserved curse does not come to rest" (Proverbs 26:2).

In modern religious and family settings, spells may appear less like rituals and more like manipulative declarations. A leader says, "If you leave this church, disaster will follow." A parent declares, "You will never succeed." A false prophet insists, "You cannot prosper unless I cover you." These are spoken enchantments, attempts to govern identity through fear. They may wound emotionally, but they cannot penetrate the spirit of one anchored in Christ.

Understanding How Spiritual Networks Work

To understand why enchantments cannot reach the believer, it helps to consider a familiar analogy: communication networks. Just as a phone connects through a provider to transmit signals, spiritual life operates through alignment and authority. Every person lives under influence according to connection. Some networks transmit life and peace. Others carry fear and bondage. The decisive question is not whether one is connected, but to whom.

Occult practitioners operate within unauthorized networks. Through rituals, vows, ancestral pacts, and hidden agreements, they align themselves with systems outside God's authority. Those who continue in occult activity, conceal unrepentant sin, or maintain secret spiritual agreements may remain connected to those channels without fully understanding the danger.

But the believer in Christ lives under a different authority. There are no shared towers, no roaming agreements, and no spiritual interoperability between the kingdom of Christ and the kingdom of darkness. When you belong to Christ, your identity and protection are secured under His authority. Witchcraft may attempt transmission, but it finds no legitimate access. That is why Scripture declares, "No weapon formed against you shall prosper" (Isaiah 54:17). This is not poetic exaggeration. It describes incompatible jurisdictions. Darkness cannot possess what Christ has sealed.

Living Without Fear

When God exposes witchcraft, the response is not panic, but clarity. Those still practicing darkness are not ultimate threats. They are captives within corrupted systems. They need truth, deliverance, and invitation, not intimidation. Because you are in Christ, you are not available to darkness. Your life is not open territory. Your identity cannot be hijacked by curses, declarations, rituals, or hidden powers. As you walk in that awareness, peace itself becomes part of your witness.

Witchcraft operates through fear-based spiritual systems. The believer lives under divine authority, secure, sealed, and covered in Christ. There is no shared signal, no open gateway, and no spiritual roaming. You are under full coverage in Him.

The preceding pages have established a necessary truth: those who dwell in Christ do not live under threat, but under covering. Fear loses its authority when divine protection is properly understood. Yet once fear is addressed, another responsibility emerges. The Church must not only resist darkness outside itself; it must also examine how authority, discernment, and perception are being formed within its own life. At this point, the question shifts from what cannot touch the believer to what is shaping the believer.

Experience, not theory, gave birth to this book. While serving within the Church, I witnessed a slow and painful change in our culture. I watched pastors and leaders move from *we* to *me*, as collaboration withered into competition and trust was replaced by suspicion. Perhaps the lowest point was realizing that when a leader fell, the reaction was not always sorrow. At times, it was a quiet satisfaction. This book grew out of that sobering mirror. The problem is not merely a few broken people. It is the atmosphere we have allowed to settle over the house of prayer and worship.

At first, the change did not arrive loudly. It crept in through whispers about motives, debates over who was "truly spiritual," and sermons that condemned more than they healed. We began arguing over who was anointed, which titles belonged to whom, and who carried the greater authority. We stopped moving toward a single Christ-centered mission and fractured into factions, often following personalities, platforms, or private agendas while quietly weakening the Church's witness.

We began living in an atmosphere of spiritual loopholes. The enemy exploited human weakness, stirring pride, jealousy, resentment, and rivalry. Nonessential matters, including politics, cultural preferences, traditions, and personal loyalties, were elevated into tests of righteousness. Fear did not always announce itself as fear. It often arrived disguised as vigilance, caution, or discernment, quietly training the Church to react rather than remain rooted.

Gradually, the pulpit that once broke chains began to build walls. Discernment became confused with accusation. Authority was expressed through exposure rather than restoration. Deliverance began to resemble performance. The Church, called to be a lighthouse, began to feel like a courtroom. That climate is the true concern of this book.

At the core of that climate is fear, not the fear of the Lord, which produces wisdom and humility, but a cultivated fear of exposure, loss, contamination, and displacement. Fear reshapes discernment into suspicion. It trains believers to scan for threats rather than test truth. It accelerates judgment, rewards certainty, and punishes patience. Once fear becomes the governing emotion, authority no longer requires wisdom to function. It requires only reaction. Accusation thrives in such an atmosphere because fear supplies its urgency, its justification, and its moral confidence.

This is why authority must be understood clearly. Authority is not merely a title, office, pulpit, collar, platform, or spiritual gift. Authority is the power to shape perception. It tells people what to fear, whom to trust, how to interpret danger, and where to place loyalty. When authority is healthy, it protects, clarifies, corrects, and restores. When it is distorted, it becomes a prison of fear and accusation.

The occult is easier to recognize when there are altars, incantations, rituals, and visible contracts. But the deeper danger is more subtle. A person can leave the outward tools of bondage behind and still carry a captive way of seeing. This book argues that the spirit of accusation does not need a ritual to thrive. It can live comfortably in leadership meetings, church pews, sermons, private conversations, and digital platforms. It stops looking like witchcraft and begins to sound like spirituality. It teaches people to judge one another while believing they are defending God.

That is why the testimonies matter. Marie Michel's story was included not to sensationalize darkness, but to reveal structure. Her journey made one truth undeniable: deliverance without compassion becomes cruelty, and discernment without love becomes deception. The believers who stood with her were not celebrities. They were faithful people who loved without fear. Her testimony exposed how darkness operates through mechanics and leverage, but it also revealed how easily the Church can mishandle the wounded, either exploiting them for spectacle or exiling them through suspicion.

Bachon's testimony carried the conversation further inward. It showed that when external altars fall, conflict often relocates into interpretation, memory, perception, and the inner ear. Even after deliverance is real, captivity can reappear as a question of governance: who defines reality, what is treated as authoritative, and whether a believer remains anchored in shared truth or becomes trapped in private certainty. This is where ecclesiastical accusation thrives most efficiently, because accusation does not require altars to function. It requires only fear, isolation, and untested perception.

This is also why the language of this manuscript has been intentionally rich in metaphor. A single metaphor would fail the task because the problem is not singular. Captivity rarely announces itself in one form. It migrates from altar to mind, from ritual to perception, from external power to internal authority. The metaphors are not the message. They are lenses. They help modern believers recognize ancient patterns without requiring a shared cultural vocabulary. They are scaffolding, meant to steady the discussion while the foundation is rebuilt: Christ's lordship, Scripture's governance, and love as the atmosphere of freedom.

Before concluding, the argument must be stated plainly. We have entered a season in which spiritual authority is increasingly measured by visibility rather than character, certainty rather than humility, and exposure rather than restoration. Digital platforms have become altars of attention. Fear has discipled many believers more deeply than Scripture. Political ideology has intensified suspicion. In that unstable air, accusation multiplies. Sometimes it wears prophetic language. Sometimes it wears discernment. Sometimes it wears concern. Yet it produces the same fruit: division, mistrust, and the slow erosion of shared truth.

This book is not written to cultivate fear or teach suspicion. It is written to call the Church back to clarity, balance, and confidence in Christ. True discernment does not imagine enemies everywhere. It recognizes truth steadily. It does not humiliate the wounded. It restores them. It does not rely on panic to function. It requires pastoral authority shaped by humility, courage formed by compassion, and a community disciplined enough to test perception in the light.

The chapters you have just read were not a detour from that mission. They were evidence of it. Now, as we move toward conclusion, the question is no longer, *How dark can darkness be?* The question is, *What kind of Church will we become in response?* A Church of suspicion, or a Church of restoration? A people trained to hunt shadows, or a people trained to carry light? A community governed by private certainty, or one governed by Scripture, tested truth, and love?

The argument must now widen, not away from the Church, but toward the world forming around it. We stand at a threshold where the ancient and the imminent collide. We are no longer merely using tools. We are inhabiting an atmosphere in which technology increasingly mediates truth, authority, identity, and even spiritual imagination. For the rising generation, technology is not simply a device in the hand. It is often a layer over the eyes, a secondary nervous system through which they encounter information, belonging, conflict, and meaning. Many do not come to sacred questions through cathedral doors, but through the glass of a screen, seeking guidance in spaces that are decentralized, anonymous, and constantly moving.

In this landscape, ecclesiastical accusation finds one of its most efficient laboratories. Whispers that once traveled through church hallways now move at the speed of the feed, propelled by algorithms that reward engagement more than truth. Digital platforms have become altars of attention, where the courtroom is always open and the jury is global. A generation is being discipled by the frantic pace of the timeline rather than the steady rhythm of the Spirit. Discernment is increasingly confused with reaction, and authority is measured not by the weight of character, but by the visibility of a profile.

A quieter migration is also underway. As artificial intelligence begins to mirror human thought, it offers simulated wisdom: a voice that can counsel without presence, advise without accountability, and inform without incarnation. The danger is not that the machine will replace God, but that it may replace the need for embodied community, reducing the mystery of the Body of Christ to private, curated certainty.

This generation stands at the edge of a profound tension where the biological and the technological converge. The Church must answer a question it can no longer postpone: what remains of the image of God when human identity is continually mediated, optimized, and reshaped by human invention? If we do not recover spiritual orientation now, we risk leaving the next generation in a world where captivity has survived the destruction of outward tools and migrated into the architecture of identity itself.

The call, therefore, is not to retreat into a pre-digital past, but to occupy this new atmosphere with a weight of glory technology cannot replicate. The Church must offer what the algorithm never can: the uncompromising lordship of Christ, the unhurried governance of Scripture, and a love so embodied and sacrificial that it breaks the mirrors of the self.

The assurance already affirmed remains essential: no enchantment, spell, or hidden power can ultimately prevail against those protected in Christ. That truth steadies the soul. It reminds the believer that the victory of Christ is not fragile, temporary, or dependent on human vigilance. Where God covers, darkness cannot intrude. Where Christ reigns, fear has no final authority.

Yet this assurance raises a more searching question. If the people of God are protected, why does fear still shape so much of the Church's life? If enchantment cannot prevail, why do suspicion, accusation, and spiritual fragmentation persist among communities that confess Christ's victory? The answer does not lie in the strength of darkness, but in the way fear is interpreted, managed, and exercised once protection is assumed.

Divine covering secures the believer, but it does not excuse the Church from the responsibility of discernment. Protection guards the soul; it does not automatically heal perception. A people may be covered and still misread one another. A Church may be protected and still allow fear to govern its understanding of authority, testimony, and threat. When fear is no longer directed outward toward enchantment but inward toward one another, the danger shifts from spiritual attack to ecclesial distortion.

It is here that the focus must turn. Having established what cannot prevail against the protected, we must now examine what has quietly taken root within the Church itself. What follows does not question divine power. It questions human posture. It does not return to darkness outside the Church, but addresses fear within it. To move forward faithfully, the Church must return, not to anxiety, not to accusation, but to the heart of the matter.

CHAPTER 19

TOWARD THE HEART OF THE MATTER

Here, the argument takes a stand to re-anchor the discussion before the conclusion, not because the argument has wandered, but because it has deepened. Having seen how fear operates in lived experience, how it recruits authority, and how it produces accusation, we are now prepared to face the more difficult work ahead: discerning what kind of authority heals rather than harms, what kind of fear is biblically formative rather than corrosive, and what kind of Church can resist the gravitational pull of accusation without retreating into denial.

Stories have been told not to provoke fascination, but to establish record. Patterns have been traced not to accuse individuals, but to expose a climate. And yet, having walked this far, it becomes necessary to pause, not to summarize what has been said, but to return deliberately to what this book has been about from the beginning.

This book was never written to catalogue spiritual phenomena, nor to elevate testimony for its own sake. It was written to confront a condition. *The Age of Ecclesiastical Accusation* is not a momentary controversy or a series of isolated failures. It is a governing posture that emerges when fear is allowed to interpret reality, authority is permitted to operate without restraint, and discernment is displaced by suspicion. Everything the reader has encountered, every narrative, theological frame, and pastoral warning, has been moving toward this central concern: how fear reshapes perception until accusation feels like wisdom and control masquerades as protection.

The testimony of Marie Michel did not interrupt the argument of this book; it clarified it. Her story functioned as evidence because fear leaves fingerprints. It organizes behavior, restricts speech, fragments identity, and trains the conscience to obey threat rather than truth. What unfolded in her life was not extraordinary because it was dramatic, but because it was consistent. The same mechanics that governed her captivity are present, in quieter and more respectable forms, wherever fear is granted interpretive authority within the Church. When fear is left unchallenged, it does not remain internal. It seeks validation. It looks for language. It recruits authority. Eventually, it demands accusation.

What complicates this age, however, is that fear no longer travels alone. It is now engineered, amplified, and ritualized through modern ecclesiastical practices that appear spiritually active while quietly bypassing discernment. Fear does not originate in technology, platforms, or ecclesiastical systems. It precedes them, emerging in seasons of uncertainty, loss of trust, cultural instability, and spiritual anxiety. It is the originating condition, not the final product. Before fear becomes visible in practices or language, it exists as atmosphere, felt more than named, endured more than examined. When fear remains unaddressed, it begins to search for relief.

That search gives rise to *Engineered Spirituality*. Rather than discipling fear through patience, testing, and formation, institutions often attempt to manage it. *Engineered Spirituality* responds to anxiety by offering certainty, speed, and control. It favors outcomes over formation, reaction over discernment, and visibility over accountability. Fear is not removed; it is organized. What once required slow spiritual maturity is replaced by techniques that produce immediate clarity. In this way, anxiety is converted into structure, urgency into virtue, and control into spiritual responsibility.

The digital altar intensifies this process. Online platforms do not create fear, but they reward it. They amplify urgency, elevate certainty, and accelerate accusation. Authority in these spaces is formed through repetition and reach rather than proximity and accountability. What once unfolded within pastoral relationships now takes place publicly, detached from communal testing. Fear gains traction not because it is true, but because it performs well. Accusation travels faster than understanding, and reaction is mistaken for discernment.

Over time, as *Engineered Spirituality* and the digital altar take hold, they begin to generate more fear than they initially received. Fear returns to the Church amplified, validated, and repeated until it appears self-evident. Leaders react defensively. Discernment collapses into vigilance. Questions harden into charges. Accusation becomes policy rather than exception. At this stage, fear is no longer merely an atmosphere; it becomes a system that sustains itself.

This is how the Age of Ecclesiastical Accusation takes form. Fear comes first. It is then managed through *Engineered Spirituality* and amplified through the digital altar. Together, they reshape interpretation, redefine authority, and normalize suspicion. What began as anxiety ends as structure. What might have been healed through truth is preserved through control. Until this order is recognized, repentance will remain misdirected and restoration delayed.

This is the heart of the matter: fear does not merely distort individuals; it restructures institutions. Once fear becomes normative, accusation becomes inevitable. Questions harden into charges. Discernment collapses into vigilance. Leaders begin to act less as shepherds and more as sentinels, guarding against imagined threats while overlooking real wounds. Communities learn to read one another through suspicion rather than charity, and spiritual authority is exercised not to heal but to contain. In such an environment, harm is rarely acknowledged because fear has already decided who is dangerous and who must be protected.

What makes this age particularly insidious is not the presence of fear. Fear has always existed. The danger is the way fear now presents itself as faithfulness. It borrows theological language, adopts moral urgency, and cloaks itself in the rhetoric of purity and protection. Accusation, in this climate, is framed as responsibility. Silence is labeled wisdom. Questioning is treated as rebellion. Those who are harmed are often rendered invisible by the very structures meant to guard them. The result is a Church that appears active yet anxious, decisive yet brittle, orthodox yet internally eroded.

To move toward the heart of the matter is to recognize that the problem is not merely what has been done, but how reality is being read. The crisis addressed in this book is interpretive before it is behavioral. Fear teaches people what to see, what to ignore, and how to explain what they do not understand. Once fear governs interpretation, repentance becomes impossible because accusation has already assigned guilt elsewhere. Restoration is delayed because control feels safer than trust.

Authority, left unexamined, becomes self-justifying.

This chapter stands here to re-anchor the reader before the conclusion, not because the argument has wandered, but because it has deepened. Having seen how fear operates in lived experience, how it recruits authority, and how it produces accusation, the reader is now prepared to face the more difficult work ahead: discerning what kind of authority heals rather than harms, what kind of fear is biblically formative rather than corrosive, and what kind of Church can resist the gravitational pull of accusation without retreating into denial.

Everything that follows depends on this clarity. The goal is not to leave the reader wary, but wise, not suspicious, but discerning, not armed with accusations, but anchored in truth. Only by returning to the heart of the matter can the Church begin to imagine a future not governed by fear, but ordered by light, accountability, and restoration.

At this point, the task before us can no longer remain theoretical. What has been exposed now demands response. If fear can be engineered, amplified, and sanctified, then it can also be named, resisted, and undone, but only through authority that submits itself to light rather than control, and through discernment that refuses the ease of accusation. The conclusion that follows does not offer spectacle or resolution by force. It calls the Church to reckon with what it has normalized, what it has excused, and what it must now unlearn. Having seen how fear shapes interpretation and accusation reshapes authority, we are finally prepared to ask the most consequential question of all: what kind of Church will emerge when fear no longer governs its reading of truth, power, or one another?

CONCLUSION

THE LIGHT THAT OUTLIVES FEAR

"The people who walked in darkness have seen a great light; on those who dwelt in the land of the shadow of death, light has dawned" (Isaiah 9:2).

This book began with a question that could no longer be avoided: what has happened to discernment in the Church, and why has fear been allowed to reshape it into accusation? The testimonies, histories, metaphors, and frameworks encountered along the way were never offered to magnify darkness or elevate conflict. They were gathered to trace a single, unsettling trajectory, how authority, once rooted in humility and love, can drift into control, suspicion, and fragmentation when fear becomes its unseen guide. The stories were not detours. They were evidence. They revealed that the greatest threat facing the Church in this age is not occult power, cultural hostility, or technological change, but the quiet erosion of shared truth when discernment is severed from compassion and authority is exercised without restoration as its aim.

The journey opened in a fog, an atmosphere shaped by excess voices, competing revelations, untested authority, and spiritual urgency without anchoring. In that fog, discernment weakened, suspicion sharpened, and fear learned to wear the garments of holiness. What many called vigilance was, in truth, anxiety baptized in religious language. What sounded like spiritual alertness often concealed insecurity, mistrust, and the need to control what could not be understood.

As the pages unfolded, it became clear that the problem before us was not a collection of isolated errors, but a structure patiently assembled over time. The Age of Ecclesiastical Accusation did not arrive suddenly. It was constructed through fear rewarded with influence, urgency mistaken for authority, and exposure confused with faithfulness. Over time, this structure trained the Church to see threat before truth, danger before dignity, and suspicion before relationship. Sanctuaries became courtrooms. Shepherds became prosecutors. The wounded were examined rather than restored.

Yet clarity does not emerge by destroying everything. This book did not dismantle belief in spiritual reality, reverence for holiness, or the necessity of discernment. It dismantled something far more dangerous: a fear-driven system of interpretation that distorted those very things. And as that system was exposed, a quieter truth emerged. Fear, no matter how spiritual it sounds, cannot outlast light. It never has. It never will.

For this reason, the darkness has not won. The Church, though bruised by division and suspicion, is not broken. Beneath the noise and fracture, she still carries the seed of restoration.

What We Have Learned to See Clearly

One of the quiet transformations this book has invited is a change in vision. Not the sharpening of suspicion, but the recovery of sight. Along the way, many may have recognized themselves, not only in moments of courage, but in moments of fatigue, confusion, and restraint shaped more by fear than by trust. This recognition is not an indictment. It is an awakening. Fear often disguises itself as responsibility, and weariness can masquerade as wisdom. To see this clearly is not to fail. It is to begin again.

What we have learned to see is that fear rarely announces itself as fear. It enters subtly, through caution that hardens into distance, through discernment that loses patience, through authority exercised defensively rather than relationally. Many leaders did not choose suspicion; they inherited it. Many communities did not seek accusation; they adapted to it. Over time, the Church learned to read itself through threat rather than promise, through damage control rather than hope. This book has asked us to pause long enough to notice that shift and to name it honestly.

Such seeing carries grief with it. There is grief in realizing how much fear has cost us, how many conversations were never finished, how many people were misread, how many wounds were left untreated because they felt inconvenient or dangerous. There is grief in acknowledging how often love was delayed while certainty was defended. This grief is not something to rush past. Scripture does not hurry lament. It treats it as a form of truth-telling, a necessary clearing of the ground before restoration can take root.

Yet what we have learned to see is not only loss, but possibility. Fear's power has always depended on remaining unnamed. Once exposed to light, it weakens. The Church's future does not depend on perfect leaders, flawless discernment, or constant vigilance. It depends on a people willing to see again, to see one another as neighbors before threats, as wounded before dangerous, as redeemable before suspect. This shift in sight is not dramatic, but it is decisive. It marks the difference between a Church that reacts and a Church that restores.

To learn to see this way is to recover spiritual maturity. Maturity does not rush to judgment, nor does it deny the reality of evil. It learns to hold truth and love together without collapsing one into the other. It resists the false comfort of accusation and chooses the harder labor of discernment practiced in community. In this sense, what the Church needs now is not sharper eyes, but steadier ones, eyes trained by patience, humility, and hope.

This, then, is one of the gifts this book seeks to leave behind: not a new set of suspicions, but a renewed capacity to see clearly without fear. Such sight does not promise ease, but it makes restoration possible. It allows leaders to lead without panic, believers to trust without naivety, and communities to heal without denial. And where sight is restored, light follows.

What began as education became illumination. Information alone cannot free a people shaped by fear. Understanding is necessary, but revelation is transformative. As Scripture, history, pastoral experience, cultural realities, and testimony converged, a deeper pattern came into view: fear is not neutral. Once permitted to govern discernment, it reshapes language, distorts perception, and alters spiritual posture.

In response, this book has labored to restore order where fear had produced chaos. Discernment was returned to its rightful place, not as a private weapon, but as a communal discipline shaped by humility, patience, love, and accountability. Testimony was restored to its proper role, not as spectacle or proof of power, but as witness interpreted under Scripture and pastoral restraint. Authority was recentered in its true source, not proximity to darkness, but conformity to the character of Christ.

These truths are not abstract. They take form in real lives. And if the theology of this book finds flesh and blood expression anywhere, it is in the story of Marie Michel. Her life was not a parable constructed for teaching, but a collision between fear and faith, counterfeit power and restoring grace. Her freedom did not glorify darkness; it revealed the sufficiency of Christ. It reminds the Church that its most decisive victories often leave no public record. They happen in rooms without cameras, in prayers without applause, in love without witnesses.

Seen in this light, the larger pattern becomes unmistakable. Fear reshaped discernment. Discernment hardened into judgment. Vigilance slipped into suspicion. In such an environment, accusation multiplied because fear required targets. What this book dismantled was that logic. What it restored was responsibility, the responsibility to discern without destroying, to correct without humiliating, to confront without abandoning. The measure of spiritual authority is not how quickly darkness is named, but how faithfully the wounded are escorted back into light.

Because restoration is fragile, it must be protected. The Church must guard discernment from collapsing into absolutism, testimony from becoming spectacle, and authority from mutating into control. It must guard its language, for words are never neutral. When fear governs language, accusation follows. When love governs language, restoration becomes possible.

The question now is no longer what has been exposed, but what will be passed on. Fear has ruled too long. It has shaped theology, distorted worship, and trained generations to associate God with anxiety rather than trust. The time has come to leave another inheritance.

Let us raise believers confident that Christ's victory is complete and His protection secure.
Let us form leaders who pray without pride, teach without theatrics, and walk without fear.
Let us build churches that cultivate maturity rather than manufacture moments.

This is not idealism. This is restoration. This is revival. And it begins wherever believers choose to love more than they fear, to discern without suspicion, to pray with authority without arrogance, and to lead with purity without pride. That is the future this book longs for: a Church where the spell of fear is broken and the light of discernment burns steadily once more.

This is not idealism.
This is restoration.
This is revival.
And it begins wherever believers choose to love more than they fear.

FINAL PRAYER AND BENEDICTION

Father,
I come before You with gratitude. I thank You for the wisdom, courage, discernment, and inspiration You entrusted to me to write this book. It was not written out of curiosity or ambition, but out of obedience, out of a burden to protect Your people, restore clarity where fear had settled, and speak truth with care and restraint.

Lord, I began this journey in the shadow of fear, and You led me patiently into light. You showed me how confusion divides families, how accusation wounds the Church, and how truth, when carried with humility, restores what fear has scattered.

Now I ask You to make me, and all who encounter these pages, builders of peace, carriers of compassion, and keepers of discernment. Heal our families from superstition and inherited fear. Deliver our churches from accusation, suspicion, and the misuse of spiritual authority.

Teach every leader to walk with humility rather than urgency, and every believer to rest in the assurance of Your protection. Let our homes become sanctuaries of light, places where peace governs perception and love sets the atmosphere.

Let everyone who reads this book, and every hand that touches it, be blessed by Your presence. May each heart be awakened, each mind be steadied, and each life become a beacon of light in places where fear once ruled. Let Your people find their way back to You, not through panic or accusation, but through truth, mercy, and love.

Guard us from confusing emotion with power, intensity with authority, or fear with faith. Train us to measure fruit rather than spectacle, character rather than noise, and obedience rather than influence.

And Lord, I ask that the next generation would inherit not our panic, not our suspicion, not our wounds, but Your peace, Your clarity, and Your confidence. Make us sons and daughters of light, fearless, faithful, and free, anchored in Christ and resting in Your truth.

I place this work, and every life it touches, back into Your hands.

Amen.

Blessing

May El Shaddai, God Almighty, the God of Abraham, Isaac, and Jacob, spread His covering over you. May He fortify what has been weakened, heal what has been fractured, and abundantly supply every grace required for the path set before you.

May Yahweh Shalom, the Lord who is Peace, quiet every fear, silence every accusation, and establish His wholeness within your heart, your home, and your calling. May His peace guard your mind and steady your steps.

May El Gibbor, the Mighty Warrior, stand before you and behind you. May He disarm every opposing force, uphold you in truth, and secure your freedom in Christ. May His strength not drive you into striving, but anchor you in confidence and rest.

And may the light of God go with you, remain upon you, and flow through you, so that your life becomes a refuge for the weary and a testimony of restoration for many.

In the name of Jesus,

Amen.

FREQUENTLY ASKED QUESTIONS

The Age of Ecclesiastical Accusation

1. Is this book claiming that fear is more dangerous than sin, heresy, or demonic activity?

No. The book argues that fear is often the mechanism through which sin, deception, and misuse of authority become normalized. Fear is not treated as an isolated emotion but as a formative force that reshapes perception, language, and judgment. When fear governs discernment, even sincere attempts at holiness can become accusatory and destructive.

2. Does this book deny the reality of spiritual warfare?

No. The book affirms the reality of spiritual warfare as taught in Scripture, but it rejects sensationalized and fear-driven interpretations of it. Spiritual warfare is presented as sustained faithfulness, discernment, and obedience—not constant confrontation, spectacle, or obsession with darkness.

3. Is the author suggesting that deliverance ministry is harmful or unnecessary?

No. Deliverance is affirmed as real and sometimes necessary. What the book critiques is deliverance divorced from discipleship, compassion, and accountability. Deliverance that humiliates, performs, or instills fear is not rejected because it is supernatural, but because it contradicts the character and ministry of Christ.

4. Does the book promote psychology over Scripture?

No. Scripture remains the final authority throughout the book. Psychological insights are used descriptively, not doctrinally, to help explain how fear embeds itself in human perception, memory, and behavior. Psychology is treated as a tool of understanding, not a replacement for biblical truth.

5. Does this book spiritualize trauma or mental illness?

No. The book explicitly states that it does not replace professional counseling, mental-health care, or medical treatment. It acknowledges trauma as a real psychological reality while examining how fear—when left unexamined—can shape spiritual interpretation and community responses to suffering.

6. Is this book anti-charismatic or anti-prophetic?

No. The book does not critique spiritual gifts; it critiques unaccountable authority, fear-driven prophecy, and spectacle without discernment. Biblical prophecy is always subject to testing, community discernment, and the fruit it produces. The book calls for prophetic humility, not prophetic silence.

7. Does the book encourage skepticism or distrust toward church leaders?

No. It encourages discernment rooted in relationship, not suspicion. The book challenges systems that train believers to read leadership through fear rather than fruit. Its goal is to restore trust by restoring integrity, not to undermine pastoral authority.

8. Is this book an attack on the modern Church?

No. It is written from within the Church, not against it. The tone is pastoral, corrective, and restorative. The book confronts patterns and systems—not individuals or denominations—with the aim of healing rather than exposure.

9. Does the book equate cultural practices (such as Vodou) with demonic activity?

No. The book does not accuse cultures, nor does it reduce complex spiritual systems to simplistic labels. It makes a careful distinction between culture, ancestral memory, survival systems, colonial distortion, and spiritual captivity. Cultural practices are treated as lived responses to history, trauma, and meaning-making—not as moral failures.

At the same time, the book refuses to collapse all spiritual phenomena into the category of "ancestral reverence" without examination. Even outside Christianity, the claim that certain extreme manifestations represent ancestral spirits encounters serious anthropological limits. Ancestors, understood across cultures, are human spirits and retain human constraints. Behaviors involving the loss of personal agency, physical domination, trance-induced violence, and the consumption of raw blood exceed what is typically associated with remembrance of the dead or ancestral honor.

For this reason, anthropologists and former practitioners themselves describe such phenomena not merely as ancestor veneration, but as spirit possession, a category that denotes external spiritual control rather than cultural memory or symbolic ritual alone.

10. Is this book about Vodou?

No. Vodou appears as one historical and cultural case study, not the subject of the book. The central theme is fear and ecclesiastical accusation within Christian contexts. Cultural analysis serves the thesis; it does not replace it.

11. Why does the book use so many metaphors (legal, architectural, technological, medical)?

Because Scripture itself uses multiple metaphors to describe spiritual reality. No single metaphor can carry the full weight of truth. The book explicitly explains its metaphorical method and places clear safeguards against taking any metaphor literally or absolutizing it.

12. Are the testimonies meant to prove theological claims?

No. Theology is established before testimony appears. Testimonies function as witness and evidence of fruit, not as doctrinal proof or emotional leverage. They illustrate patterns already grounded in Scripture and theology.

13. Does the book minimize the reality of evil or darkness?

No. Evil is acknowledged as real but never portrayed as equal, autonomous, or creative. Darkness is always shown as secondary and derivative. The book refuses to magnify darkness beyond its biblical limits.

14. Is fear presented as the only problem facing the Church today?

No. Fear is presented as a governing atmosphere that intensifies other problems—division, control, misuse of authority, paranoia, and accusation. Addressing fear clarifies many secondary issues; it does not deny their complexity.

15. Why does the book critique exposure culture and public confrontation?

Because Scripture consistently prioritizes restoration over humiliation. Exposure without responsibility produces spectacle, not healing. The book challenges practices that treat wounded people as evidence rather than neighbors.

16. Does this book discourage naming sin or confronting error?

No. It distinguishes between biblical correction and fear-driven accusation. Confrontation is necessary, but it must be governed by truth, proportion, love, and communal accountability.

17. Is the book politically motivated or partisan?

No. Political references are used illustratively to describe atmospheric pressure and information saturation, not to promote ideology. The book critiques how political language and fear can distort spiritual authority across all ideological lines.

18. Is this book academic or pastoral?

It is intentionally both. It integrates theology, pastoral experience, cultural analysis, and lived testimony. This hybrid form reflects the reality of ministry rather than forcing artificial separation.

19. Who should not read this book?

Those seeking spiritual spectacle, hidden knowledge, or confirmation of fear-based authority structures may find this book unsettling. It is written for readers willing to reflect, slow down, and examine how fear shapes perception.

20. What is the book ultimately calling the Church to do?

To recover discernment without suspicion, authority without fear, and restoration without spectacle. The book calls the Church to lead from light rather than anxiety, from love rather than accusation.

DOCTRINAL AND THEOLOGICAL ASSURANCE STATEMENT

The Age of Ecclesiastical Accusation is written within the bounds of historic Christian orthodoxy and affirms the core doctrines of the Christian faith as confessed by the global Church across generations and traditions. This work upholds the authority of Holy Scripture as the inspired Word of God and the final normative standard for Christian faith, doctrine, and discernment. All theological reflection, cultural analysis, and pastoral application presented herein are intentionally grounded in Scripture and offered in continuity with its teaching.

The book affirms the sovereignty of God, the supremacy of Jesus Christ as Lord and Savior, and His life and ministry as the definitive model of spiritual authority. It further affirms the ongoing work of the Holy Spirit in guiding, sanctifying, and equipping believers for faithful Christian living. Spiritual gifts, discernment, and deliverance are acknowledged as realities attested in Scripture and the life of the Church, while consistently being presented as subordinate to the character and lordship of Christ, governed by love, and exercised within appropriate accountability, sobriety, and humility.

This work does not deny the reality of spiritual evil or the existence of spiritual conflict as described in Scripture. At the same time, it explicitly rejects fear-based theological frameworks, spiritual sensationalism, ritualized expressions of Christianity, and any practice or posture that elevates darkness, accusation, or intimidation above the authority, peace, and sufficiency of Christ. References to deliverance and discernment are presented as pastoral ministries oriented toward restoration, discipleship, and spiritual wholeness, rather than toward performance, spectacle, or perpetual suspicion.

Cultural, historical, and religious contexts—including African and Caribbean spiritual systems—are discussed descriptively and analytically for purposes of theological understanding and pastoral clarity. Such discussion is not intended as endorsement, promotion, or validation of these systems, but is consistently framed within a Christian theological worldview that affirms the exclusive lordship of Jesus Christ and rejects syncretism in all its forms.

The Church is presented throughout this work as the Body of Christ—imperfect yet beloved, continually in need of discernment and renewal, yet never abandoned, replaced, or negated. Any critiques offered within the manuscript are directed toward identifiable patterns, postures, and systems of fear-driven authority or practice, rather than toward specific individuals, congregations, denominations, or the biblical offices Christ has established. Pastoral and ecclesial authority is affirmed as a sacred trust, to be exercised in alignment with Christ's example of truth, restraint, humility, and redemptive love.

In summary, The Age of Ecclesiastical Accusation is offered as a pastoral and theological contribution intended to strengthen discernment, restore proportion, and encourage forms of Christian authority that rest in Christ rather than react in fear. The author affirms that this work stands within the theological boundaries of orthodox Christian faith and is presented in service to the life, witness, and health of the Church.

GUIDANCE FOR USING THIS RESTORATION MANUAL

As you conclude this book, you carry with you more than information. You carry responsibility—toward the wounded, the confused, and those still bound in quiet ways. The Reader's Study Guide and the Pastoral Restoration Checklist that follow are not meant to remain on the page. They are designed to move these truths into the fabric of your life, your leadership, and your ministry.

Before you engage those tools, however, a final exhortation must be offered—one that concerns posture more than process.

Deliverance is not a performance.

Restoration is not a process of scrutiny.

One of the greatest dangers in the Age of Ecclesiastical Accusation is the misuse of discernment—when it is wielded as a weapon to expose rather than a balm to heal. Tools meant for restoration can become instruments of harm if they are applied without humility, restraint, and love.

Before you use these guides, hold firmly to three governing principles:

Deliverance Is Holy Ground.

Every soul's struggle is a private war. Those who seek freedom entrust you with sacred territory. Approach them with the same confidentiality, reverence, and care you would desire for your own deepest wounds.

Love Is the Prerequisite.

No degree of authority can replace compassion. A restorer's maturity is not measured by how loudly they command darkness to leave, but by how quietly they lead a person into the light.

Discipleship Is the Goal.

Deliverance is the doorway, not the destination. The goal is a life furnished by truth, anchored in Scripture, and sustained within a safe, accountable community.

Use these guides to build lighthouses, not courtrooms.

Let them help you raise a generation grounded in the assurance that Christ's victory is final, His authority is complete, and His protection is absolute.

SELECTED BIBLIOGRAPHY

I. Biblical Texts and Primary Scriptural Resources

Holy Bible. *English Standard Version.* Wheaton, IL: Crossway Bibles, 2001.

Holy Bible. *New International Version.* Grand Rapids, MI: Zondervan, 2011. Originally published 1973.

Holy Bible. *New King James Version.* Nashville, TN: Thomas Nelson, 1982.

Beale, G. K. *The Book of Revelation: A Commentary on the Greek Text.* New International Greek Testament Commentary. Grand Rapids, MI: Eerdmans, 1999.

Keener, Craig S. *The IVP Bible Background Commentary: New Testament.* Downers Grove, IL: InterVarsity Press, 1993.

Peterson, Eugene H. *Reversed Thunder: The Revelation of John and the Praying Imagination.* San Francisco: HarperOne, 1988.

Wright, Christopher J. H. *Old Testament Ethics for the People of God.* Downers Grove, IL: IVP Academic, 2004.

II. Testimonies, Oral Histories, and Ministerial Archives

Bachon. "The Architecture of Spiritual Captivity: Testimony and Exposure of Destructive Works." Public testimony delivered at Église Chrétienne Évangélique de la Grâce (ECEG), Port-au-Prince, Haiti, 1996.

Demosthene, Jean Maxi. "Oral History and Ministerial Legacy of Reverend Jean Maxi Demosthene (known as 'Baron')." Personal testimony and archival materials. Global Reach Evangelical Missionary Church (GREMC), n.d.

Michel, Marie. *The Video Chronicles of Transformation:* Recorded Testimonies. Video recordings, n.d.

POINT D'ACCORD. "Mon pasteur est dans une secte." Interview with Roland Sombo. Lumière du Monde Télévision (Abidjan, Côte d'Ivoire), August 14, 2023.

POINT D'ACCORD. "Prophétesse, je vis l'enfer dans mon foyer." Television broadcast and online streaming. Lumière du Monde Télévision, May 17, 2024. YouTube video, https://www.youtube.com/live/AMXNe9n1Uns.

Editorial note: Oral histories, testimonies, and broadcasts are cited as primary source material, not as doctrinal authorities.

III. Works by Simon Demosthene

Demosthene, Simon. *The Age of Ecclesiastical Accusation.* 1st ed. Boston, MA, 2026.

———. "Glossary of Terms and Themes." In The Age of Ecclesiastical Accusation, 344.

———. "Appendix B: Pastoral Restoration Checklist." In The Age of Ecclesiastical Accusation, 336.

———. *The Gods Inside My Brain.* Forthcoming.

———. *L'Importance de comprendre la possession démoniaque (The Importance of Understanding Demonic Possession).* Forthcoming.

IV. Spiritual Authority, Ethics, and Church Conflict

Blue, Ken. *Healing Spiritual Abuse: How to Break Free from Bad Church Experience.* Downers Grove, IL: InterVarsity Press, 1993.

Enroth, Ronald M. Churches *That Abuse.* Grand Rapids, MI: Zondervan, 1992.

Haugk, Kenneth C. *Antagonists in the Church: How to Identify and Deal with Destructive Conflict.* Minneapolis: Augsburg Fortress, 1988.

Keller, Timothy. *Center Church: Doing Balanced, Gospel-Centered Ministry in Your City.* Grand Rapids, MI: Zondervan, 2012.

Oakley, Lisa, and Justin Humphreys. *Escaping the Maze of Spiritual Abuse.* London: SPCK, 2019.

Tripp, Paul David. *Dangerous Calling: Confronting the Unique Challenges of Pastoral Ministry.* Wheaton, IL: Crossway, 2012.

Trull, Joe E., and James E. Carter. *Ministerial Ethics: Moral Formation for Church Leaders.* Grand Rapids, MI: Baker Academic, 2004.

V. Global Theology, Mission, and Postcolonial Studies

Arnold, Clinton E. *Powers of Darkness: Principalities and Powers in Paul's Letters.* Downers Grove, IL: InterVarsity Press, 1992.

Bonhoeffer, Dietrich. *Life Together.* New York: Harper & Row, 1954.

Bosch, David J. *Transforming Mission: Paradigm Shifts in Theology of Mission.* Maryknoll, NY: Orbis Books, 1991.

Fanon, Frantz. *Black Skin, White Masks.* New York: Grove Press, 1967.

Fee, Gordon D. *God's Empowering Presence: The Holy Spirit in the Letters of Paul.* Peabody, MA: Hendrickson, 1994.

Jenkins, Philip. *The Next Christendom: The Coming of Global Christianity.* Oxford: Oxford University Press, 2011.

Mbiti, John S. *African Religions and Philosophy*. London: Heinemann, 1969.

Sugirtharajah, R. S. *Postcolonial Reconfigurations: An Alternative Way of Reading the Bible*. St. Louis: Chalice Press, 2002.

Walls, Andrew F. *The Missionary Movement in Christian History*. Maryknoll, NY: Orbis Books, 1996.

Ward, Pete. *Participation and Mediation: A Practical Theology for the Liquid Church*. London: SCM Press, 2008.

Wright, N. T. *Paul and the Faithfulness of God*. Minneapolis: Fortress Press, 2013.

Yoder, John Howard. *The Politics of Jesus*. Grand Rapids, MI: Eerdmans, 1994.

VI. Anthropology, Vodou, and Haitian History

Brown, Karen McCarthy. *Mama Lola: A Vodou Priestess in Brooklyn*. Berkeley: University of California Press, 1991.

Desmangles, Leslie G. *The Faces of the Gods: Vodou and Roman Catholicism in Haiti*. Chapel Hill: University of North Carolina Press, 1992.

Dubois, Laurent. *Avengers of the New World: The Story of the Haitian Revolution*. Cambridge, MA: Harvard University Press, 2004.

Ramsey, Kate. *The Spirits and the Law: Vodou and Power in Haiti*. Chicago: University of Chicago Press, 2011.

VII. Psychology, Trauma, and Social Theory

Girard, René. *Things Hidden Since the Foundation of the World*. Stanford, CA: Stanford University Press, 1987.

Herman, Judith Lewis. *Trauma and Recovery: The Aftermath of Violence—from Domestic Abuse to Political Terror*. New York: Basic Books, 1992.

Pargament, Kenneth I. *Spiritually Integrated Psychotherapy*. New York: Guilford Press, 2007.

Van der Kolk, Bessel. *The Body Keeps the Score: Brain, Mind, and Body in the Healing of Trauma*. New York: Viking, 2014.

VIII. Media, Technology, and Popular Culture

Abrams, J. J., Bryan Burk, and Jeff Pinkner, executive producers. *Fringe*. Television series. Bad Robot Productions and Warner Bros. Television, 2008–2013.

Campbell, Heidi A. *Digital Religion: Understanding Religious Practice in New Media Worlds*. London: Routledge, 2013.

Carr, Nicholas. *The Shallows: What the Internet Is Doing to Our Brains*. New York: W. W. Norton, 2010.

Kirby, Danielle. *Fantasy and Belief: Alternative Religions, Popular Narratives, and Digital Culture*. London: Equinox, 2013.

Natali, Vincenzo, director. *Splice*. Film. Copperheart Entertainment and Gaumont, 2009.

Vaidhyanathan, Siva. *Antisocial Media: How Facebook Disconnects Us and Undermines Democracy*. New York: Oxford University Press, 2018.

IX. Hermeticism, Esotericism, Testimony, and Contemporary Digital Sources

Hanegraaff, Wouter J. *New Age Religion and Western Culture*. Leiden: Brill, 1996.

Kripal, Jeffrey J. *Authors of the Impossible: The Paranormal and the Sacred*. Chicago: University of Chicago Press, 2010.

Lewis, C. S. *The Screwtape Letters*. New York: HarperOne, 2001.

Partridge, Christopher. *The Re-Enchantment of the West.* London: T&T Clark, 2004.

Kawalya, James. *Delivered from Deep Darkness: My Story, My Journey from the Claw of Satan to Christ.* 2017.

Pierre, Jacques Ronald. *Libéré pour témoigner.* 2025.

AU Puits de Jacob. "Temwayaj sè #Marie Michelle – Li envite nou kache pi fon nan Kris!" YouTube video, October 23, 2023. https://www.youtube.com/@aupuitsdejacob4487.

AU Puits de Jacob. "Temwayaj sè #Marie Michelle. Rèn sanpwèl la ak bouwo mouri nan plas ti fi a. Pisans Bondye te nan li." YouTube video, November 1, 2022. https://www.youtube.com/@aupuitsdejacob4487.

Ansanm Nou Valab. "Temwayaj Sr. Marie Michelle kap esplike koman li te leve yon zonbi. Sa vreman tris anpil." YouTube video, June 7, 2020. https://www.youtube.com/@ansanmnouvalab3534.

Vadener des Ravines. "Sr. Marie Michelle, gen koze wi (Soul Capture)." YouTube video, February 2, 2022. https://www.youtube.com/@vadenerdesravines3014.

"YouTube." "Sœur Marie Michelle: Ansyen *manbo* nan yon Temwayaj." YouTube video, 2023. https://youtu.be/PLhyc0dISfo.

jchery2556. "Témoignage de Marie Michelle, Parts 1–10." YouTube video, September 28, 2010. https://youtu.be/MK-6PpN0iL8.

X. Theology, Authority, and Biblical Interpretation

Csordas, Thomas J. *Language, Charisma, and Creativity: The Ritual Life of a Religious Movement.* Berkeley: University of California Press, 1997.

Smith, Christian. *The Bible Made Impossible: Why Biblicism Is Not a Truly Evangelical Reading of Scripture.* Grand Rapids: Brazos Press, 2011.

Smith, James K. A. *Desiring the Kingdom: Worship, Worldview, and Cultural Formation.* Grand Rapids, MI: Baker Academic, 2009.

Taylor, Charles. A *Secular Age.* Cambridge, MA: Harvard University Press, 2007.

Vanhoozer, Kevin J. *The Drama of Doctrine: A Canonical-Linguistic Approach to Christian Theology.* Louisville: Westminster John Knox Press, 2005.

Weber, Max. *Economy and Society: An Outline of Interpretive Sociology.* Vol. 1. Berkeley: University of California Press, 1978.

READER'S STUDY GUIDE

A Guided Path for Reflection and Practice

This guide is not an exam, a checklist, or a diagnostic tool. It is a companion meant to walk alongside you as you process the themes of this book. You are not expected to complete it quickly. Some readers may linger with a single section for weeks. That is not failure; it is formation.

The questions and practices that follow are arranged as movements rather than tasks. Each movement corresponds to a major thread of the book and invites you to listen carefully—to your own fears, to the voice of God, and to the condition of the communities you inhabit.

Move slowly. Return often. Let clarity come before conclusions.

Movement One

Learning to See the Architecture of Anxiety

Fear rarely announces itself loudly. More often, it builds quietly—like walls erected over time. Many readers discover that what they call "discernment" is sometimes a refined form of caution, or that what they call "wisdom" is actually unresolved anxiety shaped by culture, history, or inherited narratives.

Begin by paying attention to the subtle places where trust has narrowed. Where have you become guarded without realizing it? Where has community slowly given way to suspicion, or openness to constant vigilance?

Consider how your upbringing—family stories, church teaching, national history, or cultural memory—has shaped the way you interpret spiritual threat. Ask yourself honestly whether fear has been taught as protection rather than as something Christ came to heal.

As you reflect, resist the urge to judge yourself. The goal is not exposure but understanding. When fear is named gently, it loses its authority.

In practice, this movement may require intentional silence. You may need to reduce the voices that constantly interpret the world for you—sermons, social media, conversations that feed anxiety rather than peace. Return to Scripture not as a source of alarms, but as a place where God sets boundaries around fear and restores proportion to reality.

Movement Two

Recognizing Counterfeit Power

Not all power liberates. Some power promises speed, clarity, and control while quietly bypassing the slow work of formation. In moments of pain or confusion, it is tempting to reach for shortcuts—practices, language, or systems that offer immediate relief without requiring surrender.

Ask yourself where you have been drawn to what feels powerful rather than what is faithful. Where does emotional resonance replace discernment? Where does intensity substitute for truth?

This is also the place to examine language. Words shape reality. Certain spiritual expressions, once rooted in covenantal meaning, can be softened or repurposed until they obscure rather than reveal truth. Pay attention to what words do in you. Do they produce freedom, or do they blur responsibility and accountability?

Practically, this movement invites a gentle but honest inventory of practices, habits, and influences—both physical and digital. Anything that claims authority over your peace, identity, or future deserves examination. Renunciation, in this sense, is not dramatic; it is clarifying. It is the quiet reassertion of exclusive allegiance to Christ.

Movement Three

The Church as an Arena of Speech

The Church does not fracture only through doctrine. It fractures through words. Accusation often travels disguised as concern, prayer, or discernment. Over time, speech shapes atmosphere, and atmosphere reshapes theology.

Reflect on how you speak about others, especially spiritual leaders or fellow believers. Have you ever shared information under the banner of prayer that was not yours to carry? Have you participated—actively or passively—in suspicion that felt justified but produced no healing?

Correction is part of formation. Yet in an age of accusation, correction is often interpreted as control. Ask yourself how you receive guidance. Do you instinctively brace, defend, or assume manipulation? Or are you able to discern the difference between domination and discipline?

The practice here is restraint. Commit yourself to speech that builds rather than dismantles. Scripture calls this oikodomeō—language that constructs a dwelling rather than tearing one down. Treat the struggles of others as sacred territory. Not everything revealed to you is meant to be repeated.

Movement Four

Learning from the Redeemed

Some stories cannot be managed; they must interrupt us. The testimonies in this book are not included for fascination, but for instruction. They remind us that grace does not negotiate with darkness—it displaces it.

As you reflect on these narratives, ask where in your own life you have settled for management instead of deliverance. Where have you learned to coexist with patterns God intends to break?

Stories like Marie Michel's or Fenel's confront us with a deeper question: do we understand our standing in Christ when spiritual interference arises? Or do we revert to fear, speculation, and borrowed explanations?

One of the most formative practices in this movement is intercession without investigation. Choose someone who has been labeled, misunderstood, or quietly accused. Resist the urge to analyze. Commit instead to private prayer for their restoration.

You may also find it helpful to write your own story—not as a résumé of experiences, but as a journey from fear to freedom. Naming where light displaced darkness restores coherence to memory and dignity to identity.

Movement Five

Becoming a Restorer

Every church transmits something to the next generation. The question is not whether we pass something on, but what we pass on. Fear travels easily. So does grace.

Ask yourself whether your presence in your family or congregation functions more like a hospital or a courtroom. When others fail, do you move instinctively toward restoration or toward prosecution?

This movement invites a holistic vision of healing—spiritual, emotional, relational, and functional. Healing is not the erasure of scars, but the transformation of scars into sites of service.

Begin simply. Reestablish intimacy with God not as an employee seeking approval, but as a child learning trust. Attend to unresolved pain with honesty and support. Repair relationships where accusation or silence has done damage. And finally, ask how what you have survived may become a source of healing for others.

A daily practice may help anchor this posture. Quietly affirm your identity and allegiance. Let it be simple, not dramatic. Let it remind you that your authority rests not in fear, but in belonging.

A Closing Word

This guide is not about mastery. It is about posture. If you find yourself slower, gentler, and less reactive than before, it is working. If you find fear losing its urgency and clarity gaining ground, it is bearing fruit.

Do not rush. Restoration is never hurried.

PASTORAL RESTORATION CHECKLIST

This checklist is intended for pastors and ministry leaders as a practical framework for guiding individuals transitioning from occult backgrounds or fear-based spiritual bondage. It is not a formula, but a discernment tool to be applied with patience, pastoral care, and humility.

I. The Spiritual Dimension: Rebuilding Relationship

- Renunciation and Covenant Breaking: Lead calm, specific prayers renouncing former allegiances or agreements formed in fear or ignorance. Avoid dramatization; peace and clarity mark progress.
- Identity Affirmation: Replace past labels with the biblical identity of child of God, reinforcing belonging rather than captivity.
- Theology of Coverage: Teach the principle of Divine Immunity—no shared infrastructure, roaming agreements, or identity access for darkness in Christ.
- Spiritual Disciplines: Establish a non-performance-based rhythm of Scripture and conversational prayer emphasizing relationship over vigilance.

II. The Emotional Dimension: Healing the Inner Life

- Letters of Release: Encourage private letters of forgiveness or truth-telling (not intended for delivery) to release suppressed emotion safely.
- Condemnation Audit: Use Romans 8:1 to address lingering guilt, shame, or self-accusation.
- Renewing the Mind: Identify inherited "fear signatures" and intentionally replace them with scriptural truth.
- Professional Integration: Discern when licensed mental-health support is appropriate and normalize it as wisdom.

III. The Relational Dimension: Rebuilding Community

- Confidentiality Shield: Protect personal histories as holy ground; never use them publicly without explicit consent.
- Family Bridge-Building: Provide guidance for maintaining boundaries with relatives still engaged in occult practices.
- Mentorship Assignment: Pair individuals with mature, emotionally intelligent believers for private, consistent support.
- The Hospital Welcome: Instruct leaders to treat individuals as healing, not as subjects of monitoring.

IV. The Functional Dimension: Rediscovering Purpose

- Gift Discovery: Help identify gifts previously distorted or suppressed by fear.
- Controlled Service: Introduce low-pressure service roles that allow trust and rhythm to develop.
- Testimony Readiness: Discern carefully when—and if—public sharing is appropriate.
- Raising a Restorer: Train individuals to recognize bondage in others without returning to fear-based identity.

APPENDIX C

A GUIDED POSTURE FOR DISCERNMENT WHEN ENGAGING DELIVERANCE TESTIMONIES

This appendix is offered as a posture rather than a protocol. It is meant to guide the heart of leaders who walk alongside testimonies of deliverance, not to train them in diagnosis or technique. Deliverance testimonies involve real people, real histories, and real vulnerability. How these stories are held matters as much as what they contain.

The reflections that follow are arranged as orientations rather than rules. They are designed to pace discernment, deepen wisdom, and preserve dignity. Move through them patiently. Return to them when urgency presses or clarity feels elusive.

Beginning with Testimony in Its Proper Place

Testimony is a witness, not a governor. It points toward truth; it does not establish it. Scripture alone carries doctrinal authority, and all testimony must remain submitted to that authority. When testimony begins to instruct theology rather than confirm it, discernment quietly shifts from humility to influence.

Holding testimony in its proper place protects both the Church and the person testifying. It allows stories to be honored without being elevated beyond their purpose.

Learning to Discern in Community

Discernment does not flourish in isolation. God rarely entrusts wounded lives to a single interpreter. Instead, He places them within community, where wisdom is shared and accountability is mutual. Discernment that belongs to one voice alone becomes fragile; discernment held in community becomes resilient.

Shared discernment slows conclusions. It invites prayer, listening, and collective responsibility. While this may feel inefficient, it is often the means by which harm is prevented and trust is preserved.

Allowing Relationship to Precede Interpretation

Interpretation without relationship becomes invasive. When leaders rush to assign meaning before trust has been established, people are reduced to cases rather than received as persons. Patience is not passivity; it is respect.

Relationship creates the safety in which discernment can mature. Listening before naming, presence before pronouncement, and care before clarity are not delays—they are safeguards.

Honoring Complexity Without Fear

Human lives are rarely shaped by a single cause. Trauma, culture, psychology, spiritual influence, and personal history often intersect in ways that resist simple explanations. Wisdom refuses to collapse this complexity into a single spiritual category merely because it feels decisive.

Not every struggle is demonic. Not every manifestation is spiritual. Not every breakthrough is immediate. Discernment honors complexity without becoming confused, and clarity without becoming reductionistic.

Resisting Fear-Driven Urgency

Urgency often disguises itself as spiritual responsibility. Fear whispers that action must be immediate or the moment will be lost. Yet God's authority is not threatened by patience, and truth does not weaken with time.

When discernment is driven by fear, leaders feel pressured to resolve rather than to steward. When discernment is governed by love, time becomes an ally rather than an enemy.

Protecting the Dignity of the Person

Deliverance testimonies are not teaching tools, spiritual currency, or public spectacles. They involve real people whose privacy, vulnerability, and future must be guarded. Exposure may generate attention, but it often leaves lasting wounds.

Confidentiality is not secrecy; it is pastoral care. Protecting dignity ensures that restoration is not undermined by curiosity or spiritual ambition.

Making Room for Mystery

Not every question requires an answer. Not every silence signals avoidance. Sometimes restraint is reverence. Leaders who are comfortable with mystery resist the temptation to explain what God has not yet revealed.

Silence, in these moments, is not weakness but wisdom. It acknowledges that discernment is a process, not a performance.

Measuring Fruit Over Time

True transformation reveals itself gradually. Humility, peace, restored relationships, emotional stability, and a growing love for God and others matter more than dramatic language or momentary intensity.

Fruit requires time to ripen. Discernment that measures outcomes rather than moments protects the Church from confusion and the person from misinterpretation.

A Closing Orientation

These safeguards are not limits placed on spiritual authority; they are the means by which authority remains trustworthy. When discernment is governed by love, patience, humility, and accountability, the Church becomes a place where healing is protected, restoration is nurtured, and fear loses its power to accuse.

Return to this posture whenever discernment feels rushed, exposed, or heavy. Authority held gently endures.

GLOSSARY OF TERMS AND THEMES

Editorial Note: Terms are defined according to their contextual, theological, pastoral, and cultural use within this manuscript. Definitions prioritize function and meaning over technical abstraction.

Abilities of a Hybrid Being: Extraordinary capacities attributed to individuals whose identity and physiology are believed to be integrated with non-human spiritual intelligences, enabling access to realms or abilities unavailable to ordinary practitioners.

Accusation: The act of assigning guilt, motive, or spiritual fault without relational discernment, evidence, or redemptive intent; treated in this book as a mechanism rooted in fear rather than truth.

Aesthetic Spirituality: The packaging of spiritual practices through curated visuals, rituals, and self-care language that emphasizes experience and appearance over truth, depth, and formation.

The Age of Ecclesiastical Accusation: A contemporary church climate in which fear-driven discernment mutates into suspicion, exposure, and judgment, reshaping spiritual authority into a courtroom posture rather than a restorative one.

Algorithmic Authority (Spiritual): Influence gained through digital visibility, repetition, and platform engagement rather than accountability, character, or spiritual fruit.

Ancestral Contract: A spiritual agreement or pact believed to have been made by previous generations and understood to bind descendants to specific spirits or obligations.

Ancestral Debt: Perceived spiritual obligations or inherited agreements carried through family lineages that hold descendants in patterns of bondage or service.

Ancestral Yard: A traditional Haitian living arrangement in which extended family branches share land, resources, and a unified cultural and spiritual identity.

Architectural Metaphor: A framework used throughout the book to describe spiritual realities in terms of structures, foundations, thresholds, access points, and strongholds, emphasizing how unseen systems shape lived experience.

Architecture of Spiritual Captivity: The gradual construction of internal confinement in which perception is restricted over time until freedom is no longer recognized as possible.

Auditory Spiritual Perception: The phenomenon in which an individual becomes convinced they hear specific words or conversations that others present do not perceive.

Autonomous Spiritual Identity: An identity formed around self-definition, personal experience, or cultural affirmation rather than submission to Christ.

Biological Wetware / Liquid Programming: The use of ritual substances or elixirs believed to re-map the nervous system, rendering the body a conduit for spiritual influence.

Bloodline Inheritance: The belief that spiritual covenants or declarations spoken over children by ancestors shape identity or obligation before personal choice is possible.

Breached Holiness: A condition in which sacred spaces or practices retain religious form while accommodating influences that contradict covenant faithfulness.

Clashing Truths: The coexistence of competing narratives that each claim authority, forcing interpretation to be shaped by fear or identity rather than truth.

Clean Install: A theological metaphor describing the initial act of deliverance in which a spiritual intruder is evicted and the soul is restored to its original freedom.

Correction Without Redemption: Confronting error without providing a pathway toward healing or restoration, resulting in harm rather than growth.

Counterfeit Power: Any form of spiritual influence that appears authoritative or liberating but operates through fear, manipulation, urgency, or dependency rather than surrender to Christ.

Culture (Spiritual Lens): The inherited system of meanings, stories, fears, and assumptions through which people interpret power, causality, and the unseen world.

Digital Altar: Online spaces—platforms, feeds, livestreams, and comment sections—where attention, trust, and allegiance are offered as sites of spiritual exchange.

Desperate to understand the "the failure to appear": Spiritual declarations delivered primarily through online platforms, detached from relational accountability and communal testing.

Discernment: The Spirit-guided capacity to perceive truth without suspicion, to test without paranoia, and to protect without humiliating; communal, patient, and rooted in love.

Divine Encryption: A metaphor describing the protection of a believer's identity by the blood of Christ, rendering it inaccessible to hostile spiritual systems.

Divine Immunity (Covering): The theological conviction that a believer is sealed by the Holy Spirit, establishing a covenant barrier against illegitimate spiritual claims.

Echoed Prophecy: Prophetic language repeated by others without discernment or testing, increasing perceived authority while bypassing accountability.

Edenic Pattern: The recurring biblical sequence through which deception operates—doubt, distortion, division, accusation, agreement, and destruction—first revealed in Genesis.

Engineered Spirituality: A manufactured form of devotion that mimics the Gospel while relying on emotional triggers or transactional formulas to promise results without discipleship.

Epidemic of Fear: A widespread condition in which fear becomes normalized, transmitted through religious language, and reinforced by communal expectation.

False Liberation: The illusion of freedom offered through secret knowledge, mystical shortcuts, or empowerment language that avoids surrender to Christ while reproducing bondage.

Fear (Primal / Spiritual): The foundational emotional and interpretive force that distorts perception, magnifies threat, and retrains discernment while masquerading as wisdom or vigilance.

Fear Currency: The use of fear as the primary means of sustaining influence and compliance.

Fear Economy: A system—occult or religious—in which fear is intentionally generated, sustained, and monetized to produce urgency, dependency, and control.

Hidden Syncretism: The quiet blending of incompatible beliefs within worship spaces, often unnoticed until spiritual clarity erodes.

Holorum: A specific spiritual entity referenced in Marie Michel's testimony, claiming the role of creator within a ritual system.

Hybrid Entity: An individual whose identity and physiology are believed to be integrated with non-human spiritual intelligences.

Ideological Hybridization: The internal coexistence of conflicting belief systems within an individual, producing instability in belief and practice.

Improvised Prophecy: Prophetic speech delivered without accountability, testing, or submission to Scripture.

Inheritance of Shadows: A metaphor for generational spiritual bondage received without consent or awareness.

Judicial Posture of Ministry: Approaching people primarily as suspects to be examined rather than souls to be shepherded.

Jurisdiction (Spiritual): A legal metaphor describing where authority legitimately operates; in Christ, jurisdiction belongs to God alone.

Legal Metaphor: The use of court-based language—verdicts, contracts, accusation, and immunity—to explain authority and accountability without reducing God to a legal mechanism.

Lougarou: A Creole term referring to a shape-shifting entity believed to transcend physical form.

Media-Driven Discernment: Judgment shaped primarily by news cycles, online narratives, and digital platforms rather than Scripture and spiritual maturity.

Mobile Altar: Physical objects consecrated as anchors or "hardware" for spiritual possession or influence.

Modern Mystics: Contemporary spiritual influencers who promote manifestation, spiritual technology, or hidden knowledge as alternatives to biblical discipleship.

Monetized Deliverance: Conditioning spiritual freedom upon financial contribution or transactional giving.

Noise (Spiritual / Cultural): The saturation of competing voices and narratives that overwhelm discernment and erode spiritual clarity.

Occult Residue: Inherited patterns of fear, expectation, or interpretation carried into Christian faith from prior spiritual systems.

Perception (Spiritual): The internal lens through which reality is interpreted; identified in Scripture as a primary battlefield of spiritual conflict.

Performance-Based Deliverance: Deliverance practices designed to amplify fear and spectacle rather than healing and formation.

Power Without Surrender: Seeking spiritual breakthrough while resisting repentance, obedience, and submission to God.

Prophecy as Performance: Treating prophetic expression as display rather than edification and restoration.

Restoration: The central goal of biblical authority—the healing of persons, relationships, and identity through truth, compassion, and sustained discipleship.

Sanpwèl Queen: A high-level leadership position within clandestine occult societies.

Shortcut Spirituality: The pursuit of spiritual breakthrough without the formative work of obedience and discipleship.

Sorcery (Biblical Definition): The pursuit of spiritual outcomes through manipulation rather than submission, rooted in self-will and control.

Spirit of False Liberation: A counterfeit freedom that promises autonomy while bypassing the cross and restoration.

Spiritual Bypassing (Internal): Using prophetic language or personal revelation to avoid accountability, repentance, or humility.

Spiritual Blackmail: Coercing compliance by implying negative spiritual consequences for disagreement or delay.

Spiritual Conditioning: The gradual training of perception through repeated fear-based teaching or exposure.

Spiritual Intelligence Report: A testimony offered to provide insight into perceived patterns of spiritual opposition, treated as evidence rather than authority.

Spiritual Most Wanted: High-ranking occult figures who convert to Christ and are subsequently targeted as traitors for exposing hidden systems.

Spiritual Preterm: A person delivered from bondage but left without discipleship, community, or formation.

Spiritual Residue: Non-physical remnants of past spiritual experiences that continue to influence perception and response.

Spiritual Roaming Agreements (Lack Thereof): The principle that light and darkness share no common infrastructure or jurisdiction in Christ.

Spiritual Technology: Systems or practices that promise efficient access to power while bypassing relationship and obedience.

Spoken Agreement: Aligning oneself spiritually through words with either truth or deception.

Suspicion: Fear-trained interpretation that assigns threat before understanding and fractures trust and community.

Theatrical Deliverance: A performative expression of deliverance that substitutes spectacle for healing and formation.

Theology of the Tongue: Speech understood as a theological act that participates in spiritual authority and alignment.

Threshold: Transitional spiritual moments—such as deliverance, repentance, or healing—that require discipleship to be sustained.

Transactional Prayer: Prayer treated as leverage or incantation rather than relational trust and submission.

Transactional Spirituality: Any framework that treats spiritual power as exchanged, earned, or activated rather than received through grace.

Vodou (Contextual Use): A historical and cultural spiritual system shaped by survival, trauma, and transactional logic, referenced analytically rather than devotionally.

Warfare (Spiritual): Spiritual resistance framed biblically as standing firm in truth, faith, righteousness, and peace rather than spectacle or aggression.

Zombification: A ritual practice involving substances believed to reduce victims to an externally controlled or diminished state.

ABOUT THE AUTHOR

Simon Demosthene is a pastor, educator, and ministry leader with more than three decades of experience engaging questions at the intersection of faith, culture, and spiritual formation. Raised in a Christian home in Haiti, he grew up within a complex religious environment shaped by both historic Vodou traditions and diverse Christian expressions. This early context provided him with firsthand exposure to the ways spiritual beliefs, fear, and cultural inheritance can influence identity, family life, and communal practice.

A significant influence on his spiritual formation was the life of his father, Reverend Jean Maxi Demosthene. Prior to his Christian faith, his father had been involved in ancestral spiritual systems common in Haiti. His conversion to Christianity marked a decisive break from those traditions and became a foundational moment that shaped the author's understanding of deliverance, discipleship, and restoration as long-term pastoral processes rather than dramatic events.

The author later spent more than thirty years in the United States within academically rigorous and professionally diverse environments. This experience strengthened his ability to engage a wide range of theological perspectives and cultural ideologies with discernment and care. Alongside this academic exposure, he has served in pastoral ministry within both Baptist and Pentecostal contexts, cultivating a balanced approach that values biblical orthodoxy, pastoral accountability, and spiritual maturity.

In 2009, he founded Global Reach Evangelical Missionary Church (GREMC) (GREMC), a multicultural church and community ministry serving immigrant families and individuals seeking spiritual healing, stability, and renewed purpose. His work focuses on helping people address fear-based spirituality, recover clarity of faith, and grow into a mature understanding of Christian authority grounded in Christ rather than anxiety. He continues to write and teach with a commitment to strengthening the Church's witness through discernment, restoration, and faithful leadership.

Ministry Resources & Contact Information

If you have been moved by the message of this book and are seeking prayer, further spiritual education, or connection with a community committed to restoration, you are warmly invited to reach out.

Global Reach Evangelical Missionary Church (GREMC)

- Website: www.gremc-connect.org
- Email: demostsi@gmail.com.